SO-BBB-368

# BOB MILLER'S
# MATH FOR THE GRE®
# GENERAL TEST

**Bob Miller**
Former Lecturer in Mathematics
City College of New York
New York, NY

*Research & Education Association*
Visit our website at: www.rea.com

Planet Friendly Publishing
✔ Made in the United States
✔ Printed on Recycled Paper
Text: 10%     Cover: 10%
Learn more: www.greenedition.org

At REA we're committed to producing books in an Earth-friendly manner and to helping our customers make greener choices.

Manufacturing books in the United States ensures compliance with strict environmental laws and eliminates the need for international freight shipping, a major contributor to global air pollution.

And printing on recycled paper helps minimize our consumption of trees, water and fossil fuels. This book was printed on paper made with **10% post-consumer waste**. According to Environmental Defense's Paper Calculator, by using this innovative paper instead of conventional papers, we achieved the following environmental benefits:

**Trees Saved: 9 • Air Emissions Eliminated: 1,999 pounds
Water Saved: 1,794 gallons • Solid Waste Eliminated: 590 pounds**

For more information on our environmental practices, please visit us online at **www.rea.com/green**

**To Our Readers:**

Educational Testing Service and the Graduate Record Examinations Board are revising the GRE General Test in 2011. As revisions are announced, you can count on REA to keep you up to speed at *www.rea.com/gre*.

*Research & Education Association*
61 Ethel Road West
Piscataway, New Jersey 08854
E-mail: info@rea.com

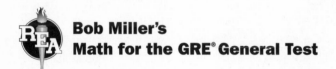

**Bob Miller's
Math for the GRE® General Test**

**Copyright © 2010 by Research & Education Association, Inc.**
Prior edition copyright © 2008 by Research & Education Association, Inc. All rights reserved. No part of this book may be reproduced in any form without permission of the publisher.

Printed in the United States of America

Library of Congress Control Number 2010920079

ISBN-13: 978-0-7386-0833-4
ISBN-10: 0-7386-0833-5

REA® is a registered trademark of
Research & Education Association, Inc.

# TABLE OF CONTENTS

# ACKNOWLEDGMENTS

I have many people to thank.

I thank my wife, Marlene, who makes life worth living, who is truly the wind under my wings.

I thank the rest of my family: children Sheryl and Eric and their spouses Glenn and Wanda (who are also like my children); grandchildren Kira, Evan, Sean, Sarah, and Ethan, my brother Jerry, and my parents, Cele and Lee, and my in-law parents, Edith and Siebeth.

I thank Larry Kling and Michael Reynolds for making this book possible.

I thank Martin Levine for making my whole writing career possible.

I have been negligent in thanking my great math teachers of the past. I thank Mr. Douglas Heagle, Mr. Alexander Lasaka, Mr. Joseph Joerg, and Ms. Arloeen Griswold, the best math teacher I ever had, of George W. Hewlett High School; Ms. Helen Bowker of Woodmere Junior High; and Professor Pinchus Mendelssohn and Professor George Bachman of Polytechnic University. The death of Professor Bachman was an extraordinary loss to our country. In a country that produces too few advanced degrees in math, every year two or three of his students would receive a Ph.D. in math, with more receiving their M.S. His teaching and writings were clear and memorable. He wrote four books and numerous papers on subjects that had never been written about or had been written so poorly that nobody could understand the material.

As usual, the last three thanks go to three terrific people: a great friend, Gary Pitkofsky; another terrific friend and fellow lecturer, David Schwinger; and my cousin, Keith Robin Ellis, the sharer of our dreams.

*Bob Miller*

---

**DEDICATION**

*To my wife, Marlene. I dedicate this book and everything else I ever do to you.*
*I love you very, very much.*

# BIOGRAPHY

I received my B.S. in the Unified Honors Program sponsored by the Ford Foundation and my M.S. in math from Polytechnic University. After the first class I taught, as a substitute for a full professor, one student said to another upon leaving the classroom, "At least we have someone who can teach the stuff." I was hooked forever on teaching. Since then, I have taught at C.U.N.Y., Westfield State College, Rutgers, and Poly. No matter how I feel, I always feel a lot better when I teach. I always feel great when students tell me they used to hate math or couldn't do math and now they like it more and can do it better.

My main blessing is my family. I have a fantastic wife in Marlene. My kids are wonderful: daughter Sheryl, son Eric, son-in-law Glenn, and daughter-in-law Wanda. My grandchildren are terrific: Kira, Evan, Sean, Sarah, and Ethan. My hobbies are golf, bowling, bridge, crossword puzzles, and Sudoku. My ultimate goals are to write a book to help parents teach their kids math, a high school text that will advance our kids' math abilities, and a calculus text students can actually understand.

To me, teaching is always a great joy. I hope that I can give some of that joy to you. I do know this book will help you get the score you need to get into the graduate school of your choice.

I really like GRE questions. I like all kinds of puzzles, both mathematical and word. To me the GRE is a game. If you win, you win the graduate school of your choice. Good luck!!!!!

# OTHER BOOKS

Bob Miller's Basic Math and Pre-Algebra for the Clueless, Second Edition
Bob Miller's Algebra for the Clueless, Second Edition
Bob Miller's Geometry for the Clueless, Second Edition
Bob Miller's Math SAT for the Clueless, Second Edition
Bob Miller's Pre-Calc with Trig for the Clueless, Third Edition
Bob Miller's High School Calc for the Clueless
Bob Miller's Calc 1 for the Clueless, Second Edition
Bob Miller's Calc 2 for the Clueless, Second Edition
Bob Miller's Calc 3 for the Clueless

# ABOUT RESEARCH & EDUCATION ASSOCIATION

Founded in 1959, Research & Education Association (REA) is dedicated to publishing the finest and most effective educational materials—including software, study guides, and test preps—for students in middle school, high school, college, graduate school, and beyond.

REA's test preparation series includes books and software for all academic levels in almost all disciplines. REA publishes test preps for students who have not yet entered high school, as well as high school students preparing to enter college. Students from countries around the world seeking to attend college in the United States will find the assistance they need in REA's publications. For college students seeking advanced degrees, REA publishes test preps for many major graduate school admission examinations in a wide variety of disciplines, including engineering, law, and medicine. Students at every level, in every field, with every ambition can find what they are looking for among REA's publications.

REA's publications and educational materials are highly regarded and continually receive an unprecedented amount of praise from professionals, instructors, librarians, parents, and students. Our authors are as diverse as the subject matter represented in the books we publish. They are well known in their respective disciplines and serve on the faculties of prestigious colleges and universities throughout the United States and Canada.

Today, REA's wide-ranging catalog is a leading resource for teachers, students, and professionals.

We invite you to visit us at *www.rea.com* to find out how "REA is making the world smarter."

# REA ACKNOWLEDGMENTS

In addition to our author, we would like to thank Larry B. Kling, Vice President, Editorial, for his overall direction; Pam Weston, Vice President, Publishing, for setting the quality standards for production integrity and managing the publication to completion; Michael Reynolds, Senior Editor, for editorial contributions and project management; Mel Friedman, Lead Mathematics Editor, for proofreading; Rachel DiMatteo, Graphic Designer, for designing this book; Christine Saul, Senior Graphic Artist, for designing our cover; Jeff LoBalbo, Senior Graphic Designer, for coordinating pre-press electronic file mapping, and Aquent Publishing Services, for typesetting this edition. Photo by Eric L. Miller.

# A NOTE ON CALCULATORS

Educational Testing Service has said it intends at some point in the future to add an online calculator to the computer-based GRE General Test. To date, the GRE General Test makes no provision for calculator usage. In the meantime, our author contends you're better off weaning yourself from the calculator anyway. Working things out in your head, or with simple scratchwork, will instill greater confidence and save valuable time on test day!

# INTRODUCTION

Congratulations to you who have graduated or are about to graduate college! You are about to begin another great adventure. Before the journey starts, however, you must take the Graduate Record Exam (GRE). This book is designed for you to maximize your GRE math score.

You can choose from two kinds of GRE. The first is a pencil-and-paper version, and the second is the computer-based test, or CBT, taken completely on a computer. The differences in test-taking strategy on these two versions are discussed in Chapter 15.

The format of the GRE is similar to that of the SAT. The GRE has multiple-choice questions with five choices. It also has quantitative comparisons in which you are given two choices, one in column A and one in column B. You answer A if A is bigger; B if B is bigger, C if they are equal, and D if you can't tell. Less than five hours after I submitted the original manuscript for this book to the publisher, the GRE surprised me with a new type of question for the CBT version: the fill-ins. You must answer these questions without being given any choices.

The GRE is different from the SAT as well. Calculators are not permitted. No formulas are given. The GRE asks many more questions on charts and graphs than does the SAT. The level of the math is lower (yes, lower) than the level on the SAT. Without permitting calculators, then, the GRE asks more arithmetic questions.

Some of you have not done much math or arithmetic for many years. I recently met with a local congressman about improving the math in this country. I hope it was successful. His uniqueness is that he had a doctorate in physics. In our discussion, he looked at some of my material and my other books in basic algebra and basic calculus. He had forgotten some of the material. If he can forget, you might also.

Each chapter of this book has three parts. First, there is a summary of the facts you need to know, together with examples. Second, there is instruction on how to do the work. In some chapters, there is very little; in others, there is more. You will be shown techniques to streamline your arithmetic. Sometimes there are ways to do no arithmetic at all, even though it appears you need to. Third, there are lots and lots of questions for you to do, together with the answers. The end of the book, Chapters 16 through 18, presents practice tests to see how well you are doing, including answer keys. Chapter 19 presents some pointers and provides a practice test for the new type of fill-in questions for the computer-based version of the GRE.

Always remember: your goal is not a perfect score. It is a score high enough to get you into the program of your choice. So, that is the goal of this book.

Good luck on the GRE!

Bob Miller

# PRO STUDY PLAN

## HOW TO USE THIS BOOK

If you need an extra boost of math prep before you feel confident enough to tackle the math portion of the GRE General, this book is for you!

Depending on where you are on your educational pathway, some of you haven't seen math in a very long time. Maybe that's why you chose this test prep—for its easy-to-understand math practice and reinforcement. As you read through this book you may find that you know the material in some of the chapters pretty well—and others, not so much. Those are the areas on which you'll need to focus.

Before you pick up your pencil and start studying, read the introduction and become familiar with the math portion of the GRE. Make sure you understand how the test is conducted, and know the type and style of questions that will be asked.

Every day, devote at least an hour (or perhaps two hours, depending on your math skills) to studying the math concepts presented in this book. At first—just like starting an exercise plan—it will be hard. But after a few days, studying will become a natural part of your routine. Find a study routine that works for you and stick to it! Some people like to get up early and study for an hour or two before going to work. Others might choose to study while commuting, on their lunch hour, at the library, or at home after work. Whatever schedule you choose, make a commitment to study every day—even on weekends.

Go through each chapter and try some of the practice problems. If you find them to be very easy, skip to the next chapter. Whenever you find a chapter that is not so easy, take your time and study the chapter in detail. After you have gone through the chapters that you think give you the most problems, go back and study the remaining chapters. Practical math tips are included in all the chapters, and they will help you solve math problems quickly and more easily.

When you have a good grasp of the material, try the first practice test. Give yourself plenty of time and work in a quiet place where you won't be disturbed. After you've finished the practice test, check your answers. If you find there are some types of questions (such as quadrilaterals) that you constantly get wrong, restudy the appropriate review chapter and practice problems.

After you've finished restudying any areas of weakness, repeat the process with the remaining two practice tests. Keep reviewing the math topics that give you trouble until you feel comfortable with the material. In just a matter of weeks, your math skills will improve and you'll be ready for the GRE!

**SUGGESTED PRO STUDY PLAN**

"*You don't need to follow any study plan except your own. Only you know how and when you study best. So work through this book at your own pace and take as much time as you need in each chapter. But, if you want some guidelines, try this 4-week Pro Study Plan. For those of you crunched for time, condense this into a 2-week schedule by combining weeks 1 and 2 together, and weeks 3 and 4 together.*"

| Week | Activity |
|------|----------|
| 1 | Read Chapter 15 and the introduction. The chapter "How to Take the GRE" explains the format of the test and offers you helpful test-taking advice. Take Practice Test 1 to determine your strengths and weaknesses. Give yourself a block of time after work, on a weekend, or at another convenient time to take the exam. You will need to concentrate, so take the practice test at a time and place where you will not be disturbed. When you take the test, try to do your best, even on sections where you may be confused. After you have finished the test, record your scores. This will help you track your progress as you study. Later in the week, study the answers for the questions you answered incorrectly. In the cases where you erred, find out why. Take notes and pay attention to sections where you missed a lot of questions. You will need to spend more time reviewing the related material. |
| 2 | Make a firm commitment to study for at least an hour a day, every day for the next few weeks. It may seem hard to find time in your busy schedule, but remember: the more you study, the better prepared you will be for the GRE General Test. This week, study review chapters 1 through 7. Do the practice exercises and check your answers for each section of the review. Pace yourself and make sure you understand the basics before moving on to the more difficult chapters. If you find yourself in need of extra review or clarification on a topic, you may want to consult your math textbook or ask a classmate or professor for additional help. |

| Week | Activity |
|------|----------|
| **3** | Keep working your way through the review chapters and practice problems. This week focus your study on chapters 8 through 14. Take your time and make sure you're familiar with all the math formulas and rules presented in the review. Pay close attention to the examples and exercises; they will show you how to solve questions you may encounter on the actual GRE exam. After you've completed the review chapters, take Practice Test 2. Record your score and see how well you did. After you've evaluated your test results, go back through each chapter and brush up on the topics you need to review. Later this week, study the answers for any questions you answered incorrectly. Make sure you understand why you answered the question wrong, so you can improve your test-taking skills. |
| **4** | After a day or two of additional study to reinforce any areas of weakness, take Practice Test 3. Don't rush! Remember what you've learned and answer every question to the best of your ability. How much has your score improved since you took the first practice exam? After the test, thoroughly review all the explanations for the questions you answered incorrectly. Later in the week, go back and review any questions you answered wrong on the previous practice tests. Spend time studying the answer explanations and re-read the relevant chapters for extra review. If you feel you need extra GRE math practice, why not review your notes during your lunch hour or on your train or bus commute? |

**Congratulations! You've worked hard and you're ready for the math portion of the GRE General!**

# CHAPTER 1: *The Basics*

"*All math begins with whole numbers. Master them and you will begin to speak the language of math.*"

**Let's** begin at the beginning. The GRE works only with **real numbers**, numbers that can be written as decimals. However, it does not always say "numbers." Let's get specific.

## NUMBERS

**Whole numbers:** 0, 1, 2, 3, 4, …

**Integers:** 0, ±1, ±2, ±3, ±4, …, where ±3 stands for both +3 and −3.

**Positive integers** are integers that are greater than 0. In symbols, $x > 0$, $x$ is an integer

**Negative integers** are integers that are less than 0. In symbols, $x < 0$, $x$ is an integer

**Even integers:** 0, ±2, ±4, ±6, …

**Odd integers:** ±1, ±3, ±5, ±7, …

## Inequalities

For any numbers represented by $a$, $b$, $c$, or $d$ on the number line:

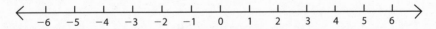

We say $c > d$ ($c$ is greater than $d$) if $c$ is to the right of $d$ on the number line.

We say $d < c$ ($d$ is less than $c$) if $d$ is to the left of $c$ on the number line.

$c > d$ is equivalent to $d < c$

$a \leq b$ means $a < b$ or $a = b$; likewise, $a \geq b$ means $a > b$ or $a = b$.

> **Example 1:**  $4 \leq 7$ is true, since $4 < 7$; $9 \leq 9$ is true, since $9 = 9$;
> but $7 \leq 2$ is false, since $7 > 2$.

**Example 2:**    Graph all integers between $-4$ and 5.

**Solution:**

Notice that the word "between" does *not* include the endpoints.

**Example 3:**    Graph all the multiples of five between 20 and 40 inclusive.

**Solution:**

Notice that "inclusive" means to include the endpoints.

## Odd and Even Numbers

**Here are some facts about odd and even integers that you should know.**

- The sum of two even integers is even.

- The sum of two odd integers is even.

- The sum of an even integer and an odd integer is odd.

- The product of two even integers is even.

- The product of two odd integers is odd.

- The product of an even integer and an odd integer is even.

- If $n$ is even, $n^2$ is even. If $n^2$ is even and $n$ is an integer, then $n$ is even.

- If $n$ is odd, $n^2$ is odd. If $n^2$ is odd and $n$ is an integer, then $n$ is odd.

# OPERATIONS ON NUMBERS

**Product** is the answer in multiplication; **quotient** is the answer in division; **sum** is the answer in addition; and **difference** is the answer in subtraction.

Since $3 \times 4 = 12$, 3 and 4 are said to be **factors** or **divisors** of 12, and 12 is both a **multiple** of 3 and a **multiple** of 4.

A prime is a positive integer with exactly two distinct factors, itself and 1. The number 1 is not a prime since only $1 \times 1 = 1$. It might be a good idea to memorize the first eight primes:

2, 3, 5, 7, 11, 13, 17, and 19.

The number 4 has more than two factors: 1, 2, and 4. Numbers with more than two factors are called **composites**. The number 28 is a **perfect** number since if you add the factors less than 28, they add to 28.

**Example 4:**   Write all the factors of 28.

**Solution:**   1, 2, 4, 7, 14, and 28.

**Example 5:**   Write 28 as the product of prime factors.

**Solution:**   $28 = 2 \times 2 \times 7$.

**Example 6:**   Find all the primes between 70 and 80.

**Solution:**   71, 73, 79. How do we find this easily? First, since 2 is the only even prime, we only have to check the odd numbers. Next, we have to know the divisibility rules:

- A number is divisible by 2 if it ends in an even number. We don't need this here because then it can't be prime.

- A number is divisible by 3 (or 9) if the sum of the digits is divisible by 3 (or 9). For example, 456 is divisible by 3 since the sum of the digits is 15, which is divisible by 3 (it's not divisible by 9, but that's okay).

- A number is divisible by 4 if the last two digits are divisible by 4. For example, 3936 is divisible by 4 since 36 is divisible by 4.

- A number is divisible by 5 if the last digit is 0 or 5.

- The rule for 6 is a combination of the rules for 2 and 3.

- It is easier to divide by 7 than to learn the rule for 7.

- A number is divisible by 8 if the last *three* digits are divisible by 8.

- A number is divisible by 10 if it ends in a zero, as you know.

- A number is divisible by 11 if the difference between the sum of the even-place digits (2nd, 4th, 6th, etc.) and the sum of the odd-place digits (1st, 3rd, 5th, etc.) is a multiple of 11. For example, for the number 928,193,926: the sum of the odd digits (9, 8, 9, 9, and 6) is 41; the sum of the even digits (2, 1, 3, 2) is 8; and $41 - 8$ is 33, which is divisible by 11. So 928,193,926 is divisible by 11.

That was a long digression!!!!! Let's get back to example 6.

We only have to check 71, 73, 75, 77, and 79. 75 is not a prime since it ends in a 5. 77 is not a prime since it is divisible by 7. To see if the other three are prime, for any number less than 100, you have to divide by the primes 2, 3, 5, and 7 only. You will quickly find they are primes.

## Rules for Operations on Numbers

**Note** *( ) are called parentheses (singular: parenthesis); [ ] are called brackets; { } are called braces.*

### Rules for adding signed numbers

1. If all the signs are the same, add the numbers and use that sign.

2. If two signs are different, subtract them, and use the sign of the larger numeral.

> **Example 7:**
>
> **a.** $3 + 7 + 2 + 4 = +16$     **c.** $5 - 9 + 11 - 14 = 16 - 23 = -7$
>
> **b.** $-3 - 5 - 7 - 9 = -24$     **d.** $2 - 6 + 11 - 1 = 13 - 7 = +6$

### Rules for multiplying and dividing signed numbers
Look at the minus signs only.

1. Odd number of minus signs—the answer is minus.

2. Even number of minus signs—the answer is plus.

> **Example 8:**     $\dfrac{(-4)(-2)(-6)}{(-2)(+3)(-1)} =$
>
> **Solution:**     Five minus signs, so the answer is minus, $-8$.

### Rule for subtracting signed numbers
The sign (−) means subtract. Change the problem to an addition problem.

> **Example 9:**   **a.** $(-6) - (-4) = (-6) + (+4) = -2$
>
> **b.** $(-6) - (+2) = (-6) + (-2) = -8$, since it is now an adding problem.

## Order of Operations

In doing a problem like this, $4 + 5 \times 6$, the **order of operations** tells us whether to multiply or add first:

1. If given letters, substitute in parentheses the value of each letter.

2. Do operations in parentheses, inside ones first, and then the tops and bottoms of fractions.

3. Do exponents next. (Chapter 3 discusses exponents in more detail.)

4. Do multiplications and divisions, left to right as they occur.

5. The last step is adding and subtracting. Left to right is usually the safest way.

**Example 10:** $4 + 5 \times 6 =$

**Solution:**   $4 + 30 = 34$

**Example 11:** $(4 + 5)6$

**Solution:**   $(9)(6) = 54$

**Example 12:** $1000 \div 2 \times 4$

**Solution:**   $(500)(4) = 2{,}000$

**Example 13:** $1000 \div (2 \times 4)$

**Solution:**   $1000 \div 8 = 125$

**Example 14:** $4[3 + 2(5 - 1)]$

**Solution:**   $4[3 + 2(4)] = 4[3 + 8] = 4(11) = 44$

**Example 15:** $\dfrac{3^4 - 1^{10}}{4 - 10 \times 2} =$

**Solution:**   $\dfrac{81 - 1}{4 - 20} = \dfrac{80}{-16} = -5$

**Example 16:** If $x = -3$ and $y = -4$, find the value:

    **a.** $7 - 5x - x^2$

    **b.** $xy^2 - (xy)^2$

**Solutions:**

    **a.** $7 - 5x - x^2 = 7 - 5(-3) - (-3)^2 = 7 + 15 - 9 = 13$

    **b.** $xy^2 - (xy)^2 = (-3)(-4)^2 - ((-3)(-4))^2 = (-3)(16) - (12)^2$
         $= -48 - 144 = -192$

Before we get to the exercises, let's talk about ways to describe a group of numbers (data).

## DESCRIBING DATA

Four of the measures that describe data are used on the GRE. The first three are measures of central tendency; the fourth, the range, measures the span of the data. Chapter 14 discusses these measures in more detail.

**Mean:**  Also called average. Add up the numbers and divide by how many numbers you have added up.

**Median:**  Middle number. Put the numbers in numeric order and see which one is in the middle. If there are two "middle" numbers,

take the average of them. This happens with an even number of data points.

**Mode:**  Most common. Which number(s) appears the most times? A set with two modes is called bimodal. There can actually be any number of modes, including that everything is a mode.

**Range:**  Highest number minus the lowest number.

**Example 17:**  Find the mean, median, mode, and range for 5, 6, 9, 11, 12, 12, and 14.

**Solutions:**  Mean: $\dfrac{5 + 6 + 9 + 11 + 12 + 12 + 14}{7} = \dfrac{69}{7} = 9\dfrac{6}{7}$

Median: 11

Mode: 12

Range: $14 - 5 = 9$

**Example 18:**  Find the mean, median, mode, and range for 4, 4, 7, 10, 20, 20.

**Solutions:**  Mean: $\dfrac{4 + 4 + 7 + 10 + 20 + 20}{6} = \dfrac{65}{6} = 10\dfrac{5}{6}$

Median: For an even number of points, it is the mean of the middle two:

$\dfrac{7 + 10}{2} = 8.5$

Mode: There are two: 4 and 20 (blackbirds?)

Range: $20 - 4 = 16$

**Example 19:**  Jim received 83 and 92 on two tests. What grade must the third test be in order to have an average (mean) of 90?

**Solution:**  There are two methods.

Method 1: To get a 90 average on three tests Jim needs 3(90) = 270 points. So far, he has 83 + 92 = 175 points. So, Jim needs 270 − 175 = 95 points on the third test.

Method 2 (my favorite): 83 is −7 from 90. 92 is + 2 from 90, and −7 + 2 = −5 from the desired 90 average. Jim needs 90 + 5 = 95 points on the third test. (Jim needs to "make up" the 5-point deficit, so add it to the average of 90.)

# EXERCISES

Finally, after a long introduction, we get to some exercises.

The GRE has two types of questions. The first type lists two columns, A and B, and you must compare the values in each. The second type is the usual multiple-choice question.

For the first type, compare the two quantities in Column A and Column B and choose:

**A.** if the quantity in Column A is greater

**B.** if the quantity in Column B is greater

**C.** if the two quantities are equal

**D.** if the relationship cannot be determined from the information given

(Q)  **Let's do some comparison exercises.**

|  | **Column A** | **Column B** |
|---|---|---|
| | $(77+1)(243) = (77)(243) + 1(243)$ | $(77)(243+1)$ |
| **Exercise 1:** | (78)(243) | (77)(244) |
| **Exercise 2:** | $\dfrac{94 \times 357 \times 10 \times 9 \times 8 \times 7}{7 \times 3 \times 2}$ | $\dfrac{7 \times 4 \times 3 \times 2 \times 357 \times 94}{9 \times 8 \times 7}$ |
| **Exercise 3:** | $x - 1$ | $x + 1$ |

| | | |
|---|---|---|
| **Exercise 4:** | $x$ | $\dfrac{1}{x}$ |
| **Exercise 5:** | $(-1)^{100}$ | $(-1)^{200}$ |
| **Exercise 6:** | $(-2)^{10}$ | $(-2)^{11}$ |
| **Exercise 7:** | $(-3)^{8}$ | $-3^{8}$ |
| **Exercise 8:** | $(59.361)^{2}$ | 3600 |
| **Exercise 9:** $n > 0$, $n$ even | prime factors of $n$ | prime factors of $2n$ |
| **Exercise 10:** $p$, $q$ primes | prime factors of $pq$ | prime factors of $2pq$ |

 **Let's look at the answers.**

**Answer 1:** Many times most or all of the arithmetic is avoidable. It is not necessary to do the arithmetic in this answer.

$(78)(243) = (77 + 1)(243) = 77(243) + 1(243)$

$(77)(244) = 77(243 + 1) = 77(243) + 1(77)$

We see that $1(243) > 1(77)$. The answer is (A).

**Answer 2:** Now here's a problem for which we never want to do any arithmetic. We don't have to. On each side, cross off all the sevens, 357, and 94.

We then get $\dfrac{10 \times 9 \times 8}{3 \times 2}$ and $\dfrac{4 \times 3 \times 2}{9 \times 8}$. The left number is greater than 1 and the other is less than 1. The answer is (A).

**Answer 3:** Cancel $x$ on both sides. The answer is (B).

**Answer 4:** Let $x = 1$, 3, and $\dfrac{1}{2}$. The answer is (D).

**Answer 5:**    Both equal 1. The answer is (C).

**Answer 6:**    $A > 0$ and $B < 0$. Positives are always bigger than negatives. The answer is (A).

**Answer 7:**    Again, $A > 0$ and $B < 0$ (one minus sign). The answer is (A).

**Answer 8:**    $3600 = (60)^2$, and $59.361 < 60$. The answer is (B).

**Answer 9:**    If $n$ is even, multiplying by 2 doesn't change the prime factors. They are the same. The answer is (C).

**Answer 10:**    This is not the same as Exercise 9. If $p$ or $q = 2$, then A and B are the same. If $p$ and $q$ are both odd, multiplying by 2 increases column B by 1 (because 2 is another prime factor). The answer is (D), you can't tell!

The second type of question on the GRE is the multiple-choice question.

**(Q) Let's do some multiple-choice questions.**

**Exercise 11:**   If $x = -5$, the value of $-3 + 4x - x^2$ is $= -3 - (-20) - 25 = 17 - 25 = -8$

     A. $-48$          D. 13

     B. $-8$          E. 4

     C. 2

**Exercise 12:**   $-0(2) - \dfrac{0}{2} - 2 =$    $0 - 0 - 2 = -2$

     A. 0          D. $-6$

     B. $-2$          E. Undefined

     C. $-4$

**Exercise 13:**  The scores on three tests were 90, 91, and 98. What does the score on the fourth test have to be in order to get exactly a 95 average (mean)?

**A.** 97          **D.** 100

**B.** 98          **E.** Not possible

**C.** 99

**Exercise 14:**  On a true-false test, 20 students scored 90, and 30 students scored 100. The sum of the mean, median, and mode is:

**A.** 300          **D.** 294

**B.** 296          **E.** 275

**C.** 295

**Exercise 15:**  If $m$ and $n$ are odd integers, which of the following is odd?

**A.** $mn + 3$          **D.** $(m + 1)(n - 2)$

**B.** $m^2 + (n + 2)^2$          **E.** $m^4 + m^3 + m^2 + m$

$O + O = E$

**C.** $mn + m + n$

**Exercise 16:**  If $m + 3$ is a multiple of 4, which of these is also a multiple of 4?

**A.** $m - 3$          **D.** $m + 9$

**B.** $m$          **E.** $m + 11$

**C.** $m + 4$

**Exercise 17:**  If $p$ and $q$ are primes, which one *can't* be a prime?

**A.** $pq$          **D.** $2pq + 1$

**B.** $p + q$          **E.** $p^2 + q^2$

**C.** $pq + 2$

**Exercise 18:**  The sum of the first $n$ positive integers is $p$. In terms of $n$ and $p$, what is the sum of the next $n$ positive integers?

**A.** $np$          **D.** $n + p^2$

**B.** $n + p$          **E.** $2n + 2p$

**C.** $n^2 + p$

$4 5 + 6 + 7 = 22$
$8 + 9 + 10 + 11 = 28$

**Exercise 19:** Let $p$ be prime, with $20p$ divisible by 6; $p$ could be

    A. 3              D. 6

    B. 4              E. 7

    C. 5

(A) **Let's look at the answers.**

**Answer 11:** $-3 - 4(-5) - (-5)^2 = -3 + 20 - 25 = -8$. The answer is (B).

**Answer 12:** $0 - 0 - 2 = -2$. The answer is (B).

**Answer 13:** $95(4) = 380$ points; $90 + 91 + 98 = 279$ points. The fourth test would have to be $380 - 279 = 101$. The answer is (E).

**Answer 14:** The median is 100; the mode is 100; for the mean we can use 2 and 3 instead of 20 and 30 since the ratio is the same:

$$\frac{2(90) + 3(100)}{5} = 96.$$ The answer is (B).

**Answer 15:** Only (C); it's the sum of three odd integers. All of the other answer choices are even.

**Answer 16:** If $m + 3$ is a multiple of 4, then $m + 3 + 8$ is a multiple of 4 since 8 is a multiple of 4. The answer is (E).

**Answer 17:** By substituting proper primes, all the others might be prime. The answer is (A).

**Answer 18:** Say $n = 5$; $p = 1 + 2 + 3 + 4 + 5$. The next five are $(1 + 5) + (2 + 5) + (3 + 5) + (4 + 5) + (5 + 5) = p + n^2$. The answer is (C).

**Answer 19:** 3 and 6 will work, but only 3 is a prime. The answer is (A).

$\frac{6}{9} = \frac{2}{3} = 66.66\%$

# CHAPTER 2: *Decimals, Fractions, and Percentages*

*"One must master the parts as well as the whole to fully understand."*

**Since** the GRE does not allow calculators, you might be spending a little more time on this chapter than you planned. Let's start with decimals.

## DECIMALS

*Rule 1:* When adding or subtracting, line up the decimal points.

> **Example 1:**   Add: 3.1416 + 234.72 + 86
>
> $$\begin{array}{r} 3.1416 \\ 234.72 \\ +\ 86. \\ \hline 323.8616 \end{array}$$

> **Example 2:**   Subtract: 56.7 − 8.82
>
> $$\begin{array}{r} 56.70 \\ -\ 8.82 \\ \hline 47.88 \end{array}$$

*Rule 2:* In multiplying numbers, count the number of decimal places and add them. In the product, this will be the number of decimal places for the decimal.

> **Example 3:**   Multiply: 45.67 × .987
>
> $$\begin{array}{rl} 45.67 & \text{(2 places)} \\ \times\ \ .987 & \text{(3 places)} \\ \hline 45.07629 & \text{(5 places)} \end{array}$$

If you're curious, the reason it's five places is that if you multiply hundredths by thousandths, you get hundred-thousandths, which is five places. Fortunately, the GRE does not ask you to do pure long multiplications like this.

***Rule 3:*** When you divide, move the decimal point in the divisor and the dividend the same number of places.

$$\overset{\text{Quotient}}{\text{Divisor}\overline{)\,\text{Dividend}}}$$

**Example 4:**     $.004\overline{)23.1} = 4\overline{)23100.}$ with quotient $5775.$

Why is this true? If we write the division as a fraction, it would be $\dfrac{23.1}{.004}$. Multiplying the numerator and denominator by 1000, we get $\dfrac{23.1}{.004} = \dfrac{23.1\times1000}{.004\times1000} = \dfrac{23100}{4}$. When you multiply by 1, the fraction doesn't change. Since $\dfrac{1000}{1000} = 1$, the fraction is the same.

***Rule 4:*** When reading a number with a decimal, read the whole part, only say the word "and" when you reach the decimal point, then read the part after the decimal point as if it were a whole number, and say the last decimal place. Whew!

**Example 5:**

| Number | Read |
|---|---|
| 4.3 | Four and three tenths |
| 2,006.73 | Two-thousand six and seventy-three hundredths |
| 1,000,017.009 | One million seventeen and nine thousandths |

**(Q)   Let's do some exercises.**

**Exercise 1:**     Which is smallest:

A. .04          D. .04444

B. .0401        E. .041

C. .04001

|  | **Column A** | **Column B** |
|---|---|---|
| **Exercise 2:** | $(.04)^2$ | $\sqrt{.04}$ |
| **Exercise 3:** | $(4.1)^2$ | $\sqrt{4.1}$ |

**Let's look at the answers.**

**Answer 1:** All choices have the same tenths (0) and hundredths (4) digits. The rest of the places of (A) are zero. The answer is (A).

**Answer 2:** $(.04)^2 = .0016$; $\sqrt{.04} = .2$. If you take the square root of a decimal and it is exact, the answer has half the number of decimal the places. The answer is (B).

**Answer 3:** (A) is bigger than 4, and (B) is less than 4. The answer is (A).

Now, let's go over fractions.

# FRACTIONS

The top of a fraction is called the **numerator**; the bottom is the **denominator**.

*Rule 1:* If the bottoms of a fraction are the same, the bigger the top, the bigger the fraction.

**Example 6:** Suppose I am a smart first grader. Can you explain to me which is bigger, $\frac{3}{5}$ or $\frac{4}{5}$?

**Solution:** Suppose we have a pizza pie. Then $\frac{3}{5}$ means we divide a pie into 5 equal parts, and I get 3. And $\frac{4}{5}$ means I get 4 pieces out of 5. So $\frac{3}{5} < \frac{4}{5}$.

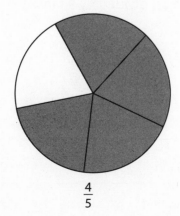

$$\frac{4}{5}$$

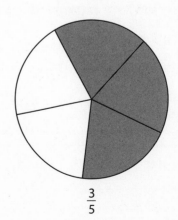

$$\frac{3}{5}$$

**Rule 2:**  If the tops of two fractions are the same, the bigger the bottom, the smaller the fraction.

**Example 7:**    Which fraction, $\frac{3}{5}$ or $\frac{3}{4}$, is bigger?

**Solution:**    Use another pizza pie example. In comparing $\frac{3}{5}$ and $\frac{3}{4}$, we get the same number of pieces (3). However, if the pie is divided into 4, the pieces are bigger, so $\frac{3}{5} < \frac{3}{4}$.

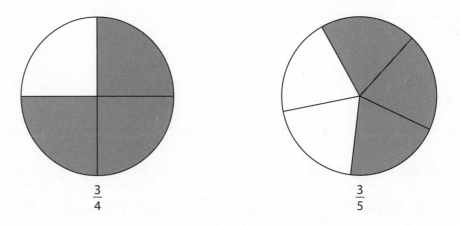

$$\frac{3}{4} \qquad\qquad\qquad \frac{3}{5}$$

**Rule 3:**  If the tops and bottoms are different, find the Least Common Denominator (LCD) and compare the tops.

Before we get into this section, the teacher in me (and maybe the purist in you) must tell you we really are talking about rational numbers, not fractions. There are two definitions.

**Definition 1:**  A **rational** number is any integer divided by an integer, with the denominator not equaling zero.

**Definition 2:**  A **rational** number is any repeating or terminating decimal.

**Note** *Technically, $\frac{\pi}{6}$ is a fraction but not a rational number. We will use the term "fraction" here instead of rational number. If it is negative, we will say "negative fraction." Note the following facts about fractions:*

$3 < 4$, but $-3 > -4$. Similarly, $\dfrac{3}{5} < \dfrac{4}{5}$, but $-\dfrac{3}{5} > -\dfrac{4}{5}$. We will do more of this later.

- A fraction is bigger than one if the numerator is bigger than the denominator.
- A fraction is less than one if the numerator is less than the denominator.
- A fraction is less than $\dfrac{1}{2}$ if the bottom is more than twice the top.
- To double a fraction, either double the top or halve the bottom.
- Adding the same number top and bottom to fraction makes it closer to 1.

**(Q)** **Let's do some more exercises.**

|  | **Column A** | **Column B** |
|---|---|---|
| **Exercise 4:** | $\dfrac{1}{6}$ | $\left(\dfrac{1}{.06}\right)^2$ |
| **Exercise 5:** | $\dfrac{\frac{1}{3}}{\frac{1}{6}}$ | $\dfrac{\frac{1}{6}}{\frac{1}{3}}$ |
| **Exercise 6:** | $\left(-\dfrac{1}{2}\right)^5$ | $\left(-\dfrac{1}{2}\right)^6$ |
| **Exercise 7:** $m, n > 2$ | $\dfrac{m}{n}$ | $\dfrac{m+1}{n+1}$ |

**(A)** **Let's look at the answers.**

**Answer 4:**   Without the square, $\dfrac{1}{.06} > 1$; square it, and it is even bigger. $\dfrac{1}{6} < 1$. In fact, $\left(\dfrac{1}{.06}\right)^2$ is more than 1000 times as big as $\dfrac{1}{6}$. The answer is (B).

**Answer 5:**   In (A), the top is bigger. In (B), the bottom is bigger. The answer is (A).

**Answer 6:**   $\left(-\dfrac{1}{2}\right)^5 < 0$ and $\left(-\dfrac{1}{2}\right)^6 > 0$. The answer is (B).

**Answer 7:**    The answer is (D), you can't tell. Substitute some numbers for $m$ and $n$ to see that this is so:

$$\text{If } m < n, \frac{3}{4} < \frac{3+1}{4+1} = \frac{4}{5}$$

$$\text{If } m = n, \frac{6}{6} = \frac{6+1}{6+1} = \frac{7}{7}$$

$$\text{If } m > n, \frac{5}{4} > \frac{5+1}{4+1} = \frac{6}{5}.$$

## Adding and Subtracting Fractions

If the denominators are the same, add or subtract the tops, keep the bottom the same, and reduce if necessary.

$$\frac{7}{43} + \frac{11}{43} - \frac{2}{43} = \frac{16}{43}$$

$$\frac{2}{9} + \frac{4}{9} = \frac{6}{9} = \frac{2}{3}$$

$$\frac{a}{m} + \frac{b}{m} - \frac{c}{m} = \frac{a+b-c}{m}$$

There is much more to talk about if the denominators are unlike.

The quickest way to add (or subtract) fractions with different denominators, especially if they contain letters or the denominators are small, is to multiply each fraction by the LCD. The LCD is really just the least common multiple, LCM. This consists of three words: multiple, common, and least.

**Example 8:**    What is the LCM of 6 and 8?

**Solution:**    **Multiples** of 6 are 6, 12, 18, 24, 30, 36, 42, 48, 54, 60, 66, 72, 78,…
**Multiples** of 8 are 8, 16, 24, 32, 40, 48, 56, 64, 72, 80,…
**Common multiples** of 6 and 8 are 24, 48, 72, 96, 120,…
The **least common multiple** of 6 and 8 is 24.

When adding or subtracting fractions, multiply the top and bottom of each fraction by the LCM divided by the denominator:

$$\frac{a}{b} - \frac{x}{y} = \left(\frac{a}{b} \times \frac{y}{y}\right) - \left(\frac{x}{y} \times \frac{b}{b}\right) = \frac{ay}{by} - \frac{bx}{by} = \frac{ay - bx}{by}$$

$$\frac{7}{20} - \frac{3}{11} = \left(\frac{7}{20} \times \frac{11}{11}\right) - \left(\frac{3}{11} \times \frac{20}{20}\right) = \frac{7(11) - 3(20)}{20(11)} = \frac{17}{220}$$

**Example 9:**   Add $\frac{5}{6} + \frac{3}{8} + \frac{2}{9}$.

**Solution:**   To find LCD, take multiples of the largest denominator, 9, and see which one is also a multiple of the others (6 and 8): 9, 18, 27, 36, 45, 54, 63, 72. The LCD is 72, so we have:

$$\frac{5}{6} = \frac{5}{6} \times \frac{12}{12} = \frac{60}{72}$$

$$\frac{3}{8} = \frac{3}{8} \times \frac{9}{9} = \frac{27}{72}$$

$$\frac{2}{9} = \frac{2}{9} \times \frac{8}{8} = \frac{16}{72}$$

Adding these, we get $\frac{103}{72}$, or $1\frac{31}{72}$. You may have to add fractions like this on the GRE.

You will not have to add fractions like the next example, ones with a large LCD. However, this is the technique to use when adding algebraic fractions. That is why the next example is here.

**Example 10:**   Add $\frac{3}{100} + \frac{5}{48} + \frac{4}{135}$.

**Solution:**   What is the LCD? We can find it by breaking the denominators into primes.

$100 = 2 \times 2 \times 5 \times 5$

$48 = 2 \times 2 \times 2 \times 2 \times 3$

$135 = 3 \times 3 \times 3 \times 5$

The LCD is the product of the most number of times a prime occurs in any one denominator. The LCD is thus $2 \times 2 \times 2 \times 2 \times 3 \times 3 \times 3 \times 5 \times 5$.

Then multiply the top numbers (numerators) by "what's missing":

$$\frac{3}{100} = \frac{3}{2 \times 2 \times 5 \times 5} = \frac{3(2 \times 2 \times 3 \times 3 \times 3)}{2 \times 2 \times 2 \times 2 \times 3 \times 3 \times 3 \times 5 \times 5} = \frac{324}{10800}$$

$$\frac{5}{48} = \frac{5}{2 \times 2 \times 2 \times 2 \times 3} = \frac{5(3 \times 3 \times 5 \times 5)}{2 \times 2 \times 2 \times 2 \times 3 \times 3 \times 3 \times 5 \times 5} = \frac{1125}{10800}$$

$$\frac{4}{135} = \frac{4}{3 \times 3 \times 3 \times 5} = \frac{4(2 \times 2 \times 2 \times 2 \times 5)}{2 \times 2 \times 2 \times 2 \times 3 \times 3 \times 3 \times 5 \times 5} = \frac{320}{10800}$$

Adding the numerators, we get 1769, so the total is $\frac{1769}{10800}$. We now must reduce this, if possible. It's not that bad because the only prime factors of 10,800 are 2, 3 and 5. Clearly 2 and 5 are not factors of 1641, but $1 + 7 + 6 + 9 = 23$, so 1769 is not divisible by 3. So $\frac{1769}{10800}$ is the final answer.

Incidentally, a trick in multiplying these kinds of numbers is to try and multiply by ten. Rearranging the denominator we get $5 \times 2 \times 5 \times 2 \times 3 \times 3 \times 3 \times 2 \times 2$. In your head, you say as you multiply, 10, 100, 300, 900, 2700, 5400, 10800.

## Multiplication of Fractions

To multiply fractions, multiply the numerators and multiply the denominators, reducing as you go. With multiplication, it is *not* necessary to have the same denominators.

$$\frac{3}{7} \times \frac{4}{11} = \frac{12}{77}$$

$$\frac{a}{b} \times \frac{c}{d} = \frac{a \times c}{b \times d}$$

$$\frac{50}{15} \times \frac{27}{8} = \frac{\cancel{50}^{25}}{15} \times \frac{27}{\cancel{8}_4} = \frac{25}{\cancel{15}_5} \times \frac{\cancel{27}^9}{4} = \frac{\cancel{25}^5}{5_1} \times \frac{9}{4} = \frac{5}{1} \times \frac{9}{4} = \frac{45}{4} \text{ or } 11\frac{1}{4}$$

To **invert** a fraction means to turn it upside down. The new fraction is called the **reciprocal** of the original fraction.

The reciprocal of $\frac{2}{3}$ is $\frac{3}{2}$; the reciprocal of $-5$ is $-\frac{1}{5}$; the reciprocal of $a$ is $\frac{1}{a}$ if $a \neq 0$.

## Division of Fractions

To divide fractions, invert the second fraction and multiply, reducing if necessary. For example,

$$\frac{3}{4} \div \frac{11}{5} = \frac{3}{4} \times \frac{5}{11} = \frac{15}{44}$$

$$\frac{m}{n} \div \frac{p}{q} = \frac{m}{n} \times \frac{q}{p} = \frac{m \times q}{n \times p}$$

$$\frac{1}{4} \div 5 = \frac{1}{4} \times \frac{1}{5} = \frac{1}{20}$$

**Example 11:**  <u>Problem</u>                                                     <u>Solution</u>

a. $\dfrac{7}{9} - \dfrac{3}{22} =$ $\qquad$ $\dfrac{127}{198}$

b. $\dfrac{3}{4} + \dfrac{5}{6} - \dfrac{1}{8} =$ $\qquad$ $\dfrac{35}{24}$, or $1\dfrac{11}{24}$

c. $\dfrac{3}{10} + \dfrac{2}{15} - \dfrac{4}{5} =$ $\qquad$ $\dfrac{-11}{30}$

d. $\dfrac{1}{4} + \dfrac{1}{8} + \dfrac{7}{16} =$ $\qquad$ $\dfrac{13}{16}$

e. $2 + \dfrac{2}{3} + \dfrac{2}{9} + \dfrac{2}{27} =$ $\qquad$ $2\dfrac{26}{27}$, or $\dfrac{80}{27}$

f. $\dfrac{5}{24} - \dfrac{7}{18} =$ $\qquad$ $-\dfrac{13}{72}$

g. $\dfrac{10}{99} - \dfrac{9}{100} =$ $\qquad$ $\dfrac{109}{9900}$

h. $\dfrac{5}{36} + \dfrac{5}{27} + \dfrac{7}{24} =$ $\qquad$ $\dfrac{133}{216}$

i. $\dfrac{2}{45} + \dfrac{1}{375} + \dfrac{8}{27} =$ $\qquad$ $\dfrac{1159}{3375}$

j. $\dfrac{3}{10,000} + \dfrac{1}{180} + \dfrac{5}{12} =$ $\qquad$ $\dfrac{38,027}{90,000}$

k. $\dfrac{7}{9} \times \dfrac{5}{3} =$ $\qquad$ $\dfrac{35}{27}$, or $1\dfrac{8}{27}$

l. $\dfrac{11}{12} \div \dfrac{9}{11} =$ $\qquad$ $\dfrac{121}{108}$, or $1\dfrac{13}{108}$

m. $\dfrac{5}{9} \times \dfrac{6}{7} =$ $\qquad$ $\dfrac{10}{21}$

n. $\dfrac{12}{13} \div \dfrac{8}{39} =$ $\qquad$ $\dfrac{9}{2}$, or $4\dfrac{1}{2}$

o. $\dfrac{4}{9} \times \dfrac{63}{122} =$ $\qquad$ $\dfrac{14}{61}$

p. $\dfrac{10}{12} \div \dfrac{15}{40} =$ $\qquad$ $\dfrac{20}{9}$, or $2\dfrac{2}{9}$

q. $\dfrac{100}{350} \times \dfrac{49}{8} =$ $\qquad$ $\dfrac{7}{4}$, or $1\dfrac{3}{4}$

r. $\dfrac{2}{3} \div 12 =$ $\qquad$ $\dfrac{1}{18}$

s. $\dfrac{2}{3} \times \dfrac{3}{4} \times \dfrac{4}{5} \times \dfrac{5}{6} \times \dfrac{6}{7} =$ $\qquad$ $\dfrac{2}{7}$

t. $\dfrac{5}{8} \times \dfrac{7}{6} \div \dfrac{35}{24} =$ $\qquad$ $\dfrac{1}{2}$

Notice all the cancellations in problem s.

## Changing from Decimals to Fractions and Back

To change from a decimal to a fraction, you read it and write it.

**Example 12:**  Change 4.37 to a fraction.

**Solution:**    You read it as 4 and 37 hundredths: $4\dfrac{37}{100} = \dfrac{437}{100}$, if necessary. That's it.

**Example 13:** Change to decimals:

a. $\dfrac{7}{4}$          b. $\dfrac{1}{6}$

**Solution:** For the fractions on the GRE, the decimal will either terminate or repeat.

a. Divide 4 into 7.0000: $7.0000 \div 4 = 1.75$

b. Divide 6 into 1.0000: $1.0000 \div 6 = .1666\ldots = .1\overline{6}$

The bar over the six means it repeats forever; for example, $.3454545\ldots = .3\overline{45}$ means 45 repeats forever, but not the 3.

# PERCENTAGES

% means hundredths: $1\% = \dfrac{1}{100} = .01$.

Follow these rules to change between percentages and decimals and fractions:

*Rule 1:* To change a percentage to a decimal, move the decimal point two places to the left and drop the % sign.

*Rule 2:* To change a decimal to a percentage, move the decimal point two places to the right and add a % sign.

*Rule 3:* To change from a percentage to a fraction, divide by 100% and simplify, or change the % sign to $\dfrac{1}{100}$ and multiply.

*Rule 4:* To change a fraction to a percentage, first change to a decimal, and then to a percentage.

**Example 14:** Change 12%, 4%, and .7% to decimals.

**Solutions:** $12\% = 12.\% = .12$; $4\% = 4.\% = .04$; $.7\% = .007$.

**Example 15:** Change .734, .2, and 34 to percentages.

**Solutions:** $.734 = 73.4\%$; $.2 = 20\%$; $34 = 34. = 3400\%$.

**Example 16:** Change 42% to a fraction.

**Solution:** $42\% = \dfrac{42\%}{100\%} = \dfrac{21}{50}$, or $42\% = 42 \times \dfrac{1}{100} = \dfrac{42}{100} = \dfrac{21}{50}$

**Example 17:** Change $\dfrac{7}{4}$ to a percentage.

**Solution:** $\dfrac{7}{4} = 1.75 = 175\%$

Two hundred years ago, when I was in elementary school, we had to learn the following decimal, fraction, percent equivalents. Since there is no calculator on this test, it may be in your best interest to memorize the following. At worst, it will help you when you go shopping for anything to see if you get the correct discounts.

| Fraction | Decimal | Percentage | Fraction | Decimal | Percentage |
|---|---|---|---|---|---|
| $\frac{1}{10}$ | .1 | 10% | $\frac{5}{8}$ | .625 | $62\frac{1}{2}\%$ |
| $\frac{1}{8}$ | .125 | $12\frac{1}{2}\%$ | $\frac{2}{3}$ | .6666… | $66\frac{2}{3}\%$ |
| $\frac{1}{6}$ | .1666… | $16\frac{2}{3}\%$ | $\frac{7}{10}$ | .7 | 70% |
| $\frac{1}{5}$ | .2 | 20% | $\frac{3}{4}$ | .75 | 75% |
| $\frac{1}{4}$ | .25 | 25% | $\frac{4}{5}$ | .8 | 80% |
| $\frac{3}{10}$ | .3 | 30% | $\frac{5}{6}$ | .8333… | $83\frac{1}{3}\%$ |
| $\frac{1}{3}$ | .3333… | $33\frac{1}{3}\%$ | $\frac{7}{8}$ | .875 | $87\frac{1}{2}\%$ |
| $\frac{3}{8}$ | .375 | $37\frac{1}{2}\%$ | $\frac{9}{10}$ | .9 | 90% |
| $\frac{2}{5}$ | .4 | 40% | 1 | 1.0 | 100% |
| $\frac{1}{2}$ | .5 | 50% | $1\frac{1}{2}$ | 1.5 | 150% |
| $\frac{3}{5}$ | .6 | 60% | 2 | 2.0 | 200% |

If you are good at doing percentage problems, skip this next section. Otherwise, here's a really easy way to do percentage problems. Make the following pyramid:

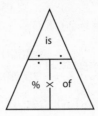

**Example 18:** What is 12% of 1.3?

**Solution:**

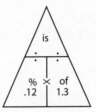

Put .12 in the % box (always change to a decimal in this box) and 1.3 in the "of" box. It tells you to multiply .12 × 1.3 = .156. That's all there is to it.

**Example 19:** 8% of what is 32?

**Solution:**

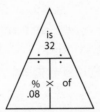

.08 goes in the % box. 32 goes in the "is" box. 32 ÷ .08 = 400.

**Example 20:** 9 is what % of 8?

**Solution:**

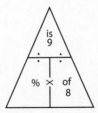

9 goes in the "is" box. 8 goes in the "of" box. 9 ÷ 8 × 100% = 112.5%. The goal is to be able to do percentage problems without using the pyramid.

**Example 21:**  In ten years, the population increases from 20,000 to 23,000. Find the actual increase and the percentage increase.

**Solution:**  The actual increase is 23,000 − 20,000 = 3,000.

The percentage increase is $\dfrac{3000}{20,000} \times 100\% = 15\%$ increase

**Example 22:**  The cost of producing widgets decreased from 60 cents to 50 cents. Find the actual decrease and percentage decrease.

**Solution:**  60 − 50 = 10 cent decrease; $\dfrac{10}{60} = 16\dfrac{2}{3}\%$ decrease.

**Note** *Percentage increases and decreases are figured on the original amount.*

**Example 23:**  The cost of a $2000 large-screen TV set is decreased by 30%. If there is 7% sales tax, how much do you pay?

**Solution:**  $2000 × .30 = $600 discount. $2000 − $600 = $1400 cost.

$1400 × .07 is $98. The total price is $1400 + $98 = $1498.

**Note** *If you took 70% of $2000 (100% − 30%), you would immediately get the cost.*

There is an interesting story about why women wear miniskirts in London, England. It seems that the sales tax is 12½% on clothes! But children's clothes are tax exempt. A girl's dress is any dress where the skirt is less than 24 inches, so that is why women in London wear miniskirts!

**Q  Let's do some exercises.**

**Exercise 8:**  The product of 2 and $\dfrac{1}{89}$ is

A. $2\dfrac{1}{89}$

B. $1\dfrac{88}{89}$

C. 172

D. $\dfrac{2}{89}$

E. $\dfrac{1}{172}$

**Exercise 9:**    $\dfrac{1}{50}$ of 2% of .02 is

    A. .08                D. .000008

    B. .008               E. .00000008

    C. .0008

**Exercise 10:**   30% of 20% of a number is the same as 40% of what percentage of the same number?

    A. 10                D. 18

    B. $12\dfrac{1}{2}$           E. Can't be determined without the number

    C. 15

**Exercise 11:**   A fraction between $\dfrac{3}{43}$ and $\dfrac{4}{43}$ is

    A. $\dfrac{1}{9}$           D. $\dfrac{7}{86}$

    B. $\dfrac{3}{28}$          E. $\dfrac{9}{1849}$

    C. $\dfrac{5}{47}$

**Exercise 12:**   The reciprocal of $2 - \dfrac{3}{4}$ is

    A. $\dfrac{1}{2} - \dfrac{4}{3}$         D. $\dfrac{5}{4}$

    B. $-\dfrac{5}{4}$         E. $\dfrac{4}{5}$

    C. $-\dfrac{4}{5}$

**Exercise 13:**   A price increase of 20% followed by a decrease of 20% means the price is

    A. Up 4%          D. Down 2%

    B. Up 2%          E. Down 4%

    C. The original price

**Exercise 14:**   A price decreases 20% followed by a 20% increase. The final price is

      **A.** Up 4%            **D.** Down 2%

      **B.** Up 2 %           **E.** Down 4%

      **C.** The original price

| | **Column A** | **Column B** |
|---|---|---|
| **Exercise 15:** | The mean of $\frac{1}{4}$ and $\frac{1}{8}$ | $\frac{1}{6}$ |
| **Exercise 16:** | Holiday discount of 50% followed by another 20% discount | 65% discount |
| **Exercise 17:** | $\frac{2}{3}$ of $37\frac{1}{2}$% | $33\frac{1}{3}$% of $\frac{3}{4}$ |
| **Exercise 18:** | A 10% discount followed by a 10% charge to send item | Original price |
| **Exercise 19:** $8 \le x \le 10$, $4 \le y \le 6$ | Largest value of $\frac{x}{y}$ | 2.5 |

**Let's look at the answers.**

**Answer 8:**   $\frac{2}{1} \times \frac{1}{89} = \frac{2}{89}$. The correct answer is (D).

**Answer 9:**   $.02 \times .02 \times .02 = .000008$. The answer is (D).

**Answer 10:**   You can forget the number and forget the percentages. $(30)(20) = (40)(?)$. $? = 15$. The answer is (C).

**Answer 11:**   $\frac{3}{43} = \frac{6}{86}$; $\frac{4}{43} = \frac{8}{86}$; between is $\frac{7}{86}$. The answer is (D). As another example like this one, to get nine fractions between $\frac{3}{43}$ and $\frac{4}{43}$, multiply both fractions, top and bottom, by 10, and the fractions in between would be $\frac{31}{430}, \frac{32}{430}, \frac{33}{430}$, etc.

**Answer 12:**   $2 - \dfrac{3}{4} = \dfrac{5}{4}$. Its reciprocal is $\dfrac{4}{5}$. The answer is (E).

**Answers 13 and 14:**   The answer is (E) for both. Suppose you have \$100. Increased by 20%, you have \$120. But another 20% less (now on a larger amount) is \$24 less. We are at \$96, down 4%. Suppose we take 20% off first. We are at \$80. 20% up (now on a smaller amount) is \$16. We are again at \$96 or again down 4%.

**Answer 15:**   $\dfrac{1}{2}\left(\dfrac{2}{8} + \dfrac{1}{8}\right) = \dfrac{3}{16} > \dfrac{1}{6}$. The answer is (A).

**Answer 16:**   Suppose you spend \$100. 50% discount puts you at \$50. A further discount of 20% (\$10) means you pay \$40, or a 60% discount. The answer is (B). That is why the January sales advertise 50% followed by 20%. It sounds like 70%, but it really is 60%.

**Answer 17:**   $\dfrac{2}{3} \times \dfrac{3}{8} = \dfrac{1}{3} \times \dfrac{3}{4} = \dfrac{1}{4}$. The answer is (C).

**Answer 18:**   This is similar to Example 23. The answer is (B).

**Answer 19:**   The largest value of a fraction occurs when we have the largest top and smallest bottom. It occurs when $x = 10$, and $y = 4$; $\dfrac{10}{4} = 2.5$, and the answer is (C).

Let's do some algebra now. We will see these topics throughout the book.

# CHAPTER 3: *Exponents*

"*The power of exponents will bring you strength and knowledge.*"

**Exponents** are a very popular topic on the GRE. They are a good test of knowledge and thinking, are short to write, and it is relatively easy to make up new problems. Let's review some basic rules of exponents.

| **Rule** | **Examples** |
|---|---|
| 1. $x^m x^n = x^{m+n}$ | $x^6 x^4 x = x^{11}$ and $(x^6 y^7)(x^4 y^{10}) = x^{10} y^{17}$ |
| 2. $\dfrac{x^m}{x^n} = x^{m-n} = \dfrac{1}{x^{n-m}}$ | $\dfrac{x^8}{x^6} = x^2, \dfrac{x^3}{x^7} = \dfrac{1}{x^4},$ and $\dfrac{x^4 y^5 z^9}{x^9 y^2 z^9} = \dfrac{y^3}{x^5}$ |
| 3. $(x^m)^n = x^{mn}$ | $(x^5)^7 = x^{35}$ |
| 4. $(xy)^n = x^n y^n$ | $(xy)^3 = x^3 y^3$ and $(x^7 y^3)^{10} = x^{70} y^{30}$ |
| 5. $\left(\dfrac{x}{y}\right)^n = \dfrac{x^n}{y^n}$ | $\left(\dfrac{x}{y}\right)^6 = \dfrac{x^6}{y^6}$ and $\left(\dfrac{y^4}{z^5}\right)^3 = \dfrac{y^{12}}{z^{15}}$ |

You should also recall the following.

| **Rule** | **Examples** |
|---|---|
| 1. $x^{-n} = \dfrac{1}{x^n}$ and $\dfrac{1}{x^{-m}} = x^m$ | $2^{-3} = \dfrac{1}{2^3} = \dfrac{1}{8}, \ \dfrac{1}{4^{-3}} = 4^3 = 64,$ $\dfrac{x^{-4} y^{-5} z^6}{x^{-6} y^4 z^{-1}} = \dfrac{x^6 z^6 z^1}{x^4 y^4 y^5} = \dfrac{x^2 z^7}{y^9}$ , and $\left(\dfrac{x^3}{y^{-4}}\right)^{-2} = \left(\dfrac{y^{-4}}{x^3}\right)^2 = \dfrac{y^{-8}}{x^6} = \dfrac{1}{x^6 y^8}$ |
| 2. $x^0 = 1, x \neq 0; \ 0^0$ is indeterminate | $(7ab)^0 = 1$ and $7x^0 = 7(1) = 7$ |

Because there are no calculators allowed on the GRE, it might pay to remember the following:

| | | | |
|---|---|---|---|
| $2^3 = 8$ | $2^4 = 16$ | $2^5 = 32$ | $2^6 = 64$ |
| $2^7 = 128$ | $2^8 = 256$ | $2^9 = 512$ | $2^{10} = 1024$ |
| $3^3 = 27$ | $4^3 = 64$ | $5^3 = 125$ | $6^3 = 216$ |

Here are some exponential examples.

**Example 1:**    Simplify the following:

<u>Problem</u>                                                    <u>Solution</u>

**a.** $(-3a^4bc^6)(-5ab^7c^{10})(-100a^{100}b^{200}c^{2000}) =$          $-1500a^{105}b^{208}c^{2016}$

**b.** $(10ab^4c^7)^3 =$          $1000a^3b^{12}c^{21}$

**c.** $(4x^6)^2(10x^3)^3 =$          $16000x^{21}$

**d.** $((2b^4)^3)^2 =$          $64b^{24}$

**e.** $(-b^6)^{101}$          $-b^{606}$

**f.** $(-ab^8)^{202} =$          $+a^{202}b^{1616}$

**g.** $\dfrac{24e^9f^7g^5}{72e^9f^{11}g^7} =$          $\dfrac{1}{3f^4g^2}$

**h.** $\dfrac{(x^4)^3}{x^4} =$          $x^8$

**i.** $\left(\dfrac{m^3n^4}{m^7n}\right)^5 =$          $\dfrac{n^{15}}{m^{20}}$

**j.** $\left(\dfrac{(p^4)^3}{(p^6)^5}\right)^{10} =$          $\dfrac{1}{p^{180}}$

**k.** $(-10a^{-4}b^5c^{-2})(4a^{-7}b^{-1}) =$          $\dfrac{-40b^4}{a^{11}c^2}$

**l.** $(3ab^{-3}c^4)^{-3} =$          $\dfrac{b^9}{27a^3c^{12}}$

**m.** $(3x^4)^{-4}\left(\left(\dfrac{1}{9x^8}\right)^{-1}\right)^2 =$    1

**n.** $(2x^{-4})^2(3x^{-3})^{-2} =$    $\dfrac{4}{9x^2}$

**o.** $\left(\dfrac{(2y^3)^{-2}}{(4x^{-5})}\right)^{-2} =$    $\dfrac{256\,y^{12}}{x^{10}}$

**Also recall the following facts for reciprocals.**

If $0 < x < 1$, then $\dfrac{1}{x} > 1$, and if $x > 1$, then $0 < \dfrac{1}{x} < 1$.

If $-1 < x < 0$, then $\dfrac{1}{x} < -1$, and if $x < -1$, then $-1 < \dfrac{1}{x} < 0$.

**In addition, use these hints for doing comparisons:**

- If there are only numbers in the problem, the answer is never (D) (you can't tell).
- If there are only letters in the problem, the answer is almost always (C) or (D), as we see in Exercise 1.
- If there are only letters, the more specific the value of the letter (such as $1 < x < 3$), the more likely the answer is (A) or (B).
- If there are both letters and numbers in the comparison, the answer could be anything.

**Q** **Let's try some exercises.**

|  |  | **Column A** | **Column B** |
|---|---|---|---|
| **Exercise 1:** |  | $x$ | $x^2$ |
| **Exercise 2:** | $-32 < x < -7$ | $x^2$ | $x^3$ |
| **Exercise 3:** | $-1 < x < 0$ | $\dfrac{-1}{x^3}$ | $\dfrac{-1}{x^4}$ |
| **Exercise 4:** | $a, b \neq 0$ | $(3ab^2)^3$ | $3a^3b^6$ |
| **Exercise 5:** | $x < 0$ | $x$ | $\dfrac{-1}{x^3}$ |

**Exercise 6:**            $3a^2b^6$                    $3(ab^3)^2$

**Exercise 7:**            $3^{-2}$                     $\dfrac{-1}{9}$

**Exercise 8:**   $x^2 = y^2$        $x^2$              $xy$

**Exercise 9:**   $0 < x < 1$: Arrange in order of smallest to largest: $x, x^2, x^3$.

    **A.** $x < x^2 < x^3$        **D.** $x^3 < x^2 < x$

    **B.** $x < x^3 < x^2$        **E.** $x^3 < x < x^2$

    **C.** $x^2 < x < x^3$

**Exercise 10:**   $-1 < x < 0$: Arrange in order largest to smallest: $x^2, x^3, x^4$

    **A.** $x^4 > x^3 > x^2$        **D.** $x^2 > x^3 > x^4$

    **B.** $x^4 > x^2 > x^3$        **E.** $x^2 > x^4 > x^3$

    **C.** $x^3 > x^4 > x^2$

**Exercise 11:**   $0 < x < 1$.

    **I:** $x > \dfrac{1}{x^2}$

    **II:** $\dfrac{1}{x^2} > \dfrac{1}{x^4}$

    **III:** $x - 1 > \dfrac{1}{x - 1}$

    Which statement(s) are always true?

    **A.** None        **D.** Statement III

    **B.** Statement I        **E.** All

    **C.** Statement II

**Exercise 12:**   $(5ab^3)^3$

    **A.** $15ab^6$        **D.** $125a^3b^6$

    **B.** $75ab + 6$        **E.** $125a^3b^9$

    **C.** $125ab^9$

**Exercise 13:** $\dfrac{(2x^5)^3(3x^{10})^2}{6x^{15}}$

    **A.** 1

    **B.** $x^{20}$

    **C.** $2x^{20}$

    **D.** $12x^{20}$

    **E.** $12x^{210}$

**Exercise 14:** $\left(\dfrac{12x^6}{24x^9}\right)^3$

    **A.** $1728x^{27}$

    **B.** $\dfrac{1}{1728x^{27}}$

    **C.** $\dfrac{1}{6x^9}$

    **D.** $\dfrac{1}{8x^9}$

    **E.** $\dfrac{1}{8x^{27}}$

**Exercise 15:** $\dfrac{(4x^4)^3}{(8x^6)^2}$

    **A.** $\dfrac{1}{2}$

    **B.** 1

    **C.** $\dfrac{1}{2}x^{28}$

    **D.** $x^{28}$

    **E.** $\dfrac{1}{2x}$

**Exercise 16:** $-1 \le x \le 5$. Where is $x^2$ located?

    **A.** $-1 \le x^2 \le 5$

    **B.** $0 \le x^2 \le 25$

    **C.** $1 \le x^2 \le 5$

    **D.** $1 \le x^2 \le 10$

    **E.** $1 \le x^2 \le 25$

**Exercise 17:** $2^m + 2^m =$

    **A.** $2^{m+1}$

    **B.** $2^{m+2}$

    **C.** $2^{m+4}$

    **D.** $2^{m^2}$

    **E.** $4^m$

**Exercise 18:**  $\dfrac{m^{-5}n^6p^{-2}}{m^{-3}n^9p^0} =$

A.  $m^2n^3p^2$

D.  $\dfrac{1}{m^2n^3p^2}$

B.  $\dfrac{1}{m^2n^3}$

E.  None of these

C.  $\dfrac{m^2}{n^3p^2}$

**Exercise 19:**  If $8^{2n+1} = 2^{n+18}$; $n =$

A.  3

D.  13

B.  7

E.  17

C.  10

**Exercise 20:**  $p = 4^n$; $4p =$

A.  $4^{n+1}$

D.  $16^p$

B.  $4^{n+2}$

E.  $64^p$

C.  $3^{n+4}$

Ⓐ  **Let's look at the answers.**

**Answer 1:**  The answer is (D); you can't tell. It is essential that you know why:

If $x > 1$, then $x^2 > x$, since $4^2 > 4$.

If $x = 1$, then $x^2 = x$, since $1^2 = 1$.

If $0 < x < 1$, then $x > x^2$, since $\dfrac{1}{2} > \left(\dfrac{1}{2}\right)^2 = \dfrac{1}{4}$ !!

If $x = 0$, then $x = x^2$, since $0 = 0^2$.

If $x < 0$, then $x^2 > x$, since the square of a negative number is a positive number.

**Answer 2:**  The answer is (A). (A) is always positive, and (B) is always negative.

**Answer 3:**  The answer is (A). This exercise is similar to answer 2.

**Answer 4:**    The answer is (D). (A) multiplied out is $27a^3b^6$. Say $a = 2$; then (A) is definitely bigger than (B). But if $a = -3$, (A) is negative and (B) is positive.

**Answer 5:**    The answer if (B) since (B) $> 0$ and (A) $< 0$.

**Answer 6:**    The answer is (C). They are equal.

**Answer 7:**    The answer is (A). $3^{-2} = \dfrac{1}{9}$; a negative exponent means reciprocal, not necessarily less than 0.

**Answer 8:**    The answer is (D); you can't tell. It depends on whether $y$ is positive or negative.

**Answer 9:**    The answer is (D). If $0 < x < 1$, the higher the power, the smaller the number.

**Answer 10:**    Take, for example, $x = -\dfrac{1}{2}$. $\left(-\dfrac{1}{2}\right)^2 = \dfrac{1}{4}$; $\left(-\dfrac{1}{2}\right)^3 = -\dfrac{1}{8}$; $\left(-\dfrac{1}{2}\right)^4 = \dfrac{1}{16}$.

Be careful! This exercise asks for largest to smallest. The answer is (E). Notice that $x^3$ has to be the smallest because it is the only negative number, so the answer choices were reduced to two, (B) and (E).

**Answer 11:**    **Statement I:** $0 < x < 1$; so $\dfrac{1}{x} > 1$ and $\dfrac{1}{x^2} > 1$ also. Let $x = \dfrac{1}{2}$; then $\dfrac{1}{x^2} = \dfrac{1}{\frac{1}{4}} = 4$. Statement I is false.

     **Statement II:** $x^2 > x^4$; so $\dfrac{1}{x^2} < \dfrac{1}{x^4}$. Statement II is false.

     **Statement III:** $0 < x < 1$; so $-1 < x - 1 < 0$; this means $\dfrac{1}{x-1} < -1$. Statement III is true.

     The answer is (D).

**Answer 12:**    $5^3a^3(b^3)^3 = 125a^3b^9$. The answer is (E).

**Answer 13:**    $\left(\dfrac{8 \times 9}{6}\right)x^{15+20-15} = 12x^{20}$. The answer is (D).

**Answer 14:**   $\left(\dfrac{1}{2x^3}\right)^3 = \dfrac{1}{8x^9}.$ The answer is (D).

**Answer 15:**   The numerator and denominator of the fraction each equal $64x^{12}$. The answer is (B).

**Answer 16:**   This is very tricky. Since 0 is between $-1$ and 5, and $0^2 = 0$, the answer is (B).

**Answer 17:**   This is one of the few truly hard problems because it is an addition problem.

$2^m + 2^m = (1)(2^m) + (1)(2^m) = (2)(2^m) = 2^1 2^m = 2^{m+1}.$ The answer is (A)!

Similarly, $3^m + 3^m + 3^m = 3^{m+1}$ and four $4^m$ terms added equal $4^{m+1}$.

**Answer 18:**   $\dfrac{m^{-5}n^6 p^{-2}}{m^{-3}n^9 p^0} = \dfrac{m^3 n^6}{m^5 n^9 p^2} = \dfrac{1}{m^2 n^3 p^2}.$ The answer is (D).

**Answer 19:**   $8^{2n+1} = (2^3)^{2n+1} = 2^{n+18}$. By the property of $1-1$ (if you care), if the bases are equal, the exponents must be equal. $3(2n+1) = n + 18; n = 3$. The answer is (A).

**Answer 20:**   $p = 4^n$; $4p = 4(4^n) = 4^1 4^n = 4^{n+1}$. The answer is (A).

Now let's go to a radical chapter.

*"We must go to the root of the problem to be enlightened."*

**The** square root symbol ($\sqrt{\phantom{x}}$) is probably the one symbol most people actually like, even for people who don't like math. How else can you explain the square root symbol on a business calculator? I have yet to find a use for it. Here are some basic facts about square roots that you should know.

1. You should know the following square roots:

   $\sqrt{0} = 0$      $\sqrt{1}=1$      $\sqrt{4}=2$      $\sqrt{9}=3$      $\sqrt{16}=4$      $\sqrt{25}=5$

   $\sqrt{36}=6$      $\sqrt{49}=7$      $\sqrt{64}=8$      $\sqrt{81}=9$      $\sqrt{100}=10$

   The numbers under the radicals (square root signs) are called perfect squares because their square roots are whole numbers.

2. $\sqrt{2} \approx 1.4$ (actually it is 1.414...), and $\sqrt{3} \approx 1.73$ (actually it is 1.732..., the year George Washington was born).

3. $\sqrt{\dfrac{a}{b}}=\dfrac{\sqrt{a}}{\sqrt{b}}$, so    $\sqrt{\dfrac{25}{9}}=\dfrac{5}{3}$      $\sqrt{\dfrac{7}{36}}=\dfrac{\sqrt{7}}{6}$      $\sqrt{\dfrac{45}{20}}=\sqrt{\dfrac{9}{4}}=\dfrac{3}{2}$

4. A method of simplification involves finding all the prime factors:
   $\sqrt{200}=\sqrt{(2)(2)(2)(5)(5)}=(2)(5)\sqrt{2}=10\sqrt{2}$

5. Adding and subtracting radicals involves combining like radicals:
   $4\sqrt{7}+5\sqrt{11}+6\sqrt{7}-9\sqrt{11}=10\sqrt{7}-4\sqrt{11}$

6. Multiplication of radicals follows this rule:
   $a\sqrt{b}\times c\sqrt{d}=ac\sqrt{bd}$
   Therefore, $3\sqrt{13} \times 10\sqrt{7}=30\sqrt{91}$ and

   $10\sqrt{8}\times3\sqrt{10}=10\times3\sqrt{2\times2\times2\times2\times5}=10\times3\times2\times2\sqrt{5}=120\sqrt{5}$

7.  If a radical appears in the denominator of a fraction, rationalize the denominator by multiplying both numerator and denominator by the radical:

$$\frac{20}{7\sqrt{5}} = \frac{20}{7\sqrt{5}} \times \frac{\sqrt{5}}{\sqrt{5}} = \frac{20\sqrt{5}}{35} = \frac{4\sqrt{5}}{7} \text{ and } \frac{7}{\sqrt{45}} = \frac{7}{3\sqrt{5}} \times \frac{\sqrt{5}}{\sqrt{5}} = \frac{7\sqrt{5}}{15}$$

8.  If $c, d > 0$, $\sqrt{c} + \sqrt{d} > \sqrt{c+d}$. Why? If you square the right side, you get $c + d$. If you square the left side you get $c + d +$ the middle term $(2\sqrt{cd})$.

9.  The square root varies according to the value of the radicand:

    If $a > 1$, $a > \sqrt{a}$. For example, $9 > \sqrt{9}$.

    If $a = 1$, $a = \sqrt{a}$ since the square root of 1 is 1.

    If $0 < a < 1$, $a < \sqrt{a}$. When you take the square root of a positive number, it becomes closer to 1. So $\sqrt{\frac{1}{4}} = \frac{1}{2} > \frac{1}{4}$.

    If $a = 0$, $a = \sqrt{a}$ since the square root of 0 is 0.

    If $a > 0$ and $\sqrt{a} < 1$, then $\frac{1}{\sqrt{a}} > 1$. Also, if $\sqrt{a} > 1$, then $\frac{1}{\sqrt{a}} < 1$.

10. The square root of a negative number is imaginary. So far, the GRE does not bother with imaginary numbers.

**Note**  $\sqrt{9} = 3$, $-\sqrt{9} = -3$, but $\sqrt{-9}$ is imaginary. The equation $x^2 = 9$ has two solutions, $\pm\sqrt{9}$, or $\pm 3$, which stands for both $+3$ and $-3$.

The GRE often uses square roots in comparison problems.

**Q  Let's try some exercises.**

**Exercise 1:**  $\left(\sqrt{12} + \sqrt{27}\right)^2 =$

A. 15          D. 225

B. 39          E. 675

C. 75

**Exercise 2:**    Suppose $0 < a < 1$.

I:      $a^2 > \sqrt{a}$

II:     $\sqrt{a} > \sqrt{a^3}$

III:    $\sqrt{a} > \dfrac{1}{\sqrt{a^7}}$

**A.** Statement I is correct        **D.** Statements I and III are correct

**B.** Statement II is correct       **E.** Statements II and III are correct

**C.** Statement III is correct

|  | **Column A** | **Column B** |
|---|---|---|
| **Exercise 3:** | $\dfrac{1}{\sqrt{c}}$ | $\dfrac{\sqrt{c}}{c}$ |
| **Exercise 4:** $c > 0$ | $\sqrt{c+2}$ | $\sqrt{c+4}$ |
| **Exercise 5:** $c > 0$ | $\sqrt{c}$ | $\dfrac{1}{\sqrt{c}}$ |
| **Exercise 6:** $0 < d < 1$ | $\sqrt{d}+1$ | $\dfrac{1}{\sqrt{d}+1}$ |

**Exercise 7:**    $c = \left(\dfrac{1}{17}\right)^2 - \sqrt{\dfrac{1}{17}}$. Which answer choice is true for $c$?

**A.** $c < -2$              **D.** $0 < c < 1$

**B.** $-2 < c < -1$        **E.** $1 < c < 2$

**C.** $-1 < c < 0$

**Exercise 8:**    $0 < m < 1$. Arrange in order, smallest to largest, $a = \dfrac{1}{m}, b = \dfrac{1}{m^2}, c = \dfrac{1}{\sqrt{m}}$.

**A.** $a < b < c$          **D.** $b < a < c$

**B.** $a < c < b$          **E.** $c < a < b$

**C.** $b < c < a$

**Let's look at the answers.**

**Answer 1:**    $\sqrt{12}=\sqrt{2\times2\times3}=2\sqrt{3}$ and $\sqrt{27}=\sqrt{3\times3\times3}=3\sqrt{3}$. Adding, we get $5\sqrt{3}$. Squaring, we get $25\sqrt{9}=25\times3=75$. The answer is (C).

**Answer 2:**    Let's look at the statements one by one.

     **Statement I:** If you square a number between 0 and 1, you make it closer to 0. If you take the square root of the same number, you make it closer to 1. Statement I is wrong.

     **Statement II:** From the previous chapter, if $0<a<1$, $a>a^3$. So are its square roots. So statement II is true.

     **Statement III:** $\sqrt{a}<1$. $a^7<1$. So $\sqrt{a^7}<1$. Then $\dfrac{1}{\sqrt{a^7}}>1$. Statement III is false.

     The answer to the question is (B).

**Answer 3:**    The answer is (C). Column B is just column A rationalized.

**Answer 4:**    The answer is (A). Since $\sqrt{4}=2$, and $c>0$, we know $\sqrt{x}+\sqrt{y}>\sqrt{x+y}$, or $\sqrt{c}+\sqrt{4}>\sqrt{c+4}$.

**Answer 5:**    The answer is (D) since we don't know if $c<1$, $c=1$, or $c>1$, and the answer is different for each case.

**Answer 6:**    $\sqrt{d}+1>1$; so $\dfrac{1}{\sqrt{d}+1}<1$. The answer is (A).

**Answer 7:**    $\dfrac{1}{17}$ squared is less than $\dfrac{1}{17}$, the square root is more than $\dfrac{1}{17}$, and both numbers are between 0 and 1. Subtracting the larger from the smaller, the answer must be (C).

**Answer 8:**    If we take $m=\dfrac{1}{4}$, we see that $\sqrt{m}>m>m^2$. That makes $\dfrac{1}{\sqrt{m}}<\dfrac{1}{m}<\dfrac{1}{m^2}$, or $c<a<b$. The answer is (E).

Notice that with these exercises, just knowing the properties of square roots will help you avoid much and sometimes all of the arithmetic.

# CHAPTER 5:  *Algebraic Manipulations*

"*Along our journey, we must learn to do.
It will help us to become truly happy.*"

**Algebraic** manipulative skills such as those in this chapter are areas that high school courses have tended to de-emphasize since 1985. It is necessary to show you how to do these problems and give you extra problems to practice. Of course, included will be the kind of questions the GRE asks.

## COMBINING LIKE TERMS

**Like terms** are terms with the same letter combination (or no letter). The same letter must also have the same exponents.

> **Example 1:**   Are the following terms like or unlike?
>
> > **a.** $4x$ and $-5x$
> >
> > **b.** $4x$ and $4x^2$
> >
> > **c.** $xy^2$ and $x^2y$
>
> **Solutions:**
>
> > **a.** $4x$ and $-5x$ are like terms even though their numerical coefficients are different.
> >
> > **b.** $4x$ and $4x^2$ are unlike terms.
> >
> > **c.** $xy^2$ and $x^2y$ are unlike; $xy^2 = xyy$ and $x^2y = xxy$.

**Combining like terms** means adding or subtracting their numerical coefficients; exponents are unchanged. Unlike terms cannot be combined.

**Example 2:**   Simplify:

Problem                                          Solution

**a.** $3m + 4m + m =$                            $8m$

**b.** $8m + 2n + 7m - 7n =$                      $15m - 5n$

**c.** $3x^2 + 4x - 5 - 7x^2 - 4x + 8 =$          $-4x^2 + 3$

## DISTRIBUTIVE LAW

The **Distributive Law** states:

$$a(x + y) = ax + ay$$

**Example 3:**   Perform the indicated operations:

Problem                                          Solution

**a.** $4(3x - 7) =$                              $12x - 28$

**b.** $5(2a - 5b + 3c) =$                        $10a - 25b + 15c$

**c.** $3x^4(7x^3 - 4x - 1) =$                    $21x^7 - 12x^5 - 3x^4$

**d.** $4(3x - 7) - 5(4x - 2) =$                  $12x - 28 - 20x + 10 = -8x - 18$

## BINOMIAL PRODUCTS

A **binomial** is a two-term expression, such as $x + 2$. We use the **FOIL method** to multiply a binomial by a binomial. FOIL is an acronym for First, Outer, Inner, Last. This means to multiply the first two terms, then the outer terms, then the inner terms, and finally the last two terms.

**Example 4:**   Multiply $(x + 4)(x + 6)$

**Solution:**

Multiplying, we get $x^2 + 6x + 4x + 24 = x^2 + 10x + 24$.

**Example 5:**   Perform the indicated multiplications:

Problem | Solution
--- | ---
**a.** $(x + 7)(x + 4) =$ | $x^2 + 4x + 7x + 28 = x^2 + 11x + 28$
**b.** $(x - 5)(x - 2) =$ | $x^2 - 7x + 10$
**c.** $(x + 6)(x - 3) =$ | $x^2 + 3x - 18$
**d.** $(x + 6)(x - 8) =$ | $x^2 - 2x - 48$
**e.** $(x + 5)(x - 5) =$ | $x^2 - 5x + 5x - 25 = x^2 - 25$
**f.** $(x + 5)^2 =$ | $(x + 5)(x + 5) = x^2 + 10x + 25$
**g.** $(x - 10)^2 =$ | $x^2 - 20x + 100$
**h.** $(2x + 5)(3x - 10) =$ | $6x^2 - 5x - 50$
**i.** $3(x + 4)(x + 5) =$ | $3(x^2 + 9x + 20) = 3x^2 + 27x + 60$
**j.** $7(4x + 3)(4x - 3) =$ | $7(16x^2 - 9) = 112x^2 - 63$

You should know the following common binomial products:

$$(a + b)(a - b) = a^2 - b^2$$

$$(a - b)(a - b) = a^2 - 2ab + b^2$$

$$(a + b)(a + b) = a^2 + 2ab + b^2$$

**Note** *For a perfect square $(a + b)^2$, the first term of the resulting trinomial is the first term squared ($a^2$), and the third term of the resulting trinomial is the last term squared ($b^2$). The middle term is twice the product of the two terms of the binomial (2ab), so*

$$(a + b)^2 = a^2 + 2ab + b^2$$

**Example 6:**    Perform the indicated multiplications:

<u>Problem</u>                                   <u>Solution</u>

**a.** $(a + 4)(a + 7)$                         $a^2 + 11a + 28$

**b.** $(b + 5)(b + 6)$                         $b^2 + 11b + 30$

**c.** $(c + 1)(c + 9)$                         $c^2 + 10c + 9$

**d.** $(d + 4)(d + 8)$                         $d^2 + 12d + 32$

**e.** $(e + 11)(e + 10)$                       $e^2 + 21e + 110$

**f.** $(f - 6)(f - 2)$                         $f^2 - 8f + 12$

**g.** $(g - 10)(g - 20)$                       $g^2 - 30g + 200$

**h.** $(h - 4)(h - 3)$                         $h^2 - 7h + 12$

**i.** $(i - 1)(i - 7)$                         $i^2 - 8i + 7$

**j.** $(j - 3)(j - 5)$                         $j^2 - 8j + 15$

**k.** $(k + 5)(k - 2)$                         $k^2 + 3k - 10$

**l.** $(m + 5)(m - 8)$                         $m^2 - 3m - 40$

**m.** $(n - 6)(n + 2)$                         $n^2 - 4n - 12$

**n.** $(p - 8)(p + 10)$                        $p^2 + 2p - 80$

**o.** $(q - 5r)(q + 2r)$                       $q^2 - 3qr - 10r^2$

**p.** $(s + 3)^2$                              $s^2 + 6s + 9$

**q.** $(t - 4)^2$                              $t^2 - 8t + 16$

**r.** $(3u + 5)^2$                             $9u^2 + 30u + 25$

**s.** $(5v - 4)^2$                             $25v^2 - 40v + 16$

**t.** $(ax + by)^2$           $a^2x^2 + 2abxy + b^2y^2$

**u.** $(be - ma)^2$         $b^2e^2 - 2\,beam + m^2a^2$

**v.** $(w + x)\,(w - x)$      $w^2 - x^2$

**w.** $(a - 11)\,(a + 11)$     $a^2 - 121$

**x.** $(am - 7)\,(am + 7)$    $a^2m^2 - 49$

**y.** $(a^2b + c)\,(a^2b - c)$    $a^4b^2 - c^2$

**z.** $3(x + 5)\,(x - 2)$      $3x^2 + 9x - 30$

**aa.** $-4(2x - 5)\,(3x - 4)$    $-24x^2 + 92x - 80$

**bb.** $x(2x - 5)\,(4x + 7)$    $8x^3 - 6x^2 - 35x$

**cc.** $5(x - 5)\,(x + 5)$     $5x^2 - 125$

 **Let's do some exercises.**

| | **Column A** | **Column B** |
|---|---|---|
| **Exercise 1:** | $6(2x + 2)$ | $2(6x + 6)$ |
| **Exercise 2:** | $x(2x + 3)$ | $2(x^2 + 2x)$ |
| **Exercise 3:** $x^2 + y^2 = 20, xy = -6$ | $(x + y)^2$ | 10 |
| **Exercise 4:** | $(x + y)^2$ | $(x - y)^2 + 4xy$ |

**Exercise 5:**    $x^2 - y^2 = 24.\ 3(x + y)\,(x - y) =$

A. 8           D. 72

B. 24         E. 13,824

C. 27

**Exercise 6:**   $x + y = m; x - y = \dfrac{1}{m}; x^2 - y^2 =$

   A. $m^2$                    D. $\dfrac{1}{m}$

   B. $m$                      E. $\dfrac{1}{m^2}$

   C. 1

**Exercise 7:**   $\left(x + \dfrac{1}{x}\right)^2 = 64; x^2 + \dfrac{1}{x^2} =$

   A. 9                        D. 65

   B. 62                       E. 66

   C. 64

 **Let's look at the answers.**

**Answer 1:**   They both equal $12x + 12$. The answer is (C).

**Answer 2:**   The answer depends on whether $x$ is negative, zero, or positive, or whether $3x > 4x$, $3x = 4x$, or $3x < 4x$. Since we don't have a value for $x$, the answer is (D).

**Answer 3:**   $(x + y)^2 =$ (rearranging the terms) $x^2 + y^2 + 2xy = 20 + 2(-6) = 8$, and $8 < 10$. The answer is (B).

**Answer 4:**   They both equal $x^2 + 2xy + y^2$. The answer is (C).

**Answer 5:**   $3(x + y)(x - y) = 3(x^2 - y^2) = 3(24) = 72$. The answer is (D).

**Answer 6:**   $(x + y)(x - y) = x^2 - y^2 = \dfrac{m}{1} \times \dfrac{1}{m} = 1$. The answer is (C).

**Answer 7:**   $\left(x + \dfrac{1}{x}\right)\left(x + \dfrac{1}{x}\right) = x^2 + 2(x)\left(\dfrac{1}{x}\right) + \dfrac{1}{x^2} = x^2 + \dfrac{1}{x^2} + 2 = 64.$

   So $x^2 + \dfrac{1}{x^2} = 64 - 2 = 62$. The answer is (B).

Let's go on to factoring.

# FACTORING

**Factoring** is the reverse of the distributive law. There are three types of factoring you need to know: largest common factor, difference of two squares, and trinomial factorization.

If the distributive law says $x(y + z) = xy + xz$, then taking out the largest common factor says $xy + xy = x(y + z)$. Let's demonstrate a few factoring examples.

**Example 7:**    Factor:

| Problem | Answer | Explanation |
|---|---|---|
| **a.** $4x + 6y - 8$ | $2(2x + 3y - 4)$ | 2 is the largest common factor. |
| **b.** $8ax + 12ay - 40az$ | $4a(2x + 3y - 10z)$ | 4 is the largest common factor; $a$ is also a common factor. |
| **c.** $10a^4y^6z^3 - 15a^7y$ | $5a^4y(2y^5z^3 - 3a^3)$ | The largest common factor and the lowest power of each common variable is factored out. $a^4$ and $y$; but not $z$ because it is not in both terms. |
| **d.** $x^4y - xy^3 + xy$ | $xy(x^3 - y^2 + 1)$ | Factor out the lowest power of each common variable. Three terms in the original give three terms in parentheses. Note that $1 \times xy = xy$. |
| **e.** $9by + 12be + 4ye$ | prime | Some expressions cannot be factored. |

## Difference of Two Squares

Since $(a + b)(a - b) = a^2 - b^2$, factoring tells us that $a^2 - b^2 = (a + b)(a - b)$.

**Example 8:**

| Problem | Answer | Explanation |
|---|---|---|
| **a.** $x^2 - 25$ | $(x + 5)(x - 5)$ or $(x - 5)(x + 5)$ | Either order is OK. |
| **b.** $x^2 - 121$ | $(x + 11)(x - 11)$ | |
| **c.** $9a^2 - 25b^2$ | $(3a + 5b)(3a - 5b)$ | |

**d.** $5a^3 - 20a$        $5a(a^2 - 4) = 5a(a + 2)(a - 2)$        Factor out largest common factor first, then use the difference of two squares.

**e.** $x^4 - y^4$        $(x^2 + y^2)(x^2 - y^2) =$        This is the difference of two squares where the square roots in the factors are also squares. Sum of two squares doesn't factor, but use the difference of two squares again.

$(x^2 + y^2)(x + y)(x - y)$

**Example 9:**    Factor completely:

<u>Problem</u>                                <u>Solution</u>

**a.** $12am + 18an$                    $6a(2m + 3n)$

**b.** $6at - 18st + 4as$              $2(3at - 9st + 2as)$

**c.** $10ax + 15ae - 16ex$          Prime

**d.** $18a^5c^6 - 27a^3c^8$          $9a^3c^6(2a^2 - 3c^2)$

**e.** $25a^4b^7c^9 - 75a^8b^9c^{10}$    $25a^4b^7c^9(1 - 3a^4b^2c)$

**f.** $a^4b^5 + a^7b - ab$            $ab(a^3b^4 + a^6 - 1)$

**g.** $9 - x^2$                        $(3 + x)(3 - x)$

**h.** $x^4 - 36y^2$                    $(x^2 + 6y)(x^2 - 6y)$

**i.** $2x^3 - 98x$                    $2x(x + 7)(x - 7)$

**j.** $a^4 - 81b^2$                    $(a^2 + 9b)(a^2 - 9b)$

**k.** $x^2 - 49y^6$                    $(x + 7y^3)(x - 7y^3)$

**l.** $5z^2 - 25$                      $5(z^2 - 5)$

**m.** $a^4 - c^8$                      $(a^2 + c^4)(a + c^2)(a - c^2)$

**n.** $2a^9 - 32a$                    $2a(a^4 + 4)(a^2 - 2)(a^2 + 2)$

**Let's do some exercises.**

**Exercise 8:**    $8x + 6y = 30$. Then $20x + 15y =$

A. 15                    D. 75

B. 30                    E. 150

C. 60

**Exercise 9:**    $x^2 - 4 = 47 \times 43$; $x =$

A. 41                    D. 47

B. 43                    E. 49

C. 45

 **Let's look at the answers.**

**Answer 8:**    $8x + 6y = 2(4x + 3y) = 30$; so $4x + 3y = 15$. $20x + 15y = 5(4x + 3y)$
= $5 \times 15 = 75$. The answer is (D).

**Answer 9:**    $x^2 - 4 = (x + 2)(x - 2) = 47 \times 43$, or $(45 + 2)(45 - 2)$. So $x = 45$. The
answer is (C).

Later in this chapter and in later chapters, we will see more GRE comparison questions. For
now, let's do trinomial factoring.

## Factoring Trinomials

Factoring trinomials is a puzzle, a game, which is rarely done well in high school and even
more rarely practiced. Let's learn the factoring game.

First, let's rewrite the first four problems and solutions found in Example 5 (see page 45)
backward and look at them.

A. $x^2 + 11x + 28 = (x + 7)(x + 4)$

B. $x^2 - 7x + 10 = (x - 5)(x - 2)$

C. $x^2 + 3x - 18 = (x + 6)(x - 3)$

D. $x^2 - 2x - 48 = (x + 6)(x - 8)$

Each term starts with $x^2(= +1x^2)$, so the first sign is $+$. We'll call the sign in front of the $x$ term
the middle sign, and we'll call the sign in front of the number term the last sign.

Let's look at **A** and **B** above to state some rules of the game:

1.  If the last sign (in the trinomial) is +, then both signs (in the parentheses) must be the same. The reason? $(+) \times (+) = +$, and $(-) \times (-) = +$.

2.  Only if the last sign is +, look at the sign of the middle term. If it is +, both factors have a + sign (as in A); if it is −, both factors have a − sign (as in B).

3.  If the last sign is −, the signs in the two factors must be different.

Now, let's play the game:

**Example 10:** Factor: $x^2 - 16x + 15$.

**Solution:**

1.  The last sign + means both signs are the same. The middle sign − means both are −.

2.  The only factors of $x^2$ are $(x)(x)$. Look at the number term 15. The factors of 15 are (3)(5) and (1)(15). So $(x - 5)(x - 3)$ and $(x - 15)(x - 1)$ are the only possibilities. We have chosen the first and last terms to be correct, so we only do the middle term. The first, $-8x$, is wrong; the second, $-16x$, is correct.

3.  The answer is $(x - 15)(x - 1)$. If neither worked, the trinomial couldn't be factored.

**Example 11:** Factor completely: $x^2 - 4x - 21$.

**Solution:**

1.  Last sign negative means the signs are different in the factors.

2.  $x^2 = x(x)$ and the factors of 21 are 7 and 3, or 1 and 21. We want the pair that totals the middle number; so 7 and 3 are correct; 7 gets the minus sign!

3.  The answer is $(x - 7)(x + 3)$.

**Note** *If you multiply the inner and outer terms and get the right number but the wrong sign, both signs in the parentheses must be changed.*

The game gets more complicated if the coefficient of $x^2$ is not 1.

**Example 12:** Factor completely: $4x^2 + 4x - 15$.

**Solution:**

1. Last sign is $-$, so the signs of the factors must be different.

2. The factors of $4x^2$ are $(4x)(x)$ or $(2x)(2x)$.

3. The factors of 15 are 3 and 5 or 1 and 15. Let's write out all the possibilities and the resulting middle terms. We are looking for terms whose difference is $4x$.

   $(4x \quad 3) (x \quad 5)$: middle terms are $3x$ and $20x$, no way to get $4x$.

   $(4x \quad 5) (x \quad 3)$: middle terms are $5x$ and $12x$, and again, there is no way again to get $4x$.

   $(4x \quad 15) (x \quad 1)$: middle terms $15x$ and $4x$, wrong!

   $(4x \quad 1) (x \quad 15)$: middle terms $1x$ and $60x$, the next county.

   $(2x \quad 1) (2x \quad 15)$: middle terms $2x$ and $30x$, wrong again!

   $(2x \quad 3) (2x \quad 5)$: middle terms $6x$ and $10x$, correct, whew!

4. The minus sign goes in front of the 3 and the plus sign goes in front of the 5. The answer is $(2x - 3)(2x + 5)$.

**Example 13:** Factor completely: $3x^2 + 15x + 12$

**Solution:** Take out the common factor first.

$3x^2 + 15x + 12 = 3(x^2 + 5x + 4) = 3(x + 4)(x + 1)$.

**Example 14:** Factor completely; coefficients may be integers only.

| Problem | Solution |
|---|---|
| a. $x^2 + 11x + 24$ | $(x + 3) (x + 8)$ |
| b. $x^2 - 11x - 12$ | $(x - 12) (x + 1)$ |
| c. $x^2 + 5x - 6$ | $(x + 6) (x - 1)$ |
| d. $x^2 - 20x + 100$ | $(x - 10)^2$ |
| e. $x^2 - x - 2$ | $(x - 2) (x + 1)$ |

f. $x^2 - 15x + 56$                    $(x - 7)(x - 8)$

g. $x^2 + 8x + 16$                    $(x + 4)^2$

h. $x^2 - 6x - 16$                    $(x - 8)(x + 2)$

i. $x^2 - 17x + 42$                    $(x - 14)(x - 3)$

j. $x^2 + 5xy + 6y^2$                    $(x + 2y)(x + 3y)$

k. $3x^2 - 6x - 9$                    $3(x - 3)(x + 1)$

l. $4x^2 + 16x - 20$                    $4(x + 5)(x - 1)$

m. $x^3 - 12x^2 + 35x$                    $x(x - 7)(x - 5)$

n. $2x^8 + 8x^7 + 6x^6$                    $2x^6(x + 3)(x + 1)$

o. $x^4 - 10x^2 + 9$                    $(x + 3)(x - 3)(x + 1)(x - 1)$

p. $x^4 - 8x^2 - 9$                    $(x^2 + 1)(x + 3)(x - 3)$

q. $2x^2 - 5x + 3$                    $(2x - 3)(x - 1)$

r. $2x^2 + 5x - 3$                    $(2x - 1)(x + 3)$

s. $5x^2 - 11x + 2$                    $(5x - 1)(x - 2)$

t. $9x^2 + 21x - 8$                    $(3x + 8)(3x - 1)$

u. $3x^2 - 8x - 3$                    $(3x + 1)(x - 3)$

v. $6x^2 - 13x + 6$                    $(3x - 2)(2x - 3)$

w. $6x^2 + 35x - 6$                    $(6x - 1)(x + 6)$

x. $9x^2 + 71x - 8$                    $(9x - 1)(x + 8)$

y. $9x^4 + 24x^3 + 12x^2$                    $3x^2(3x + 2)(x + 2)$

**Let's do a couple of exercises.**

**Exercise 10:** $x^2 + 5x + 4 = 27$; $3(x + 1)(x + 4) =$

    A. 9      D. 81

    B. 24      E. 243

    C. 30

|  | Column A | Column B |
|---|---|---|
| **Exercise 11:** $x^2 + 11x + 24 = 0$ | $x^2 + 11x$ | 24 |

 **Let's look at the answers.**

**Answer 10:** $x^2 + 5x + 4 = (x + 1)(x + 4) = 27$; $3(x + 1)(x + 4) = 3(27) = 81$. The answer is (D).

**Answer 11:** It looks like you have to factor but you don't. $(x^2 + 11x) + 24 = 0$; so $x^2 + 11x$ has to equal $-24$! The answer is (B).

Again, later on, we will have more problems involving trinomial factoring.

## ALGEBRAIC FRACTIONS

Except for adding and subtracting, the techniques for algebraic fractions are easy to understand. They must be practiced, however.

### Reducing Fractions

Factor the top and bottom; cancel factors that are the same.

**Example 15:** Reduce the following fractions:

<u>Problem</u>

 a. $\dfrac{x^2 - 9}{x^2 - 3x}$

 b. $\dfrac{2x^3 + 10x^2 + 8x}{x^4 + x^3}$

 c. $\dfrac{x - 9}{9 - x}$

<u>Solution</u>

$\dfrac{(x + 3)(x - 3)}{x(x - 3)} = \dfrac{x + 3}{x}$

$\dfrac{2x(x + 4)(x + 1)}{x^3(x + 1)} = \dfrac{2(x + 4)}{x^2}$

$\dfrac{(x - 9)}{-1(x - 9)} = -1$

**Let's do some more exercises.**

|  | **Column A** | **Column B** |
|---|---|---|
| **Exercise 12:** | $\dfrac{16x + 4}{4}$ | $4x$ |
| **Exercise 13:** | $\dfrac{x^2 - 16}{x - 4}$ | $2x + 4$ |
| **Exercise 14:** | $\dfrac{2x^2 + 10x + 12}{2x + 6}$ | $x$ |

 **Let's look at the answers.**

**Answer 12:** $\dfrac{16x + 4}{4} = \dfrac{4(4x + 1)}{4} = 4x + 1 > 4x$. The answer is (A). Alternatively,

$\dfrac{16x + 4}{4} = \dfrac{16x}{4} + \dfrac{4}{4} = 4x + 1$.

**Answer 13:** $\dfrac{(x + 4)(x - 4)}{x - 4} = x + 4$. Comparing $x + 4$ to $2x + 4$ or $x$ to $2x$ is impossible, since we don't know if $x > 0$, $x = 0$, or $x < 0$. The answer is (D).

**Answer 14:** $\dfrac{2(x + 2)(x + 3)}{2(x + 3)} = \dfrac{2(x + 2)}{2} = x + 2 > x$. The answer is (A).

## Multiplication and Division of Fractions

Algebraic fractions use the same principle as multiplication and division of numerical fractions except we factor all tops and bottoms, canceling one factor in any top with its equivalent in any bottom. In a division problem, we must remember to invert the second fraction first and then multiply.

**Example 16:** $\dfrac{x^2 - 25}{(x + 5)^3} \times \dfrac{x^3 + x^2}{x^2 - 4x - 5} =$

**Solution:** $\dfrac{(x + 5)(x - 5)}{(x + 5)(x + 5)(x + 5)} \times \dfrac{x^2(x + 1)}{(x - 5)(x + 1)} = \dfrac{x^2}{(x + 5)^2}$

**Example 17:** $\dfrac{x^4 + 4x^2}{x^6} \div \dfrac{x^4 - 16}{x^2 + 3x - 10} =$

**Solution:** $\dfrac{x^2(x^2 + 4)}{x^6} \times \dfrac{(x + 5)(x - 2)}{(x^2 + 4)(x - 2)(x + 2)} = \dfrac{x + 5}{x^4(x + 2)}$

## Adding and Subtracting Algebraic Fractions

It might be time to review the section in Chapter 2 on adding and subtracting fractions. Follow these steps:

1. If the bottoms are the same, add the tops, reducing if necessary.

2. If the bottoms are different, factor the denominators.

3. The LCD is the product of the most number of times a prime appears in any one denominator.

4. Multiply top and bottom by "what's missing."

5. Add (subtract) and simplify the numerators; reduce, if possible.

**Example 18:** $\dfrac{x}{36 - x^2} - \dfrac{6}{36 - x^2} =$

**Solution:** $\dfrac{x - 6}{36 - x^2} = \dfrac{x - 6}{(6 - x)(6 + x)} = \dfrac{-1}{x + 6}$

**Example 19:** $\dfrac{5}{12xy^3} + \dfrac{9}{8x^2y} =$

**Solution:** $\dfrac{5}{2 \times 2 \times 3xyyy} + \dfrac{9}{2 \times 2 \times 2xxy} = \dfrac{5(2x)}{2 \times 2 \times 2 \times 3xxyyy} +$

$\dfrac{9(3yy)}{2 \times 2 \times 2 \times 3xxyyy} = \dfrac{10x + 27y^2}{24x^2y^3}$

**Example 20:** $\dfrac{2}{x^2 + 4x + 4} + \dfrac{3}{x^2 + x + 6} =$

**Solution:** $\dfrac{2}{(x + 2)(x + 2)} + \dfrac{3}{(x + 2)(x + 3)} = \dfrac{2(x + 3)}{(x + 2)(x + 2)(x + 3)} +$

$\dfrac{3(x + 2)}{(x + 2)(x + 3)(x + 2)} = \dfrac{5x + 12}{(x + 2)(x + 2)(x + 3)}$

## Simplifying Complex Fractions

This is a topic the GRE is asking quite a bit more recently. Some examples will help you to understand how to simplify complex fractions.

**Example 21:** Simplify $\dfrac{2 - \frac{5}{6}}{\frac{2}{3} + \frac{7}{8}}$

**Solution:** Find the LCD of all the terms (24) and multiply each term by it.

$$\frac{\frac{2}{1} \times \frac{24}{1} - \frac{5}{6} \times \frac{24}{1}}{\frac{2}{3} \times \frac{24}{1} + \frac{7}{8} \times \frac{24}{1}} = \frac{48 - 20}{16 + 21} = \frac{28}{37}$$

**Note** *When you multiply each term by 24, all the fractions disappear except for the major one.*

**Example 22:** Simplify $\dfrac{\frac{1}{y^2} - \frac{1}{z^2}}{\frac{1}{y} - \frac{1}{z}}$

**Solution:** The LCD is $y^2z^2$.

$$\frac{\frac{1}{y^2} \times \frac{y^2z^2}{1} - \frac{1}{z^2} \times \frac{y^2z^2}{1}}{\frac{1}{y} \times \frac{y^2z^2}{1} - \frac{1}{z} \times \frac{y^2z^2}{1}} = \frac{z^2 - y^2}{yz^2 - y^2z} = \frac{(z - y)(z + y)}{yz(z - y)} = \frac{z + y}{yz}$$

This is my favorite problem in the whole world because it is relatively short with lots of skills. I've noticed it's a favorite of a number of other authors.

**Example 23:** Simplify $\dfrac{1 - \frac{25}{x^2}}{1 - \frac{10}{x} + \frac{25}{x^2}}$.

**Solution:** The LCD is $x^2$.

$$\frac{x^2\left(1 - \frac{25}{x^2}\right)}{x^2\left(1 - \frac{10}{x} + \frac{25}{x^2}\right)} = \frac{x^2 - 25}{x^2 - 10x + 25} = \frac{(x + 5)(x - 5)}{(x - 5)(x - 5)} = \frac{x + 5}{x - 5}$$

**Q** **Let's do some more exercises.**

**Exercise 15:** The reciprocal of $2 - \dfrac{1}{4}$ is

A. $\dfrac{1}{2} - 4$

B. $-\dfrac{4}{7}$

C. $-\dfrac{4}{9}$

D. $\dfrac{4}{9}$

E. $\dfrac{4}{7}$

**Exercise 16:** $x, y, z > 0.\ x + \dfrac{1}{y + \frac{1}{z}} =$

A. $\dfrac{x + y}{z}$     D. $\dfrac{x + y + z}{xyz + 1}$

B. $\dfrac{xyz + y + z}{yz}$     E. $\dfrac{xyz + x + z}{yz + 1}$

C. $\dfrac{xz + yz + 1}{yz}$

**Exercise 17:** $y = \dfrac{1}{x}.$ Then $\dfrac{1 - x}{1 - y} =$

A. $-x$     D. $(1 - x)$

B. $x$     E. $(x - 1)$

C. $1$

| **Column A** | **Column B** |
|---|---|
| **Exercise 18:** $\dfrac{1}{6 + \frac{1}{3 + \frac{1}{2}}}$ | $\dfrac{1}{2 + \frac{1}{5 + \frac{1}{4}}}$ |
| **Exercise 19:** $\dfrac{5}{3 - \frac{3}{2}} + \dfrac{5}{\frac{3}{2} - 3}$ | $0$ |

 **Let's look at the answers.**

**Answer 15:** $2 - \dfrac{1}{4} = \dfrac{7}{4}.$ Its reciprocal is $\dfrac{4}{7}.$ The answer is (E).

**Answer 16:** $x + \dfrac{z \times 1}{z\left(y + \frac{1}{z}\right)} = \dfrac{x}{1} + \dfrac{z}{yz + 1} = \dfrac{x}{1} \times \dfrac{yz + 1}{yz + 1} + \dfrac{z}{yz + 1} = \dfrac{xyz + x + z}{yz + 1}.$

The answer is (E).

**Answer 17:** $\dfrac{1 - x}{1 - y} = \dfrac{1 - x}{1 - \frac{1}{x}} = \dfrac{x(1 - x)}{x\left(1 - \frac{1}{x}\right)} = \dfrac{x(1 - x)}{(x - 1)} = -x.$ The answer is (A)

since $\dfrac{1 - x}{x - 1} = -1.$

The secret of this problem is *not* to multiply out the top.

**Answer 18:** This looks like Exercise 16, and it can be done that way. However, there is a much easier way. Fraction A is $\dfrac{1}{6+m}$ , where $0 < m < 1$. So $\dfrac{1}{7} < A < \dfrac{1}{6}$. Fraction B is $\dfrac{1}{2+n}$, where $0 < n < 1$. So $\dfrac{1}{3} < B < \dfrac{1}{2}$. B is larger. Again, the idea is to do as little arithmetic as possible. The answer is (B).

**Answer 19:** Again, the problem looks like simplifying a complex fraction. However, the first fraction in A is the negative of the second fraction. When added, the sum is 0. The answer is (C).

" *The equations here are the equations for life. Master them, and it will bring you joy.* "

## FIRST-DEGREE EQUATIONS

**In** high school, the topic of first-degree equations was probably the most popular of all. The GRE asks questions that are usually not too long and usually not too tricky. To review, here are the steps to solving first-degree equations. If you get good at these, you will know when to use the steps in another order.

To solve for $x$, follow these steps:

1.  Multiply by the LCD to get rid of fractions. Cross-multiply if there are only two fractions.
2.  If the "$x$" term appears only on the right, switch the sides.
3.  Multiply out all parentheses by using the distributive law.
4.  On each side, combine like terms.
5.  Add the opposite of the $x$ term on the right to each side.
6.  Add the opposite of the non-$x$ term(s) on the left to each side.
7.  Factor out the $x$. This step occurs only if there is more than one letter in a problem.
8.  Divide each side by the whole coefficient of $x$, including the sign.

Believe it or not, it took a long time to get the phrasing of this list just right.

 *Note* *The **opposite** of a term is the same term with its opposite sign. So the opposite of 3x is $-3x$, the opposite of $-7y$ is $+7y$, and the opposite of 0 is 0. The technical name for "opposite" is **additive inverse**.*

Let's do some examples.

**Example 1:**    Solve for $x$: $7x - 2 = 10x + 13$

**Solution:**    Steps 1–4 are not present.

| | |
|---|---|
| $7x - 2 = 10x + 13$ | Step 5: Add $-10x$ to each side. |
| $-3x - 2 = +13$ | Step 6: Add $+2$ to each side. |
| $-3x = 15$ | Step 8: Divide each side by $-3$. |
| $x = -5$ | Solution |

**Example 2:**    Solve for $x$: $7 = 2(3x - 5) - 4(x - 6)$

**Solution:**    

| | |
|---|---|
| $7 = 2(3x - 5) - 4(x - 6)$ | No Step 1. Step 2: Switch sides. |
| $2(3x - 5) - 4(x - 6) = 7$ | Step 3: Multiply out the parentheses. |
| $6x - 10 - 4x + 24 = 7$ | Step 4: Combine like terms on each side. |
| $2x + 14 = 7$ | No Step 5. Step 6: Add $-14$ to each side. |
| $2x = -7$ | Step 8: Divide each side by 2. |
| $x = -\dfrac{7}{2}$ | The answer doesn't have to be an integer |

**Example 3:**    Solve for $x$: $\dfrac{x}{4} + \dfrac{x}{6} = 1$

**Solution:**    

| | |
|---|---|
| $\dfrac{x}{4} + \dfrac{x}{6} = 1$ | Step 1: Multiply each term by 12 |
| $3x + 2x = 12$ | Step 4: Combine like terms |
| $5x = 12$ | Step 8: Divide each side by 5 |
| $x = \dfrac{12}{5}$ | Solution |

**Example 4:**    Solve for $x$: $y = \dfrac{3x - 5}{x - 7}$

**Solution:**    

| | |
|---|---|
| Write $y = \dfrac{y}{1}$: $\dfrac{y}{1} = \dfrac{3x - 5}{x - 7}$ | Step 1: Cross-multiply |
| $(x - 7)y = 1(3x - 5)$ | Step 3: Distribute |

$$xy - 7y = 3x - 5 \qquad \text{Step 5: Add } -3x \text{ to each side}$$

$$xy - 3x - 7y = -5 \qquad \text{Step 6: Add } 7y \text{ to each side}$$

$$xy - 3x = 7y - 5 \qquad \text{Step 7: Factor out the } x \text{ from the left}$$

$$x(y - 3) = 7y - 5 \qquad \text{Step 8: Divide each side by } y - 3$$

$$x = \frac{7y - 5}{y - 3}$$

**Q** **Let's do some GRE–type exercises.**

**Exercise 1:**   $2x - 6 = 4; x + 3 =$

   A. 5          D. 8

   B. 6          E. 9

   C. 7

**Exercise 2:**   $x - 9 = 9 - x; x =$

   A. 0          D. 13.5

   B. 4.5        E. 18

   C. 9

**Exercise 3:**   $4x - 17 = 32; 12x - 51 =$

   A. $12\frac{1}{4}$          D. 96

   B. $36\frac{3}{4}$          E. 288

   C. 64

**Exercise 4:**   $\dfrac{xy}{y - x} = 1; x =$

   A. $\dfrac{1}{2}$          D. $\dfrac{y}{y - 1}$

   B. 1          E. $\dfrac{y}{1 - y}$

   C. $\dfrac{y}{y + 1}$

**Let's go over the answers.**

**Answer 1:**    $x = 5$, but the question asks for $x + 3 = 8$. The answer is (D).

**Note** *Tests such as the GRE often ask for x + something instead of just x. Be careful—give what the test wants.*

**Answer 2:**    $2x = 18$; $x = 9$. The answer is (C). It actually can be solved just by looking, since $9 - 9 = 9 - 9$ (or $0 = 0$).

**Answer 3:**    We do not solve this equation. We recognize that $12x - 51 = 3(4x - 17) = 3(32) = 96$. The answer is (D).

**Answer 4:**    By cross-multiplying, we get $xy = y - x$. Then $xy + x = y$, which factors to $x(y + 1) = y$. Therefore, $x = \dfrac{y}{y + 1}$. The answer is (C).

## LINEAR INEQUALITIES

**To review some facts about inequalities:**

$a < b$ (read, "$a$ is less than $b$") means $a$ is to the left of $b$ on the number line.

$a > b$ (read, "$a$ is greater than $b$") means $a$ is to the right of $b$ on the number line.

$x > y$ is the same as $y < x$.

The notation $x \geq y$ (read, "$x$ is greater than or equal to $y$") means $x > y$ or $x = y$.

Similarly, $x \leq y$ (read, "$x$ is less than or equal to $y$"), means $x < y$ or $x = y$.

We solve linear inequalities ($<, >, \leq, \geq$) the same way we solve linear equalities, except when we multiply or divide by a negative, the order reverses.

**Example 5:**    Solve for $x$: $6x + 2 < 3x + 10$

**Solution:**    $3x < 8$, so $x < \dfrac{8}{3}$.

The inequality does not switch because both sides are divided by a positive number (3).

**Example 6:**    Solve for $x$: $-2(x - 3) \leq 4x - 3 - 7$

**Solution:**    $-2x + 6 \leq 4x - 10$, or $-6x \leq -16$. Thus, $x \geq \dfrac{-16}{-6} = \dfrac{8}{3}$.

Here the inequality switches because we divided both sides by a negative number $(-6)$.

**Example 7:**    Solve for $x$: $8 > \dfrac{x - 2}{-3} \geq 5$

**Solution:**    We multiply through by $-3$, and both inequalities switch. We get $-24 < x - 2 \leq -15$. If we add 2 to each part to get a value for $x$ alone, the final answer is $-22 < x \leq -13$.

**(Q)    Now, let's do some more exercises.**

**Exercise 5:**    If $3x + 4 > 17$, $3x + 7 >$

A. $\dfrac{13}{3}$                    D. 17

B. $\dfrac{22}{3}$                    E. 20

C. 14

**Exercise 6:**    If $3x + 4y < 5$; $x <$

A. $5 - 4y - 3$                    D. $\dfrac{5 - 4y}{3}$

B. $\dfrac{5}{4}y - 3$                    E. $\dfrac{5}{3} - 4y$

C. $\dfrac{5}{12}y$

**Exercise 7:**    $x > 0$ and $y > 0$. The number of ordered pairs of whole numbers $(x, y)$ such that $2x + 3y < 9$ is

A. 1                    D. 4

B. 2                    E. 5

C. 3

**Let's look at the answers.**

**Answer 5:**    We don't actually have to solve this one. $3x + 7 = (3x + 4) + 3 > 17 + 3$, or 20. The answer is (E).

**Answer 6:**    $3x + 4y < 5$ is the same as $3x < 5 - 4y$. Dividing by 3, we get $\dfrac{5 - 4y}{3}$. The answer is (D).

**Answer 7:**    We must substitute numbers. (1,1) is okay since $2(1) + 3(1) < 9$; (2,1) is okay since $2(2) + 3(1) < 9$; (1,2) is okay since $2(1) + 3(2) < 9$; and that's all. The answer is (C).

We will do more on ordered pairs later in the book. As we have already seen, some questions overlap more than one topic.

## ABSOLUTE VALUE EQUALITIES

**Absolute value** is the magnitude, without regard to sign. You should know the following facts about absolute value:

$|3| = 3, |-7| = 7,$ and $|0| = 0$

$|u| = 6$ means that $u = 6$ or $-6$.

$|u| = 0$ always means $u = 0$.

$|u| = -17$ has no solution since the absolute value is never negative.

**Example 8:**    Solve for $x$: $|2x - 5| = 7$

**Solution:**    Either $2x - 5 = 7$ or $2x - 5 = -7$. So $x = 6$ or $x = -1$.

**Note**   *This kind of problem always has two answers.*

**Example 9:**    Solve for $x$: $|5x + 11| = 0$.

**Solution:**    $5x + 11 = 0$; $x = -\dfrac{11}{5}$.

**Note**   *This type of problem (absolute value equals 0) always has one answer.*

Those of you with some math background know there is a lot more to absolute value. This section and the next, however, are all you need for the GRE.

**Q** **Let's do a few more exercises.**

**Exercise 8:**    $|2x + 1| = |x + 5|; x =$

A. $-2$    D. 4 and $-2$

B. 0    E. 0 and 4

C. 4

**Exercise 9:**    $|x - y| = |y - x|$. This statement is true:

A. For no values    D. Only for all integers

B. Only if $x = y = 0$    E. For all real numbers

C. Only if $x = y$

**Exercise 10:**    If $4|2x + 3| = 11$; then $8|2x + 3| + 5 =$

A. $\dfrac{11}{4}$    D. 27

B. $\dfrac{31}{4}$    E. 110

C. 22

**A** **Let's look at the answers.**

**Answer 8:**    $2x + 1 = x + 5$ or $2x + 1 = -(x + 5)$. The answer is (D).

**Answer 9:**    The answer is (E).

**Answer 10:**    We don't have to solve this at all. If $4|2x + 3| = 11$; then $8|2x + 3| = 2(11) = 22$. Adding 5, we get 27. The answer is (D).

## ABSOLUTE VALUE INEQUALITIES

If we talk about integers $|u| \leq 3$, we have u $= -3, -2, -1, 0, 1, 2,$ and 3. So $|u| \leq a$ means $-a \leq u \leq a$, where $a > 0$.

**Example 10:** Solve for $x$: $|2x - 3| < 11$

**Solution:** $-11 < 2x - 3 < 11$. Adding 3 to each piece means $-8 < 2x < 14$.
Dividing by 2 gives $-4 < x < 7$.

If we talk about integers $|u| \geq 4$, we have $u = 4, 5, 6, \ldots$ and $-4, -5, -6, \ldots$ So $|u| \geq a$ means $u \geq a$ or $u \leq -a$, $a > 0$.

**Example 11:** Solve for $x$: $|x - 7| > 4$.

**Solution:** $x - 7 > 4$ or $x - 7 < -4$. The two parts of the answer are $x > 11$ or $x < 3$.

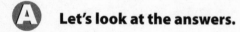 **Let's do some more excercises:**

**Exercise 11:** If $5 \leq |x| \leq 5$, $x =$

A. 0                  D. no values

B. 5                  E. all values

C. $-5$ and 5

**Exercise 12:** $|x - 5| \geq -5$ if $x =$

A. 0                  D. no values

B. 5                  E. all values

C. $-5$ and 5

**Exercise 13:** $|x + 5| \leq -5$ if $x =$

A. 0                  D. no values

B. 5                  E. all values

C. $-5$ and 5

**Let's look at the answers.**

**Answer 11:** The answer is (C).

**Answer 12:** The absolute value is always bigger than any negative number because it is always greater or equal to zero. The answer is (E).

**Answer 13:** The absolute value can't be less than a negative number. The answer is (D).

## QUADRATIC EQUATIONS

Quadratic equations, equations involving the square of the variable, can be solved in three principal ways: factoring, taking the square root, and using the quadratic formula. Another name for the solution of any equation is a **root**.

## Solving Quadratics by Factoring

Solving quadratic equations by factoring is based on the fact that if $a \times b = 0$, then either $a = 0$ or $b = 0$.

> **Example 12:**  Solve for all values of $x$: $x(x - 3)(x + 7)(2x + 1)(3x - 5)(ax + b)(cx - d) = 0$.

> **Solution:**  Setting each factor equal to 0 (better if you can do it just by looking), we get $x = 0, 3, -7, -\dfrac{1}{2}, \dfrac{5}{3}, -\dfrac{b}{a}$, and $\dfrac{d}{c}$.

## Solving Quadratics by Taking the Square Root

If the equation is of the form $x^2 = c$, with no $x$ term and $c > 0$, we just take the square root: $x = \pm\sqrt{c}$.

> **Note**  $\sqrt{9} = 3$, $-\sqrt{9} = -3$, $\sqrt{-9}$ is not real, and if $x^2 = 9$, then $x = \pm 3$!

> **Example 13:**  Solve for all values of $x$:
>
> a. $x^2 - 7 = 0$
>
> b. $ax^2 - b = c$, where $a, b, c > 0$.

> **Solutions:**  a. $x^2 = 7$; $x = \pm\sqrt{7}$
>
> b. $ax^2 = b + c$; $x^2 = \dfrac{b + c}{a}$, so $x = \pm\sqrt{\dfrac{b + c}{a}}$ or $\pm\dfrac{\sqrt{a(b + c)}}{a}$

## Solving Quadratics by Using the Quadratic Formula

The quadratic formula states that if $ax^2 + bx + c = 0$, then

$$x = \frac{-b \pm \sqrt{b^2 - 4ac}}{2a},$$

where $a$ is the coefficient of the $x^2$ term, $b$ is the coefficient of the $x$ term, and $c$ is the number term.

**Example 14:** Solve $3x^2 - 5x + 2 = 0$ by using the quadratic formula.

**Solution:**   $a = 3, b = -5, c = 2. x = x = \dfrac{-(-5) \pm \sqrt{(-5)^2 - 4(3)(2)}}{2(3)} = \dfrac{5 \pm 1}{6}.$

$x_1$ (read, "x sub one," the first answer) $= \dfrac{5 + 1}{6} = 1$; $x_2$ (read, "x sub two,"

the second answer) $= \dfrac{5 - 1}{6} = \dfrac{2}{3}.$

**Example 15:** Solve $3x^2 - 5x + 2 = 0$ by factoring.

**Solution:**   This is the same problem as Example 14. $3x^2 - 5x + 2 = (3x - 2)(x - 1)$

$= 0$, so $x = 1, \dfrac{2}{3}.$

Factoring is preferred; using the quadratic formula takes too long.

Before we go to the next set of exercises, I suppose most of you know the quadratic formula, but few have seen it shown to be true. The teacher in me has to show you, even if you don't care.

$ax^2 + bx + c = 0$                          The coefficient of $x^2$ must be 1.

$x^2 + \dfrac{b}{a}x = \dfrac{-c}{a}$                          Complete the square; this means taking half the coefficient of x, squaring it, adding it to both sides.

$x^2 + \dfrac{b}{a}x + \left(\dfrac{b}{2a}\right)^2 = \left(\dfrac{b}{2a}\right)^2 - \dfrac{c}{a}$   Take the square root of both sides.

$\left(x + \dfrac{b}{2a}\right)^2 = \dfrac{b^2}{4a^2} - \dfrac{c}{a}$

$= \dfrac{b^2}{4a^2} - \dfrac{4ac}{4a^2}$

$= \dfrac{b^2 - 4ac^2}{4a^2}$

$x + \dfrac{b}{2a} = \dfrac{\pm\sqrt{b^2 - 4ac}}{\sqrt{4a^2}}$

$= \dfrac{\pm\sqrt{b^2 - 4ac}}{2a}$

Solve for $x$ and simplify.

$$x = -\frac{b}{2a} \pm \sqrt{\frac{b^2 - 4ac}{2a}} \text{ or}$$

$$\frac{-b \pm \sqrt{b^2 - 4ac}}{2a}$$

$$\text{So } x = \frac{-b \pm \sqrt{b^2 - 4ac}}{2a}$$

The formula is really true. You should have questioned it in high school. Hopefully college has taught you to question everything.

**Ⓠ** **Let's do some GRE exercises.**

|  |  | Column A | Column B |
|---|---|---|---|
| **Exercise 14:** | $x^2 + 5x - 6 = 0$ | The sum of the two roots. | 0 |
| **Exercise 15:** | $x^2 = 11$ | Minimum root | $-4$ |
| **Exercise 16:** | $\dfrac{x^2 - 9}{x^2 - 25}$ | Maximum value to make fraction $= 0$ | 4 |
| **Exercise 17:** | $\dfrac{x^2 - 9}{x^2 - 25}$ | Minimum value to make fraction undefined | 0 |
| **Exercise 18:** | $x^3 - 4x^2 - 7x + 28 = 0$   $x^3 - 4x^2$ |  | $7x - 28$ |
| **Exercise 19:** | $\dfrac{x - 4}{x - 3} = \dfrac{x - 2}{x}$ | Root of this equation | 0 |

**Ⓐ** **Let's look at the answers.**

**Answer 14:**   $(x + 6)(x - 1) = 0$; the roots are $-6$ and $+1$. The sum is less than 0. The answer is (B).

**Answer 15:**   $-\sqrt{11} > -\sqrt{16} = -4$. The answer is (A).

**Answer 16:** For the fraction to equal 0, the top must equal 0, so $x = 3 < 4$. The answer is (B).

**Answer 17:** For the fraction to be undefined, the bottom must equal 0; the minimum value is $-5 < 0$. The answer is (B).

**Answer 18:** Move the last two terms to the other side of the equation. The answer is (C).

**Answer 19:** Cross-multiplying, we get $x(x - 4) = (x - 3)(x - 2)$. Canceling the $x^2$ terms, we get $-4x = -5x + 6$. So $x = 6 > 0$. The answer is (A).

Now let's go to a chapter that discusses word problems, always very important to the GRE (as well as the SAT).

# CHAPTER 7: *Word Problems in One Unknown*

"*It is necessary to study the words of math. Only then can you truly understand all.*"

I consider this section the most important section of the book. Although the book is filled with skills that may be on the GRE, most of the questions will not be pure math questions but will have words that you must interpret and then do some math. Unfortunately, most high schools have de-emphasized these kinds of problems. In this chapter, I will try to make these dreaded "word problems" easy to understand.

First, we'll look at the words you'll need to know. Next, we'll go over the more likely problems to show up on the GRE. We'll then go over the other types of word problems. Finally, we'll review some common measurements.

## BASICS

As we know, the answer in **addition** is the **sum**. Other words that indicate addition are **plus, more, more than, increase,** and **increased by.** You can write all sums in any order since addition is commutative.

The answer in **multiplication** is the **product.** Another word that is used is **times.** Sometimes the word **of** indicates multiplication, as we shall see shortly. **Double** means to multiply by two, and **triple** means to multiply by three. Since multiplication is also commutative, we can write any product in any order.

Division's answer is called the **quotient.** Another phrase that is used is **divided by.**

The answer in **subtraction** is called the **difference.** Subtraction can present a reading problem because $4 - 6 \neq 6 - 4$, so we must be careful to subtract in the correct order. Example 1 shows how some subtraction phrases are translated into algebraic expressions.

**Example 1:**    <u>Phrases</u>                                                  <u>Expressions</u>

    **a.** The difference between 9 and 5              $9 - 5$

        The difference between $m$ and $n$          $m - n$

    **b.** Five minus two                             $5 - 2$

        $m$ minus $n$                          $m - n$

    **c.** Seven decreased by three            $7 - 3$

        $m$ decreased by $n$               $m - n$

    **d.** Nine diminished by four             $9 - 4$

        $m$ diminished by $n$              $m - n$

    **e.** Three from five                     $5 - 3$

        $m$ from $n$                           $n - m$

    **f.** Ten less two                        $10 - 2$

        $m$ less $n$                           $m - n$

    **g.** Ten less than two;                 $2 - 10$

        $m$ less than $n$                  $n - m$

Notice in parts $f$ and $g$ of Example 1 how one word makes a difference: $a$ less $b$ means $a - b$; $a$ less than $b$ means $b - a$. $a$ is less than $b$ means $a < b$. You must read carefully!!

The following words usually indicate an equal sign: *is, am, are, was, were, the same as, equal to.*

You also must know the following phrases for inequalities: at least ($\geq$), not more than ($\leq$), over ($>$), and under ($<$).

**Example 2:**    Write the following in symbols:

    <u>Problem</u>                                                  <u>Solution</u>

    **a.** $m$ times the sum of $q$ and $r$         $m(q + r)$

    **b.** Six less the product of $x$ and $y$     $6 - xy$

    **c.** The difference between $c$ and $d$     $\dfrac{c - d}{f}$

        divided by $f$

    **d.** *b* less than the quotient of *r*            $\frac{r}{s} - b$
       divided by *s*

    **e.** The sum of *d* and *g* is the same       $d + g = hr$
       as the product of *h* and *r*

**Example 3:**   <u>Phrases</u>                           <u>Expressions</u>

    **a.** *x* is at least *y*                   $x \geq y$

    **b.** Zeb's age *n* is not more than 21     $n \leq 21$

    **c.** Let *l* = my age, I am over 30 years old    $l > 30$

    **d.** Let *p* = most people, most people are    $p < 7$
       under seven feet tall

*Warning:* The word "number" does not necessarily mean an integer or even necessarily a positive number.

# RATIOS

Comparing two numbers is called a **ratio**. The ratio of 3 to 5 is written two ways: $\frac{3}{5}$ or $3:5$ ("read, the ratio of 3 to 5").

    **Example 4:**   Find the ratio of 5 ounces to 2 pounds.

    **Solution:**    The ratio is $\frac{5}{32}$, since 16 ounces are in a pound.

    **Example 5:**   A board is cut into two pieces that are in the ratio of 3 to 4. If the board
                   is 56 inches long, how long is the longer piece?

    **Solution:**    If the pieces are in the ratio 3:4, we let one piece equal 3*x* and the other
                  4*x*. The equation, then, is $3x + 4x = 56$; so $x = 8$; and the longer piece is
                  $4x = 32$.

I have asked this problem many, many times. Almost no one has ever gotten it correct—not because it is difficult, but because no one does problems like this one anymore.

## CONSECUTIVE INTEGERS

If there are any "fun" word problems, they would have to do with consecutive integers. Let's recall the following facts about integers, most of which you know without having to even think about them:

$$\text{Integers:} \quad -3, -2, -1, 0, 1, 2, 3, 4, \ldots$$

$$\text{Evens:} \quad -6, -4, -2, 0, 2, 4, 6, 8, \ldots$$

$$\text{Odds:} \quad -5, -3, -1, 1, 3, 5, 7, \ldots$$

If we let $x =$ integer, then $x + 1$ represents the next consecutive integer, and $x + 2$ represents the next consecutive integer after that. Then $x + (x + 1) + (x + 2) = 3x + 3$ is the sum of three consecutive integers, where $x$ is the smallest and $x + 2$ is the largest in the group.

If $y =$ an even integer, then $y + 2$ is the next consecutive even integer; $y + 4$ and $y + 6$ are the next consecutive integers after that. Then the sum of four consecutive even integers is $y + (y + 2) + (y + 4) + (y + 6) = 4y + 12$.

Similarly, if $z$ is an odd integer, the next three odd integers are $z + 2$, $z + 4$, and $z + 6$. This is the same as for even integers, except we start out letting $z$ be odd instead of even.

**Example 6:**    The sum of three consecutive integers is twice the smallest. What is the smallest integer?

**Solution:**    We have $x + (x + 1) + (x + 2) = 2x$, which simplifies to $3x + 3 = 2x$. So $x = -3$. The integers are $-3$, $-2$, and $-1$; and the smallest is $-3$. Notice that integers can be negative!

Most consecutive integer problems are done by using tricks, as the next few examples show.

**Example 7:**    The sum of five consecutive even integers is 210. What is the sum of the smallest two?

**Solution:**    If you have an odd number of consecutive, consecutive even, or consecutive odd integers, the middle number is the average (the mean); So the middle number is given by $\dfrac{210}{5} = 42$. Once you know that, count backwards and forwards to get the others. The five numbers are 38, 40, 42, 44, and 46. The sum of the two smallest is $38 + 40 = 78$.

**Example 8:** The sum of four consecutive integers is $-50$. What is the sum of the two largest?

**Solution:** Dividing $-50$ by 4, we get $-12.5$. The four consecutive integers are the closest integers to $-12.5$, namely $-14$, $-13$, $-12$, and $-11$. The sum of the two largest, $-12$ and $-11$ is $-23$.

## AGE

Similar to consecutive integer problems are age problems. We just have to think about it logically.

**Example 9:** $p$ years ago, Mary was $q$ years old; in $r$ years she will be how many years old?

**Solution:** The secret is age now. If Mary was $q$ years old $p$ years ago, now she is $p + q$; so $r$ years in the future, she will be $p + q + r$. If necessary, substitute numbers for $p$, $q$, and $r$ to see how this works.

## SPEED

We are familiar with speed being given in miles per hour (mph), so it is easy to remember that $\text{speed} = \dfrac{\text{distance}}{\text{time}}$, or $r = \dfrac{d}{t}$, where $r$ stands for rate (the speed). Use this relationship, or the equivalent ones: $d = rt$ or $t = \dfrac{d}{r}$, to do word problems involving speed.

**Example 10:** Sue drives for 2 hours at 60 mph and 3 hours at 70 mph. What is her average speed?

**Solution:** Sue's average speed for the whole trip is given by $r = \dfrac{d}{t}$, where $d$ is the total distance and $t$ is the total time. Note that her average speed is *not* the average of the speeds. Use $d = rt$ for each part of her trip to get the total distance. The total distance is $60(2) + 70(3) = 330$ miles. The total time is 5 hours. So Sue's average speed is $r = \dfrac{330}{5} = 66$ mph.

**Example 11:**  Don goes 40 mph in one direction and returns at 60 mph. What is his average speed?

**Solution:**  Notice that the problem doesn't tell the distance. It doesn't have to; the distance in each direction is the same, since it is a round trip. We can take any distance, so let's choose 120 miles, the LCM of 40 and 60. Then the time going is $\frac{120}{40} = 3$ hours, and the time returning is $\frac{120}{60} = 2$ hours. The average speed is the total distance divided by the total time, $\frac{2(120)}{3+2} = \frac{240}{5} = 48$ mph.

We actually don't have to choose a number for the distance, however. We could use $x$. Just for learning's sake, we will do this same problem (Example 11) using $x$ as the distance. The time going is $\frac{x}{40}$, and the time returning is $\frac{x}{60}$. Then we have:

$$\text{Total speed} = \frac{\text{total distance}}{\text{total time}} = \frac{2x}{\frac{x}{40} + \frac{x}{60}} = \frac{120(2x)}{120(\frac{x}{40} + \frac{x}{60})} = \frac{240x}{5x} = 48 \text{ mph}$$

**Example 12:**  A plane leaves Indianapolis traveling west. A plane traveling 30 mph faster leaves Indianapolis going east. After two hours the planes are 2,000 miles apart. What is the speed of the faster plane?

**Solution:**  A chart and a picture are best for problems like this.

| | $r$ | $t$ | $d$ |
|---|---|---|---|
| W | $x$ | 2 | $2x$ |
| E | $x + 30$ | 2 | $2(x + 30)$ |

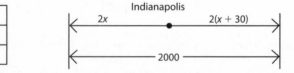

We let $x$ = the speed of the plane going west; then $x + 30$ is the speed of the eastern-going plane. The time for each is 2 hours. Since $rt = d$, the distances are as shown in the above chart. According to the picture, $2x + 2(x + 30) = 2000$. So $x = 485$; $x + 30 = 515$ mph.

The problem is the same if the planes are starting at the ends and flying toward each other.

**Example 13:** A car leaves Chicago at 2 p.m. going west. A second car leaves Chicago at 5 p.m., going 30 mph faster. At 7 p.m., the faster car hits the slower one. The accident occurred after how many miles?

**Solution:** Again, let's construct a chart and picture.

| | r | t | d |
|---|---|---|---|
| Slower | $x$ | 5 | $5x$ |
| Faster | $x + 30$ | 2 | $2(x + 30)$ |

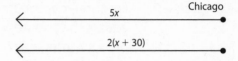

The rate of the slower car is $x$, and the time of the slower car is 7 p.m. $-$ 2 p.m., or 5 hours. The rate of the faster car is $x + 30$; and its time is 7 p.m. $-$ 5 p.m., or 2 hours. When they crashed, their distances were equal, so $5x = 2(x + 30)$. Then $x = 20$; and the total distance is $5(20)$ or $2(20 + 30) = 100$ miles.

 **Let's do some basic exercises.**

**Exercise 1:** Four more than a number is seven less than triple the number. The number is

A. 4        D. 9

B. 5.5      E. 11

C. 7

**Exercise 2:** Mike must have at least an 80 average but less than a 90 average to get a *B*. If he received 98, 92, and 75 on the first three tests, which of these grades will give him a *B*?

A. 42       D. 98

B. 54       E. 100

C. 66

**Exercise 3:** Nine less than a number is the same as the difference between nine and the number. The number is

A. 18       D. 29

B. 9        E. All numbers are correct.

C. 0

**Exercise 4:**     Seven consecutive odd numbers total −77. The sum of the largest three is

A. −21          D. −39

B. −27          E. −45

C. −33

**Exercise 5:**     For three consecutive integers, the sum of the squares of the first two equals the square of the largest. There are two sets of answers. The sum of all six integers is

A. 0            D. 12

B. 3            E. 24

C. 6

**Exercise 6:**     Ed goes 20 mph in one direction and 50 mph on the return trip. His average speed is

A. 25 mph          D. 30 mph

B. $27\frac{2}{7}$ mph          E. $30\frac{6}{7}$ mph

C. $28\frac{4}{7}$ mph

**Exercise 7:**     The angles of a triangle are in the ratio of 3:5:7. The largest angle is

A. 12°          D. 84°

B. 36°          E. 108°

C. 60°

|  | Column A | Column B |
|---|---|---|
| **Exercise 8:**   $y$ is greater than 4 less than twice $x$ | $y$ | $2x - 6$ |

**Exercise 9:**     $b$ years in the future, I will be $c$ years old. How old was I six years in the past?

A. $b - c - 6$          D. $b - c + 6$

B. $c - b - 6$          E. $b + c - 6$

C. $c - b + 6$

**Exercise 10:** Meg is six times as old as Peg. In 15 years, Meg will be three times as old as Peg. Meg's age now is

A. 10                    D. 75

B. 25                    E. 90

C. 60

**Exercise 11:** A fraction, when reduced, is $\frac{2}{3}$. If 6 is added to the numerator and 14 is added to the denominator, the fraction reduces to $\frac{3}{5}$. The sum of the original numerator and denominator is

A. 60                    D. 90

B. 70                    E. 100

C. 80

 **Let's look at the answers.**

**Answer 1:** Let's break this one down into small pieces. Four more than a number is written as $n + 4$ (or $4 + n$). Seven less than triple the number is $3n - 7$ (the only correct way). "Is" means equals, so the equation is $n + 4 = 3n - 7$. Solving, we get $n = 5.5$. The answer is (B).

**Answer 2:** The "setup" to do this problem is $80 \leq \frac{(98 + 92 + 75 + x)}{4} < 90$.

However, $80(4) = 320$ total points for a minimum, and it must be less than $90(4) = 360$ points. So far, Mike has $98 + 92 + 75 = 265$ points; $265 + 66 = 321$ points. So the answer is (C). (However, choices (D) or (E) will result in an A, and I'm sure Mike wouldn't object to that.)

**Answer 3:** $x - 9 = 9 - x$; $x = 9$. The answer is (B).

**Answer 4:**    The middle one is $-\dfrac{77}{7} = -11$. The three largest ones are thus $-9$, $-7$, $-5$, and their sum is $-21$. The answer is (A).

**Answer 5:**    $x^2 + (x + 1)^2 = (x + 2)^2$, which simplifies to $x^2 - 2x - 3 = 0$; $(x - 3)$ $(x + 1) = 0$. The solution set is $x = 3$ or $x = -1$. For $x = 3$, the integers are 3, 4, 5; for $x = -1$, the integers are $-1$, 0, 1. The sum of all six is $3 + 4 + 5 + (-1) + 0 + 1 = 12$. The answer is (D).

**Answer 6:**    If we assume a 100-mile distance, the original trip was 5 hours, and the return trip was 2 hours. $r = \dfrac{d}{t} = \dfrac{200}{7} = 28\dfrac{4}{7}$ mph. The answer is (C).

**Answer 7:**    $3x + 5x + 7x = 180$, so $x = 12°$. The largest angle is $7x = 84°$. The answer is (D).

**Answer 8:**    Since $y > 2x - 4$; and $2x - 4 > 2x - 6$, (because $-4 > -6$), then $y > 2x - 6$. The answer is (A).

**Answer 9:**    My age now is $c - b$, so six years ago it was $(c - b) - 6$. The answer is (B).

**Answer 10:**

| | Age now | Age in 15 years |
|---|---|---|
| Peg | $x$ | $x + 15$ |
| Meg | $6x$ | $6x + 15$ |

We let $x$ = Peg's (the younger one's) age. Meg's age is thus $6x$. In 15 years, Meg's age $(6x + 15)$ will be (equals) three times Peg's age $(3(x+15))$. So the equation is $6x + 15 = 3x + 45$, and $x = 10$. Meg's age now is $6x = 60$. The answer is (C).

**Answer 11:**    The fraction can be written as $\dfrac{2x}{3x}$. So $\dfrac{2x + 6}{3x + 14} = \dfrac{3}{5}$. Cross-multiplying, we get $5(2x + 6) = 3(3x + 14)$, so $x = 12$. $2x = 24$ and $3x = 36$, and their sum is $24 + 36 = 60$. The answer is (A).

# WORK

The basic idea of work problems is that if a job can be done in $x$ hours, then each hour, the amount that is done is $\frac{1}{x}$ of the job. In 4 hours, for example, a job that takes 6 hours to do is $\frac{4}{6} = \frac{2}{3}$ done. The whole job done is represented by the number 1.

**Example 14:** Rob can do a job in 8 hours and Nan can do the same job in 4 hours. Together, they can do the job in how many hours?

**Solution:** I always say there are two answers to this problem. The first is that they start watching TV and the job never gets done. However, this is how to do the real problem. If a job can be done in 8 hours, then the part done in one hour is $\frac{1}{8}$; in three hours, it is $\frac{3}{8}$; and in $x$ hours, it is $\frac{x}{8}$. The part done in $x$ hours by Rob is $\frac{x}{8}$, and similarly, the part done by Nan in $x$ hours is $\frac{x}{4}$. The part done by Rob plus the part done by Nan is the whole job, so $\frac{x}{8} + \frac{x}{4} = 1$. Thus, $x = 2\frac{2}{3}$. It would take them $2\frac{2}{3}$ hours to do the job together.

**Example 15:** Sandy takes twice as long to do a job as Randy. They finish the job together in 3 hours. How long would it take Randy to do the job alone?

**Solution:** The number of hours it takes Randy is $x$ hours, so he does $\frac{3}{x}$ of the job in 3 hours. Sandy takes $2x$ hours to do the job, so she does $\frac{3}{2x}$ of the job in 3 hours. Therefore, $\frac{3}{x} + \frac{3}{2x} = 1$ is the equation representing the work done in three hours. Multiplying by $2x$, we get $6 + 3 = 2x$, or $x = 4.5$.

It would take Randy 4.5 hours to do the job alone.

## MIXTURES

These kinds of problems are easier done with charts. The columns are cost per pound, the number of pounds, and the total cost.

**Example 16:** Walnuts selling at $6.00 a pound are mixed with 24 pounds of almonds at $9.00 a pound to give a mixture selling at $7.00 a pound. How many pounds of walnuts are used?

|  | Cost/Pound × | Number of Pounds = | Total Cost |
|---|---|---|---|
| Walnuts | 6 | $x$ | $6x$ |
| Almonds | 9 | 24 | 216 |
| Mixture | 7 | $x + 24$ | $7(x + 24)$ |

**Solution:** We set up a chart for the cost. We let $x$ equal the number of pounds of walnuts. The total pounds of walnuts plus the total pounds of almonds is the total weight of the mixture. The equation is the cost of the walnuts plus the cost of the almonds is the cost of the mixture: $6x + 216 = 7(x + 24)$, so $x = 48$ pounds of walnuts.

Coin problems are just like mixture problems, except we are working with money, not nuts and bolts (or walnuts and almonds).

**Example 17:** There are 40 coins in nickels and dimes totaling $2.80. How many nickels are there?

**Solution:**

|  | Value/Coin × | Number of Coins = | Total Value |
|---|---|---|---|
| Nickels | 5 | $x$ | $5x$ |
| Dimes | 10 | $40 - x$ | $10(40 - x)$ |
| Mixture | — | 40 | 280 |

The problem is done in pennies. The total number of coins is 40. If there are $x$ nickels, there are $40 - x$ dimes. The value of $x$ nickels is $5x$. The value of $40 - x$ dimes is $10(40 - x)$. The values of nickels plus dimes is the total value: $5x + 400 - 10x = 280$, so $x = 24$ nickels.

**Let's do some more exercises.**

**Exercise 12:**  The value of *d* dimes and *q* quarters in pennies is

A. $d + q$

B. $dq$

C. $250\,dq$

D. $10d + 25q$

E. $35dq$

**Exercise 13:**  Water is poured into a tank at the same time a pipe is opened that drains the tank. If the tank is filled in 10 hours and the tank can empty in 15 hours, and the tank starts empty, how many hours does it take to fill the tank?

A. 20

B. 30

C. 40

D. 60

E. 120

**Exercise 14:**  Adult tickets cost $10 and children's tickets cost $5. If 100 tickets are sold and $800 is taken in, how many adult tickets are sold?

A. 50

B. 60

C. 70

D. 75

E. 80

**Exercise 15:**  Sid is twice as old as Rex. Ten years ago, Sid was four times as old as Rex. How old is Sid today?

A. 5

B. 10

C. 20

D. 30

E. 60

**Exercise 16:**  The number of quarters is four more than twice the number of dimes. If the total is $7.00, how many dimes are there?

A. 10

B. 16

C. 20

D. 24

E. 34

**Exercise 17:**  Fred leaves Fort Worth by car traveling north. Two hours later, Jim also leaves Fort Worth going north, but 20 mph slower. After six more hours, they are 300 miles apart. Fred's speed is

**A.** 60 mph                  **D.** 90 mph

**B.** 70 mph                  **E.** 100 mph

**C.** 80 mph

**Exercise 18:**  Deb can do a job alone in 6 hours. After working alone for two hours, she is joined by Sue who can do the job alone in 8 hours. They work together and finish the job. How many hours did Deb work?

**A.** $3\dfrac{3}{7}$                  **D.** $4\dfrac{1}{2}$

**B.** 4                  **E.** 5

**C.** $4\dfrac{2}{7}$

 **Let's look at the answers.**

**Answer 12:**  Dimes are 10 cents each, and the value is $10d$. Similarly, the value of quarters is $25q$. The answer is (D).

**Answer 13:**  $\dfrac{x}{10} - \dfrac{x}{15} = 1$. We use a minus sign because it empties. Solving, we get $x = 30$. The answer is (B).

**Answer 14:**

|  | Value/ Tickets | × Number of Tickets | = Total Value |
|---|---|---|---|
| Adult | 10 | $x$ | $10x$ |
| Child | 5 | $100 - x$ | $5(100 - x)$ |
| Mixture | — | 100 | 800 |

As the chart indicates, this is similar to the mixture problem, Example 16 in this chapter. The equation is $10x + 500 - 5x = 800$, so $x = 60$. The answer is (B).

**Answer 15:**

|  | Age now | Age 10 years ago |
|---|---|---|
| Sid | 2x | 2x − 10 |
| Rex | x | x − 10 |

According to the chart and the problem, $2x - 10 = 4(x - 10)$, so $x = 15$. Sid's age is $2x = 30$. The answer is (D).

**Answer 16:** We could use a chart like the one for Example 15 but it probably is unnecessary. We have $x$ dimes and $(2x + 4)$ quarters. The equation is $10x + 25(2x + 4) = 700$, so $x = 10$. The answer is (A).

**Answer 17:**

|  | r × | t = | d |
|---|---|---|---|
| Fred | x | 8 | 8x |
| Jim | x − 20 | 6 | 6(x − 20) |

Fred goes at $x$ mph for 8 hours. Jim goes at $x - 20$ mph for 6 hours. Since they are going in the same direction, we get $8x - 6(x - 20) = 300$, or $x = 90$. The answer is (D). Notice that 300 is the *difference* in their distances, not the distance they traveled, so we use subtraction.

**Answer 18:** Deb can do the job in 6 hours; her part is $\frac{x}{6}$. Sue worked two hours less and can do the job in 8 hours; her part is $\frac{x - 2}{8}$. The equation is $\frac{x}{6} + \frac{x - 2}{8} = 1$, $x = 4\frac{2}{7}$. The answer is (C).

## MEASUREMENTS

You might want to review some basic measurements and how to convert a few.

Linear: 12 inches = 1 foot; 3 feet = 1 yard; 5,280 feet = 1 mile.

Liquid: 8 ounces = 1 cup; 2 cups = 1 pint; 2 pints = 1 quart; 4 quarts = 1 gallon

Weight: 16 ounces = 1 pound; 2,000 pounds = 1 ton.

Dry measure: 2 pints = 1 quart; 8 quarts = 1 peck; 4 pecks = 1 bushel. If I love you a bushel and a peck, it would be 5 pecks or 40 dry quarts.

Metric: 1,000 grams in a kilogram; 1,000 liters in a kiloliter; 1,000 meters in a kilometer; 1,000 millimeters = 1 meter; 100 centimeters = 1 meter; 10 millimeters = 1 centimeter

When doing conversions, we pay particular attention to the units, canceling them when doing the multiplications. A good guide is: to go from large to small, multiply; from small to large, divide (or multiply by the reciprocal).

**Example 18:** Change 30 kilograms 20 grams to milligrams.

**Solution:**    This is going from large to small, so multiply by the conversions:

$$\frac{30 \text{ kg}}{1} \times \frac{1000 \text{ g}}{1 \text{ kg}} \times \frac{1000 \text{ mg}}{1 \text{ g}} + \frac{20 \text{ g}}{1} \times \frac{1000 \text{ mg}}{1 \text{ g}} = 30{,}020{,}000 \text{ mg}$$

Notice how the measurements (g, kg) cancel.

**Example 19:** Change 90 miles per hour into feet per second.

**Solution:**    Now we are going from small to large, so multiply by the reciprocals (same as dividing); to change from miles to feet, though, we are going from large to small, so just multiply by $\dfrac{5{,}280 \text{ feet}}{1 \text{ mile}}$:

$$\frac{90 \text{ miles}}{\text{hour}} \times \frac{1 \text{ hour}}{60 \text{ minutes}} \times \frac{1 \text{ minute}}{60 \text{ seconds}} \times \frac{5280 \text{ feet}}{1 \text{ mile}} = \frac{132 \text{ feet}}{\text{sec}}$$

**Note** *Each fraction after the first is equivalent to 1. When you multiply by 1, the value doesn't change. Again, the measurements cancel, and you wind up with feet per second.*

# CHAPTER 8: *Working with Two or More Unknowns*

*"Understanding more complex problems will be gratifying to you."*

## SOLVING SIMULTANEOUS EQUATIONS

**We** can solve two equations in two unknowns, also known as **simultaneous equations**, in five basic ways. Only two are practical for the GRE exam: **substitution** and **elimination**. Sometimes, we use a combination of these two.

### Substitution

In substitution, we find an unknown with a coefficient of 1, solve for that variable, and substitute it in the other equation.

**Example 1:**   Solve for $x$ and $y$:     $3x + 4y = 4$      (1)

                                         $x - 5y = 14$     (2)

**Solution:**   In equation (2) $x = 5y + 14$. Substituting this into equation (1), we get $3(5y + 14) + 4y = 4$. Solving, we get $y = -2$; $x = 5y + 14 = 5(-2) + 14 = 4$. The answer is $x = 4$ and $y = -2$.

**Example 2:**   Solve for $x$ and $y$:     $3x + y = 14$      (1)

                                         $2x + 5y = 18$     (2)

**Solution:**   In equation (1), we solve for $y$: $y = 14 - 3x$, and substitute it into equation (2). Equation (2) then becomes $2x + 5(14 - 3x) = 18$. Solving this equation, we get $2x + 70 - 15x = 18$, or $-13x = -52$. So $x = 4$. Since $y = 14 - 3x$, $y = 14 - 3(4) = 2$. The answer is $x = 4$ and $y = 2$.

We can check by substituting these values into the original equations to see that they are solutions to both equations.

## Elimination

If none of the original coefficients of any of the terms is 1, it is usually better to use the elimination method. There are several ways to eliminate one of the variables, as seen in the following examples. Once we have eliminated one of the variables, we can solve for the other variable by using substitution.

**Example 3:**
$$2x + 3y = 12$$
$$5x - 3y = 9$$

**Solution:** If we add the equations, term by term, we can eliminate the $y$ term. We get $7x = 21$, so $x = 3$; substituting $x = 3$ into either equation, we get $y = 2$. So the answer is $x = 3$, $y = 2$.

**Example 4:** Solve for $x$ and $y$: 
$$3x + 2y = 12$$
$$3x - 2y = 0$$

**Solution:** Again, just add the equations. The $y$ term cancels out, and we get $6x = 12$; $x = 2$. We substitute this value for $x$ into either equation to find a value for $y$: $3x + 2y = 12$; $3(2) + 2y = 12$; $2y = 6$; so $y = 3$. The answer is $x = 2$ and $y = 3$.

**Example 5:** Solve for $x$ and $y$: 
$$4x + y = 17$$
$$x + y = 2$$

**Solution:** If adding doesn't work to eliminate one variable, try subtracting. We get $3x = 15$, so $x = 5$, and $y = -3$, by substitution into the second equation, the easier one. Mathematicians always try to do things the easiest way possible!

**Example 6:**
$$5x + 4y = 14$$
$$5x - 2y = 8$$

**Solution:** Subtracting, we get $6y = 6$; so $y = 1$; substituting, we get $x = 2$.

If adding or subtracting doesn't work, we must find two numbers that when we multiply the first equation by one of them and the second equation by the other, and then add (or subtract) the resulting equations, one letter is eliminated.

**Example 7:**              $5x + 3y = 11$          (1)

                           $4x - 2y = 22$          (2)

**Solution:**   To eliminate $x$, multiply the first equation by 4 and the second by $-5$; then add.

$4(5x + 3y) = 4(11)$          or     $20x + 12y = 44$

$-5(4x - 2y) = -5(22)$        or     $-20x + 10y = -110$

Adding, we get, $22y = -66$; so $y = -3$. We could substitute now, but we could also eliminate $y$ by multiplying the original equation (1) by 2 and equation (2) by 3. Let's do that.

$2(5x + 3y) = 2(11)$          or     $10x + 6y = 22$

$3(4x - 2y) = 3(22)$          or     $12x - 6y = 66$

Adding, we get $22x = 88$; so $x = 4$. The answer is $x = 4$, $y = -3$.

**Example 8:**   Solve for $x$ and $y$:          $5x + 4y = 11$

                                                 $2x - 3y = 9$

**Solution:**   Let's look at $5x$ and $2x$. If we multiply $5x$ by 2 and $2x$ by $-5$ and then add, the $x$ terms will disappear.

$2(5x + 4y) = 2(11)$ or $10x + 8y = 22$

$-5(2x - 3y) = (-5)(9)$ or $-10x + 15y = -45$

Adding these two new equations, we get $23y = -23$; so $y = -1$. We can then get $x$ by substitution into either original equation. Using the second equation (again, the easier one), we get $2x - 3(-1) = 9$, or $2x = 6$, so $x = 3$. The answer is $x = 3$ and $y = -1$.

## Practice in Solving Simultaneous Equations

For those of you who are curious, the other three basic ways of solving simultaneous equations are by using graphs, matrices, or determinants.

**Let's do some exercises.**

**Exercise 1:**    If $x + y = 12$ and $x - y = 18$, $y - 3 =$

    A. $-6$            D. $12$

    B. $-3$            E. $15$

    C. $0$

**Exercise 2:**    $3x + 2y = 61$ and $4x + 5y = 16$; $x + y =$

    A. $3$            D. $11$

    B. $5$            E. Can't be determined

    C. $7$

**Exercise 3:**    $6x - 7y = 42$ and $3x - 10y = 27$; $x + y =$

    A. $3$            D. $11$

    B. $5$            E. Can't be determined

    C. $7$

 *Sometimes "can't be determined" can occur as an answer; however, I've never found it could be the answer for two questions in a row.*

|  | **Column A** | **Column B** |
|---|---|---|

**Exercise 4:**    Mean of $x$ and $y$            $4$
$6x + 6y = 48$

**Exercise 5:**    If $x = y + 3$ and $y = z + 7$, $x$ (in terms of $z$) =

    A. $z - 10$            D. $z + 4$

    B. $z - 4$            E. $z + 10$

    C. $z$

**Exercise 6:**    Two apples and 3 pears cost 65 cents, and 5 apples and 4 pears cost $1.10. Find the cost of one pear:

    A. $10$            D. $25$

    B. $15$            E. $30$

    C. $20$

**Exercise 7:**    As in Exercise 6, 2 apples and 3 pears cost 65 cents, and 5 apples and 4 pears cost $1.10. Find the cost of one pear and one apple together:

A. 10                     D. 25

B. 15                     E. 30

C. 20

**Exercise 8:**    Find $x + y$:    $7x + 4y = 27$

$x - 2y = -3$

A. 1                      D. 7

B. 3                      E. 9

C. 5

**Exercise 9:**    For lunch, Ed buys 3 hamburgers and one soda for $12.50, and Mei buys one hamburger and one soda for $5.60. How much does Ed pay for his hamburgers?

A. $2.15                  D. $10.35

B. $3.45                  E. $18.10

C. $6.90

 **Let's look at the answers.**

**Answer 1:**    Adding, we get $2x = 30$. So $x = 15$. By substitution, we get $y = -3$; so $-3 - 3 = -6$. The answer is (A).

**Answer 2:**    A trick. We could solve for $x$ and $y$, but it takes a long time. The problem asks for $x + y$. Eighty percent of the time, just add the equations. Here we get $7x + 7y = 77$; so $x + y = 11$. The answer is (D).

**Answer 3:**    Another trick. We subtract the equations and get $3x + 3y = 15$; so $x + y = 5$. The answer is (B).

**Answer 4:**    $x + y = 8$; the mean is defined as $\dfrac{x + y}{2}$, so the mean is 4. The answer is (C).

**Answer 5:**    $x = y + 3 = (z + 7) + 3 = z + 10$. The answer is (E).

**Answer 6:**
$$2a + 3p = 65$$
$$5a + 4p = 110$$

In solving for $p$, eliminate $a$ by multiplying the top equation by 5 and the bottom by $-2$.

| | | |
|---|---|---|
| $5(2a + 3p) = 5(65)$ | or | $10a + 15p = 325$ |
| $-2(5a + 4p) = -2(110)$ | or | $-10a - 8p = -220$ |

Adding, we get $7p = 105$; $p = 15$. The answer is (B).

**Answer 7:**    Much more often, we get a problem like this. The equations are the same as in Exercise 6, but rather than asking for the cost of one apple or the cost of one pear, this exercise asks for the cost of one apple plus one pear. The trick is simply to add the original equations. $7a + 7p = 175$. Dividing both sides by 7, we get $a + p = 25$. The answer is (D).

**Answer 8:**    Less frequently, when adding doesn't work, try subtracting. If we subtract, the difference becomes $6x + 6y = 30$. So $x + y = 5$. The answer is (C).

**Answer 9:**    The equations are
$$3h + s = 12.50$$
$$h + s = 5.60$$

Subtracting, we get $2h = 6.90$, so $h = 3.45$. Ed's three hamburgers cost $10.35. The answer is (D).

## NEW WORD PROBLEMS

Let's try some "new" word problems. The only true difference from what we saw in Chapter 7 involves tens and units digit problems.

### Digit Problems

If we have a two-digit number, it is represented by $t$ for the tens digit and $u$ for the units digit. For example, for 68, $t = 6$ and $u = 8$. The value of the number is represented by $10t + u$. The number 68 would thus be $10(6) + 8$. The number with the digits reversed is $10u + t$, or $86 = 10(8) + 6$. The sum of the digits is $t + u$, or $6 + 8 = 14$ in this case.

**Example 9:**   In a two-digit number, the sum of the digits is 8. If the digits are reversed, the new number is 36 more than the original number. What is the number?

**Solution:**   There are two methods to answer this question:

Method A:  $t + u = 8$ is the first equation. The new number, $10u + t$ is (=) 36 more than the original number, or $10t + u + 36$. So the equation is $10u + t = 10t + u + 36$, or $9u - 9t = 36$. In this type of problem only, we can divide the equation by 9 and get $u - t = 4$. Since $t + u = 8$, adding these two equations gives $2u = 12$, or $u = 6$, so $t = 2$, and the number is 26.

Method B:  Since $t + u = 8$, the only possible answers could be 17, 26, or 35, since the number with the digits reversed is bigger. $71 - 17 \neq 38$, but $62 - 26 = 36$; so the number is 26.

## Mixture Problems

Mixture problems with two unknowns are treated similarly to how we did mixture problems with one unknown in the last chapter. It often helps to construct a chart.

**Example 10:**   How many pounds of peanuts at $3.00 a pound must be mixed with $7.00-per-pound cashews to give 20 pounds of a $6.00 mixture?

**Solution:**   Construct a chart with the given information.

|         | Cost/Pound × | Pounds = | Total Cost |
|---------|-----------|--------|-----------|
| Peanuts | 3 | $x$ | $3x$ |
| Cashews | 7 | $y$ | $7y$ |
| Mixture | 6 | 20 | 120 |

Let $x =$ pounds of peanuts and $y =$ pounds of cashews. According to the chart,

$$x + y = 20$$
$$3x + 7y = 120$$

Since we want $x$, multiply the top equation by $-7$, and add the result to the second equation.

$$-7x + -7y = -140$$
$$3x + 7y = 120$$

Adding, we get $-4x = -20$, so $x = 5$ pounds of peanuts.

## Age Problems

Age problems with two unknowns are treated similarly to how we did age problems with one unknown in the last chapter. It often helps to construct a chart.

**Example 11:**    Joan is 4 times the age of Ben. In 4 years, Joan will be $2\frac{1}{2}$ times the age of Ben. Ben will be how many years old then?

**Solution:**    Construct a chart with the given information.

|      | Age now | Age in 4 years |
|------|---------|----------------|
| Joan | $x$     | $x + 4$        |
| Ben  | $y$     | $y + 4$        |

Let $x =$ Joan's age and $y =$ Ben's age. The first equation is $x = 4y$. In 4 years, the equation is $x + 4 = \left(\frac{5}{2}\right)(y + 4)$, or $2(x + 4) = 5(y + 4)$. By the Distributive Law (Chapter 5), $2x + 8 = 5y + 20$, or $2x - 5y = 12$.

But we know $x = 4y$. So, by substitution, $2(4y) - 5y = 12$, or $3y = 12$, so $y = 4$ (Ben's present age). In 4 years, Ben will be $y + 4 = 8$ years old.

## Fraction Problems

Sometimes, trial and error finds the answer for you. Simply substitute the answer choices into the problem to see what works. But you should also be able to set up simultaneous equations. You might ask, "What is the best method?" The answer is, "Whatever gives you the answer the fastest." Everyone is different.

**Example 12:**  A fraction when reduced is $\frac{3}{4}$. If 1 is subtracted from the numerator and 2 is added to the denominator, the ratio becomes $\frac{2}{3}$. What is the original fraction?

**Solution:**  We have $\frac{x}{y} = \frac{3}{4}$, or $3y = 4x$, which gives us $-4x + 3y = 0$. We also have $\frac{x-1}{y+2} = \frac{2}{3}$, or, by cross-multiplication, $3(x - 1) = 2(y + 2)$. This gives us $3x - 2y = 7$. Our simultaneous equations are

$$-4x + 3y = 0$$
$$3x - 2y = 7$$

If we eliminate $x$ by multiplying the top equation by 3 and the bottom equation by 4 and adding the resulting equations. We get $y = 28$, and by substitution, $x = 21$. So the original fraction is $\frac{21}{28}$.

**Q  Let's do a few exercises.**

**Exercise 10:**  In a two-digit number, the tens digit is the square of the units digit. The difference between the number and the number reversed is 54. The original number is

A. 24                         D. 71

B. 39                         E. 93

C. 42

**Exercise 11:**  How many ounces of 40% alcohol must be mixed with 10 ounces of 70% alcohol to give a solution that is 45% alcohol?

A. 20                         D. 50

B. 30                         E. 60

C. 40

**Exercise 12:** May's age is twice Fay's age. In 15 years, Fay will be $\dfrac{3}{5}$ as old as May. The sum of their original ages is

A. 66

B. 75

C. 90

D. 96

E. 105

**Exercise 13:** If 4 less than $x$ is the same as 7 more than the product of 4 and $y$, which answer choice is true?

A. $x + 4y - 11 = 0$

B. $x + y + 15 = 0$

C. $x + y + 7 = 0$

D. $x + 4y - 11 = 0$

E. $4y - x + 11 = 0$

**Exercise 14:** The product of 4 and the sum of $x$ and $y$ is at least as large as the quotient of $a$ divided by $b$. This can be written as

A. $4x + y - \dfrac{a}{b} \geq 0$

B. $4x + y - \dfrac{a}{b} > 0$

C. $4(x + y) - \dfrac{a}{b} \geq 0$

D. $4(x + y) + \dfrac{a}{b} > 0$

E. $\dfrac{a}{b} - 4x + 4y < 0$

**Exercise 15:** The sum of the digits of a two-digit number is 10. The number reversed is 18 more than the original number. The original number is

A. 19

B. 28

C. 37

D. 46

E. 55

**Let's look at the answers.**

**Answer 10:** Trial and error is best for this problem. Of the answer choices, the only possible ones are 42 since $2^2 = 4$, and 93 since $3^2 = 9$. However, only for 93 is the second criterion true: $93 - 39 = 54$. The answer is (E).

**Answer 11:** This is a mixture problem. The principle is this: If we have 10 ounces of 70% alcohol, the amount of alcohol is $10(.70) = 7$ ounces of alcohol. Now construct a chart for this problem; eliminate the decimal point since all items in this will have a decimal.

|  | Ounces | × % alcohol | = Amount of Alcohol in mixture |
|---|---|---|---|
| 40% alcohol | $x$ | 40 | $40x$ |
| 70% alcohol | 10 | 70 | 700 |
| 45% alcohol mixture | $y$ | 45 | $45y$ |

We let $x =$ the amount of 40% alcohol, and $y =$ the total ounces in the mixture. We get $x + 10 = y$ and $40(x) + 10(70) = 45(y)$, since we can eliminate all decimal points in this equation. Substitute the first equation for $y$ because we want $x$: $40x + 700 = 45(x + 10)$, or $45x + 450 = 40x + 700$. Thus, $5x = 250$, and $x = 50$. The answer is (D).

**Answer 12:** Construct a chart in which May's age is $y$ and Fay's age is $x$.

|  | Age now | Age in 15 years |
|---|---|---|
| May | $x$ | $y + 15$ |
| Fay | $y$ | $x + 15$ |

From the chart $y = 2x$ and $x + 15 = \left(\dfrac{3}{5}\right)(y + 15)$, or $5(x + 15)$ $= 3(y + 15)$. Then $5x + 30 = 3y$. Substituting $y = 2x$, we get $5x + 30$ $= 3(2x)$; so $x = 30$ and $y = 60$. The sum of their ages is $x + y = 90$. The answer is (C).

**Answer 13:**  $x - 4 = 4y + 7$. When we rearrange the terms, we see that only (E) is correct.

**Answer 14:**  $4(x + y) \geq \dfrac{a}{b}$. When we rearrange the terms, we see that only (C) is correct.

**Answer 15:**  $t + u = 10$ and $10u + t = 10t + u + 18$, or $9u - 9t = 18$. Dividing both sides of this equation by 9, we get $u - t = 2$. We thus have $t + u = 10$ and $u - t = 2$. Adding these equations, we get $2u = 12$, so $u = 6$ and $t = 4$. Thus, the number is 46. The answer is (D). We could have tried trial and error for this problem.

Let's take a break from algebra and word problems now, and look at some familiar lines and shapes.

*"Your journey began from a single point. You travel in a straight line; sometimes the slope may be steep and the distance seems far, but you are now at the midpoint. The endpoint is in sight."*

**This** topic used to be part of a course called analytic geometry (algebraic geometry). We'll start at the beginning.

## POINTS IN THE PLANE

We start with a **plane**—a two-dimensional space, like a piece of paper. On this plane, we draw two perpendicular lines, or **axes**. The *x*-axis is horizontal; the *y*-axis is vertical. Positive *x* is to the right; negative *x* is to the left. Positive *y* is up; negative *y* is down. Points in the plane are indicated by **ordered pairs** (*x*, *y*). The *x* number, called the **first coordinate** or **abscissa**, is always given first; the *y* number, called the **second coordinate** or **ordinate**, is always given second. Here are some points on the plane.

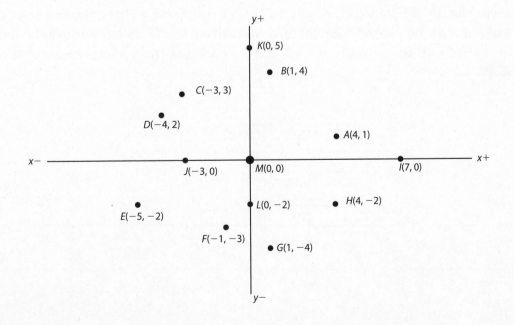

Note the following:

For any point on the *x*-axis, the *y* coordinate always is 0.

For any point on the *y*-axis, the *x* coordinate is 0.

The point where the two axes meet, (0, 0), is called the **origin**.

The axes divide the plane into four **quadrants**, usually written with roman numerals, starting in the upper right quadrant and going counterclockwise.

In quadrant I, $x > 0$ and $y > 0$.

In quadrant II, $x < 0$ and $y > 0$.

In quadrant III, $x < 0$ and $y < 0$.

In quadrant IV, $x > 0$ and $y < 0$.

```
                    y
                    |
          II        |        I
                    |
        x < 0       |     x > 0
        y > 0       |     y > 0
                    |
   x ───────────────┼─────────────── x
                    |
        x < 0       |     x > 0
        y < 0       |     y < 0
                    |
          III       |        IV
                    |
                    y
```

In the following figure, we draw the line $y = x$. For every point on this line, the first coordinate has the same value as the second coordinate, or $y = x$. If we shade the area above this line, $y > x$ in the shaded portion. Similarly, $x > y$ in the unshaded portion. Sometimes, questions on the GRE ask about this.

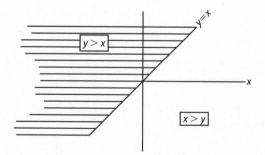

The following figure shows symmetry about the *x*-axis, *y*-axis, and the origin. Suppose (*a*, *b*) is in quadrant I. Then (−*a*, *b*) would be in quadrant II, (−*a*, −*b*) would be in quadrant III, and (*a*, −*b*) would be in quadrant IV, as pictured.

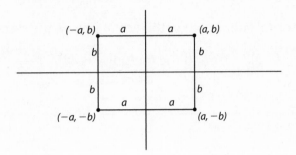

# LINES

## Distance and Midpoint

The formulas for distance and midpoint look a little complicated, but they are fairly easy to use. It just takes practice.

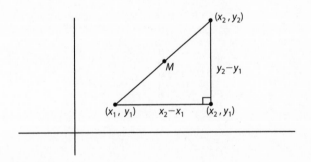

To find the **distance** between two points $(x_1, y_1)$ and $(x_2, y_2)$ on a plane, we must use the distance formula:

$$d = \sqrt{(x_2 - x_1)^2 + (y_2 - y_1)^2}$$

The distance formula is just the Pythagorean Theorem (discussed in the next chapter).

Distances are always positive. You may be six feet tall, but you cannot be minus six feet tall.

The **midpoint** of a line between two points $(x_1, y_1)$ and $(x_2, y_2)$ on a plane is given by

$$M = \left( \frac{x_1 + x_2}{2}, \frac{y_1 + y_2}{2} \right)$$

If the line is horizontal, these formulas simplify to $d = x_2 - x_1$ and $M = \dfrac{x_1 + x_2}{2}$.

Similarly, if the line is vertical, these formulas simplify to $d = y_2 - y_1$ and $M = \dfrac{y_1 + y_2}{2}$.

For example, for the horizontal line shown in the figure below, the distance between the points is $d = x_2 - x_1 = 7 - (-3) = 10$, and the midpoint is $M = \dfrac{x_1 + x_2}{2} = \dfrac{-3 + 7}{2} = 2$.

Similarly, for the vertical line shown in the figure below, the distance between the points is $d = y_2 - y_1 = -3 - (-7) = 4$, and the midpoint is $M = \dfrac{y_1 + y_2}{2} = \dfrac{(-7) + (-3)}{2} = -5$.

## SLOPE

The **slope** of a line tells by how much the line is "tilted" compared to the x-axis. The formula for the slope of a line is

$$m = \frac{\text{rise}}{\text{run}} = \frac{\text{change in } y}{\text{change in } x} = \frac{y_2 - y_1}{x_2 - x_1}$$

where $(x_1, y_1)$ and $(x_2, y_2)$ are any two points on the line.

Note the following facts about the slope of a line, as shown in the figure below:

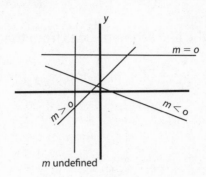

The slope is positive if the line goes from the lower left to the upper right.

The slope is negative if it goes from the upper left to the lower right.

Horizontal lines have zero slope.

Vertical lines have no slope or undefined slope or "infinite" slope.

**Example 1:**   Find the distance, slope, and midpoint for the line segment joining these points:

   **a.** (2, 3) and (6, 8)        **c.** (7, 3) and (4, 3)

   **b.** (4, −3) and (−2, 0)       **d.** (2, 1) and (2, 5)

**Solutions:**   **a.** We let $(x_1, y_1) = (2, 3) =$ and $(x_2, y_2) = (6, 8)$, although the other way around is also okay.

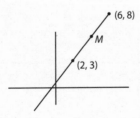

Then

$$\text{Distance} = d = \sqrt{(x_2 - x_1)^2 + (y_2 - y_1)^2}$$
$$= \sqrt{(6 - 2)^2 + (8 - 3)^2} = \sqrt{41}$$

$$\text{Slope} = m = \frac{y_2 - y_1}{x_2 - x_1} = \frac{8 - 3}{6 - 2} = \frac{5}{4}$$

$$\text{Midpoint} = M = \left(\frac{x_1 + x_2}{2}, \frac{y_1 + y_2}{2}\right) = \left(\frac{2 + 6}{2}, \frac{3 + 8}{2}\right) = (4, 5.5)$$

Notice that the slope is positive; the line segment goes from the lower left to the upper right.

**b.** We let $(x_1, y_1) = (4, -3) =$ and $(x_2, y_2) = (-2, 0)$.

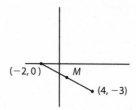

$$\text{Distance} = d = \sqrt{(-2 - 4)^2 + (0 - (-3))^2}$$
$$= \sqrt{45} = \sqrt{3 \times 3 \times 5} = 3\sqrt{5}$$

$$\text{Slope} = m = \frac{0 - (-3)}{-2 - 4} = \frac{-1}{2}$$

$$\text{Midpoint} = M = \left(\frac{4 + (-2)}{2}, \frac{-3 + 0}{2}\right) = (1, -1.5)$$

Notice that the slope is negative; the line segment goes from the upper left to the lower right.

**c.** We let $(x_1, y_1) = (7, 3) =$ and $(x_2, y_2) = (4, 3)$.

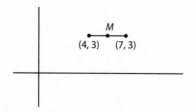

It is a one-dimensional distance, so $d = |4 - 7| = 3$

$$\text{Slope} = m = \frac{3 - 3}{4 - 7} = \frac{0}{-3} = 0$$

$$\text{Midpoint} = M = \left(\frac{7 + 4}{2}, \frac{3 + 3}{2}\right) = (5.5, 3)$$

Notice that the horizontal line segment has slope $m = 0$.

**d.** We let $(x_1, y_1) = (2, 1) =$ and $(x_2, y_2) = (2, 5)$.

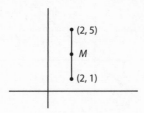

Again, this is a one-dimensional distance, so $d = |5 - 1| = 4$

$$\text{Slope} = m = \frac{5 - 1}{2 - 2} = \frac{4}{0}, \text{undefined}$$

$$\text{Midpoint} = M = \left( \frac{2 + 2}{2}, \frac{5 + 1}{2} \right) = (2, 3)$$

Notice that the slope of the vertical line segment is undefined.

 **Now let's do some exercises.**

Use the figure below for Exercises 1 and 2.

The line through $(m, n)$ and $(p, q)$ is parallel to the $x$-axis.

|            | **Column A** | **Column B** |
|------------|:------------:|:------------:|
| **Exercise 1:** | $m$ | $p$ |
| **Exercise 2:** | $n$ | $q$ |

Use the figure below for Exercises 3, 4, and 5.

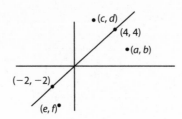

| **Exercise 3:** | $c$ | $d$ |
| --- | --- | --- |
| **Exercise 4:** | $e$ | $f$ |
| **Exercise 5:** | $\dfrac{d}{c}$ | $\dfrac{b}{a}$ |

**Exercise 6:** The coordinates of $P$ are $(j, k)$. If $s < k < j < r$, which of the points shown in the figure could have the coordinates $(r, s)$?

A. A                    D. D

B. B                    E. E

C. C

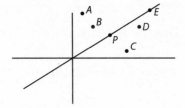

Use the figure below for Exercises 7 and 8.

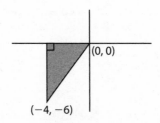

**Exercise 7:** Which of the following points is inside the triangle?

A. $(-3,6)$              D. $(-3,-4)$

B. $(-5,-5)$             E. $(-1,-3)$

C. $(-2,-5)$

**Exercise 8:**   The area of the triangle is

          **A.** 6                   **D.** 24

          **B.** 12               **E.** 48

          **C.** 18

**Exercise 9:**   $M$ is the midpoint of line segment $AB$. If the coordinates of $A$ are $(m, -n)$, then the coordinates of $B$ are

          **A.** $(m, n)$            **D.** $(n, m)$

          **B.** $(-m, n)$         **E.** $(-n, -m)$

          **C.** $(-m, -n)$

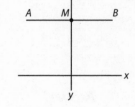

**Exercise 10:**   In the given figure, $AB \parallel x$-axis and $PQ = AB$.

          The coordinates of point $A$ are

          **A.** $(-1, 2)$          **D.** $(9, 0)$

          **B.** $(1, 2)$            **E.** $(-9, 2)$

          **C.** $(9, -8)$

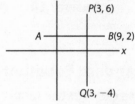

 **Let's look at the answers.**

**Answer 1:**   $p > 0$ and $m < 0$. The answer is (B).

**Answer 2:**   $n$ and $q$ are the same height. The answer is (C).

**Answer 3:**   Point $(c, d)$ is to the left and above point $(4, 4)$, so $c < 4$, but $d > 4$. The answer is (B).

**Answer 4:**   Point $(e, f)$ is to the right and below $(-2, -2)$, so $e > -2$ and $f < -2$. The answer is (A).

**Answer 5:**   Since $d$ is bigger than $c$, $\dfrac{d}{c} > 1$; since $a$ is bigger than $b$, $\dfrac{b}{a} < 1$. The answer is (A).

**Answer 6:**     For points C, D, and E, the x value is bigger than the x value of P; only point C has a y value less than the y value of P. The answer is (C).

**Answer 7:**     The answer is (D).

**Answer 8:**     We really haven't gotten to this, but I asked it because we have the picture. The area of the triangle is half the area of the rectangle.

$$A = \frac{1}{2}bh = \frac{1}{2} \times 4 \times 6 = 12$$

The answer is (B).

**Answer 9:**     Slightly tricky. Point B has the same y value as A, but its x value is the negative of the x value for A. The answer is (C).

**Answer 10:**     The length of PQ = 10. For the length of AB to be 10, A must be $(-1, 2)$ since $9 - (-1) = 10$. The answer is (A).

## Standard Equation of a Line

Let's go over the facts we need.

**Standard form** of the line: $Ax + By = C$; A, B both $\neq 0$.

The **x-intercept**, the point at which the line hits the x-axis, occurs when $y = 0$

The **y-intercept**, the point at which the line hits the y-axis, occurs when $x = 0$.

**Point-slope form** of a line: Given slope m and point $(x_1, y_1)$, the point-slope form of a line is

$$m = \frac{y - y_1}{x - x_1}$$

**Slope-intercept form** of a line: $y = mx + b$, where m is the slope and $(0, b)$ is the y-intercept.

Lines of the form:

$y$ = constant, such as $y = 2$, are lines parallel to the x-axis; the equation of the x-axis is $y = 0$.

$x$ = constant, such as $x = -3$, are lines parallel to the y- axis; the equation of the y-axis is $x = 0$.

$y = mx$ are lines that pass through the origin.

**Example 2:** For $Ax + By = C$, find the $x$ and $y$ intercepts.

**Solution:** The $y$-intercept means $x = 0$; so $y = \dfrac{C}{B}$, and the $y$ intercept is $\left(0, \dfrac{C}{B}\right)$.

The $x$-intercept means $y = 0$; so $x = \dfrac{C}{A}$, and the $x$ intercept is $\left(\dfrac{C}{A}, 0\right)$.

**Example 3:** For $3x - 4y = 7$, find the $x$ and $y$ intercepts.

**Solution:** For the $y$-intercept, $x = 0$; so $y = \dfrac{7}{-4}$, and the $y$-intercept is $\left(0, -\dfrac{7}{4}\right)$. For the $x$-intercept, $y = 0$; so $x = \dfrac{7}{3}$, and the $x$-intercept is $\left(\dfrac{7}{3}, 0\right)$.

**Example 4:** Given $m = \dfrac{3}{2}$ and point $(5, -7)$, write the equation of the line in standard form.

**Solution:** $m = \dfrac{y - y_1}{x - x_1}$, so $\dfrac{3}{2} = \dfrac{y - (-7)}{x - 5}$. Cross-multiplying, we get $3(x - 5) = 2(y + 7)$, or $3x - 2y = 29$.

**Example 5:** Given points $(3,6)$ and $(7,11)$, write the line in slope-intercept form.

**Solution:** $y = mx + b$. $m = \dfrac{11 - 6}{7 - 3} = \dfrac{5}{4}$, and we will use point $(3, 6)$, so $x = 3$ and $y = 6$. Therefore, $6 = \dfrac{5}{4}(3) + b$, and $b = \dfrac{9}{4}$. So the line is $y = \dfrac{5}{4}x + \dfrac{9}{4}$.

**Example 6:** Sketch lines $x = -3$, $y = 8$, and $y = \dfrac{2}{3}x$.

**Solution:**

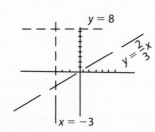

**Let's do a few more exercises.**

**Exercise 11:** A line with the same slope as the line $y = \dfrac{2}{3}x - 2$ is

    **A.** $2x = 6 - 3y$           **D.** $-2x - 3y = 6$

    **B.** $2x + 3y = 6$           **E.** $2y = 6 - 3x$

    **C.** $2x - 3y = 6$

**Exercise 12:** Find the area of the triangle formed with the positive $x$-axis, positive $y$-axis, and the line though the point (3,4) with slope $-2$. The area is

    **A.** 5           **D.** 50

    **B.** 15          **E.** 10

    **C.** 25

**A** **Let's look at the answers.**

**Answer 11:** You have to solve for $y$ in each case. The only one that works is (C).

**Answer 12:** You must draw the figure.

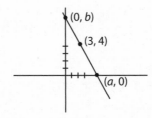

The area of the triangle is one-half the $x$-intercept times the $y$-intercept.

The equation of the line is $-2 = \dfrac{y - 4}{x - 3}$. If we let $x = 0$, the $y$-intercept is

10. If we let $y = 0$, the $x$–intercept is 5. Area $= \dfrac{1}{2}ab = \dfrac{1}{2} \times 5 \times 10 = 25$.

The answer is (C).

Let's finally get to angles and triangles.

"*Understanding the area and its perimeter will enhance your chances for success.*"

**Before** I wrote this chapter, I formulated in my head how the chapter would go. Too many of the questions on angles had to do with triangles. So I decided to write the chapters together. Let's start with some definitions.

## TYPES OF ANGLES

There are several ways to classify angles, such as by angle measure, as shown here:

**Acute angle:** An angle of less than 90°.

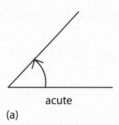

acute

(a)

**Right angle:** A 90° angle. As we will see, some other words that indicate a right angle or angles are perpendicular (⊥), altitude, and height.

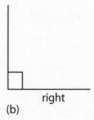

right

(b)

**Obtuse angle:** An angle of more than 90° but less than 180°.

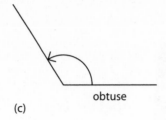

(c)

**Straight angle:** An angle of 180°.

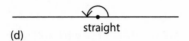

(d)          straight

**Reflex angle:** An angle of more than 180° but less than 360°.

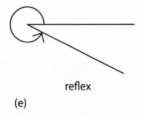

reflex

(e)

Angles are also named for their relation to other angles, such as:

**Supplementary angles:** Two angles that total 180°.

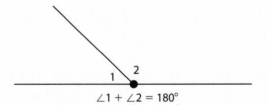

$\angle 1 + \angle 2 = 180°$

**Complementary angles:** Two angles that total 90°.

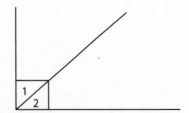

*A note of interest:* Once around a circle is 360°. The reason that it is 360° is that the ancient Babylonians, about 7000 years ago, thought there were 360 days in a year. Three hundred sixty degrees is unique to the planet Earth.

You probably learned that angles are congruent and measures of angles are equal. I am using what I learned; it is simpler and makes understanding easier. So "angle 1 equals angle 2" (or $\angle 1 = \angle 2$) means the angles are both congruent and equal in degrees.

## ANGLES FORMED BY PARALLEL LINES

Let's look at angles formed when a line crosses two parallel lines. In the figure below, $\ell_1 \parallel \ell_2$, and $t$ is a transversal, a line that cuts two or more lines. It is not important that you know the names of these angles, although many of you will. It is important only to know that angles formed by a line crossing parallel lines that look equal are equal. The angles that are not equal add to 180°. In this figure, $\angle 1 = \angle 4 = \angle 5 = \angle 8$ and $\angle 2 = \angle 3 = \angle 6 = \angle 7$. Any angle from the first group added to any angle from the second group totals 180°.

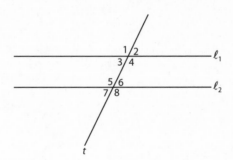

**Vertical angles**, which are the opposite angles formed when two lines cross, are equal. In the figure below, $\angle 1 = \angle 3$ and $\angle 2 = \angle 4$. Also, $\angle 1 + \angle 2 = \angle 2 + \angle 3 = \angle 3 + \angle 4 = \angle 4 + \angle 1 = 180°$.

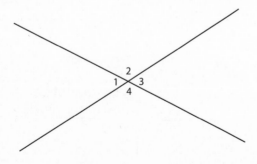

**Q** **Let's do some exercises.**

**Exercise 1:**    $\angle b =$

A. 45°          D. 105°

B. 60°          E. 135°

C. 90°

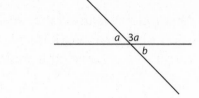

**Exercise 2:**    $\ell_1 \| \ell_2. \; m - n =$

A. 30°          D. 90°

B. 50°          E. 180°

C. 65°

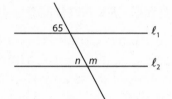

**Exercise 3:**    $y + z =$

A. $180° - x$          D. $90° + \dfrac{5x}{4}$

B. $180° - \dfrac{x}{4}$          E. $90° - \dfrac{5x}{4}$

C. $45° - \dfrac{x}{4}$

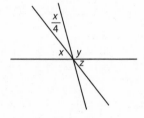

**Exercise 4:**    $180° - w =$

A. $x + w$          D. $y - z$

B. $x + y$          E. $z - w$

C. $y + z$

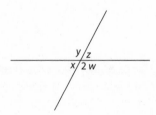

**Exercise 5:**    $b =$

A. 5.5°          D. 12.5°

B. 7°          E. Cannot be
                  determined

C. 10°

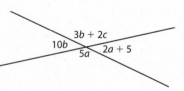

**Exercise 6:**    $y$ (in terms of $x$) $=$

A. $x$          D. $140° + x$

B. $x + 40°$          E. $320° - x$

C. $140° - x$

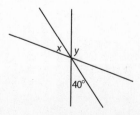

**Exercise 7:**   $\angle x =$

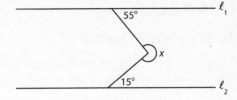

A. $70°$          D. $290°$

B. $110°$         E. $345°$

C. $210°$

 **Now let's look at the answers.**

**Answer 1:**   $3a + a = 180°$; $a = 45°$ and $b = a = 45°$. The answer is (A).

**Answer 2:**   $n = 65°$ and $n + m = 180°$; so $m = 115°$, and $m - n = 50°$. The answer is (B).

**Answer 3:**   $\dfrac{x}{4} + y + z = 180°$, so $y + z = 180° - \dfrac{x}{4}$. The answer is (B).

**Answer 4:**   Below the line, $x + 2w = x + w + w = 180°$, so $x + w = 180° - w$. The answer is (A).

**Answer 5:**   This is a toughie. Don't look at vertical angles, look at the supplementary angles. On the bottom, we have $5a + 2a + 5° = 180°$, so $7a = 175°$, and $a = 25°$. Then, on the left, $10b + 5a = 180°$. Substituting $a = 25°$, we get $10b = 180° - 125° = 55°$, or $b = 5.5°$. The answer is (A).

We could also have looked at the vertical angles, once we determined that $a = 25°$. Then $10b = 2a + 5° = 2(25°) + 5° = 55°$, so $b = 5.5°$.

**Answer 6:**   $x + y + 40° = 180°$; so $y = 140° - x$. The answer is (C).

**Answer 7:**   Draw $\ell_3 \parallel \ell_1$ and $\ell_2$. $a = 55°$, $b = 15°$, $a + b = 70°$

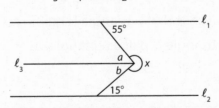

$\angle x = 360° - 70° = 290°$. The answer is (D).

So many angle questions on the GRE involve triangles that we ought to look at triangles next.

# TRIANGLES

## Basics about Triangles

A **triangle** is a polygon with three sides. Angles are usually indicated with capital letters. The side opposite the angle is indicated with the same letter, only lowercase.

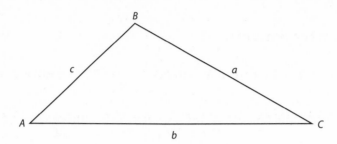

You should know the following general facts about triangles.

The **sum of the angles** of a triangle is 180°.

The **altitude,** or **height** (h), of △ABC shown below is the line segment drawn from a vertex perpendicular to the base, extended if necessary. The **base** of the triangle is AC = b.

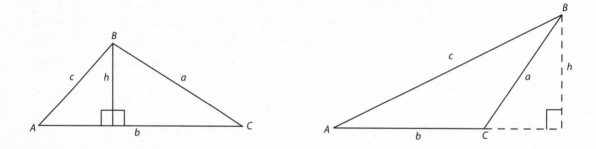

The **perimeter of a triangle** is the sum of the three sides: $p = a + b + c$.

The **area of a triangle** is $A = \frac{1}{2}bh$. The reason is that a triangle is half a rectangle. Since the area of a rectangle is base time height; a triangle is half a rectangle, as shown in the figure below.

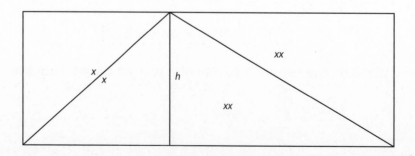

An **angle bisector** is a line that bisects an angle in a triangle. In the figure below, *BD* bisects ∠*ABC* if ∠1 = ∠2.

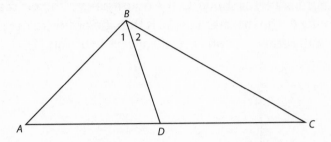

A **median** is a line drawn from any angle of a triangle to the midpoint of the opposite side. In the figure below, *BD* is a median to side *AC* if *D* is the midpoint of *AC*.

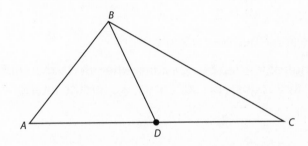

There are many kinds of triangles. One way to describe them is by their sides.

A **scalene** triangle has three unequal sides and three unequal angles.

An **isosceles** triangle has at least two equal sides. In the figure below, side *BC* (or *a*) is called the **base**; it may be equal to, greater than, or less than any other side. The **legs**, *AB* = *AC* (or *b* = *c*) are equal. Angle *A* is the **vertex angle**; it may equal the others, or be greater than or less than the others. The **base angles** are equal: ∠*B* = ∠*C*.

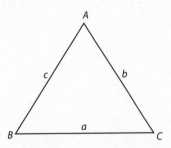

An **equilateral** triangle is a triangle with all equal sides. All angles equal 60°, so this triangle is sometimes called an **equiangular** triangle. For an equilateral triangle of side *s*, the perimeter $p = 3s$, and the area $A = \dfrac{s^2\sqrt{3}}{4}$. This formula seems to be very popular lately, and you may see it on the GRE.

Triangles can also be described by their angles.

An **acute** triangle has three angles that are less than 90°.

A **right** triangle has one right angle, as shown in the figure below. The **right angle** is usually denoted by the letter capital C. The **hypotenuse** AB is the side opposite the right angle. The **legs**, AC and BC, are not necessarily equal. $\angle A$ and $\angle B$ are always **acute** angles.

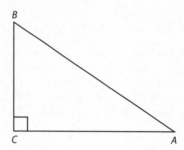

An **obtuse** triangle has one angle between 90° and 180°.

An **exterior angle** of a triangle is formed by extending one side. In the figure below, $\angle 1$ is an exterior angle. An exterior angle equals the sum of its two remote interior angles: $\angle 1 = \angle A + \angle B$.

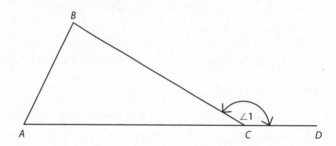

There are two other facts about triangles you should know:

1.  The sum of any two sides of a triangle must be greater than the third side.

2.  The largest side lies opposite the largest angle; and the largest angle lies opposite the largest side, as shown in the figure below.

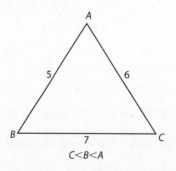

$C < B < A$

**Example 1:**     Give one set of angles for a triangle that satisfies the following descriptions:

| Description | Solution |
|---|---|
| **a.** Scalene, acute | 50°, 60°, 70° |
| **b.** Scalene, right | 30°, 60°, 90°: We will deal with this one soon. |
| **c.** Scalene, obtuse | 30°, 50°, 100° |
| **d.** Isosceles, acute | 20°, 80°, 80° |
| **e.** Isosceles, right | Only one: 45°, 45°, 90°: We will deal with this one soon also. |
| **f.** Isosceles, obtuse | 20°, 20°, 140° |
| **g.** Equilateral | Only one: three 60° angles |

Let's first do some exercises with angles. Then we'll turn to area and perimeter exercises. We'll finish the chapter with our old friend Pythagoras and his famous theorem.

 **Let's do some more exercises.**

|  |  | **Column A** | **Column B** |
|---|---|---|---|
| **Exercise 8:** |  | *a* | *b* |
| **Exercise 9:** |  | ∠1 | ∠2 |

**Exercise 10:**

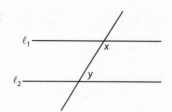

$x + y$                    180°

**Exercise 11:** If two sides of a triangle are 4 and 7, and if only integer measures are allowed for the sides, the third side must be taken from which set?

    **A.** {5, 6, 7, 8, 9, 10, 11}    **D.** {3, 4, 5, 6, 7, 8, 9, 10, 11}

    **B.** {4, 5, 6, 7, 8, 9, 10}    **E.** {1, 2, 3, 4, 5, 6, 7, 8, 9, 10, 11}.

    **C.** {3, 4, 5, 6, 7, 8, 9, 10}

**Exercise 12:** Arrange the sides in order, largest to smallest, for the figure shown below.

    **A.** $a > b > c$    **D.** $b > c > a$

    **B.** $a > c > b$    **E.** $c > a > b$

    **C.** $b > a > c$

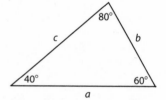

**Exercise 13:** $x = 2y; z =$

    **A.** 30°    **D.** 60°

    **B.** 40°    **E.** 90°

    **C.** 50°

**Exercise 14:** $WX$ bisects $\angle ZXY$; $\angle Z =$

    **A.** 20°    **D.** 60°

    **B.** 40°    **E.** 70°

    **C.** 50°

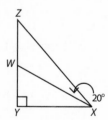

**Exercise 15:** $\angle TVW = 10x$; $x$ could be

    **A.** 3°    **D.** 16°

    **B.** 6°    **E.** 20°

    **C.** 9°

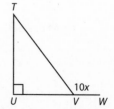

**Exercise 16:** Write $b$ in terms of $a$:

A. $a + 90°$          D. $180° - a$

B. $2a$              E. $180° - 2a$

C. $2a + 90°$

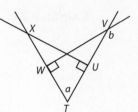

**Exercise 17:** $a + b + c + d =$

A. $90°$             D. $360°$

B. $180°$            E. $450°$

C. $270°$

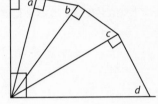

**Exercise 18:** The largest angle is

A. $30°$             D. $80°$

B. $50°$             E. $90°$

C. $70°$

**Exercise 19:** $\ell_1 \parallel AB; y =$

A. $40°$             D. $80°$

B. $60°$             E. Can't be determined

C. $70°$

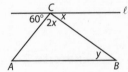

**Exercise 20:** $\ell_1 \parallel AB; y =$

A. $40°$             D. $80°$

B. $60°$             E. Can't be determined

C. $70°$

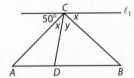

Use $\triangle ABC$ for Exercises 21 and 22.

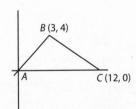

**Exercise 21:** The area of $\triangle ABC$ is

A. 18                D. 48

B. 24                E. 60

C. 36

**Exercise 22:** The perimeter of $\triangle ABC$ is

A. $17 + \sqrt{97}$      D. $\sqrt{266}$

B. 27      E. $10\sqrt{10}$

C. 32

For Exercises 23 and 24, use this figure of a square with an equilateral triangle on top of it, $AE = 20$.

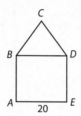

**Exercise 23:** The perimeter of $ABCDE$ is

A. 50      D. 160

B. 100      E. 200

C. 120

**Exercise 24:** The area of $ABCDE$ is

A. 600      D. 800

B. $100(4 + \sqrt{2})$      E. 1,000

C. $100(4 + \sqrt{3})$

For Exercises 25 and 26, use $\triangle ABC$ with midpoints $X$, $Y$, and $Z$.

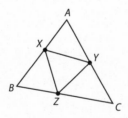

**Exercise 25:** If the perimeter of $\triangle ABC$ is 1, the perimeter of $\triangle XYZ$ is

A. $\dfrac{1}{16}$        D. $\dfrac{1}{2}$

B. $\dfrac{1}{8}$        E. 1

C. $\dfrac{1}{4}$

**Exercise 26:** If the area of $\triangle ABC$ is 1, the area of $\triangle XYZ$ is

A. $\dfrac{1}{16}$        D. $\dfrac{1}{2}$

B. $\dfrac{1}{8}$        E. 1

C. $\dfrac{1}{4}$

**Exercise 27:** In the figure shown, $BC = \dfrac{1}{3}BD$. If the area of $\triangle ABC = 10$, the area of rectangle $ABDE$ is

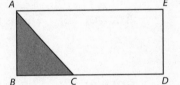

A. 30        D. 120

B. 40        E. Can't be
determined

C. 60

 **Let's look at the answers.**

**Answer 8:** Since $a$ is opposite the 50° angle, it is larger than $b$, which is opposite the 40° angle. The answer is (A). Figure not done to scale. Beware!

**Answer 9:** Since $\angle 2$ is an exterior angle, it is equal to the sum of the two remote interior angles, so it is bigger than either of them. The answer is (B).

**Answer 10:** Any two unequal angles formed in this figure total 180°. The answer is (C).

**Answer 11:**   The third side $s$ must be greater than the difference and less than the sum of the other two sides, or $> 7 - 4$ and $< 7 + 4$. Thus the third side must be between 3 and 11. The answer is (B).

**Answer 12:**   Judge the relative lengths of the sides by the size of the angles opposite them. Then $a > c > b$. The answer is (B).

  Watch out for the words "Not drawn to scale." If it is a simple figure, "not drawn to scale" usually means it truly is not drawn to scale, and you cannot assume relative sizes without being given actual measurements. However, if it is a semi-complicated or complicated figure, the figure probably *is* drawn to scale.

**Answer 13:**   $y = 30°$; $x = 60°$; and $z = 30°$. The answer is (A).

**Answer 14:**   $\angle ZXY = 40°$, so $\angle Z$ must be $50°$. The answer is (C).

**Answer 15:**   $\angle TVW$ must be between $90°$ and $180°$, so $9° < x < 18°$. Only answer (D) is correct.

**Answer 16:**   This is really tricky. $UX$ is drawn to confuse you. In $\triangle TVW$, $b$ is the exterior angle, so $b = a + 90°$. The answer is (A).

**Answer 17:**   The sum of 4 triangles is $4 \times 180° = 720°$. The sum of 5 right angles (don't forget the one in the lower left of the figure, which is the sum of four acute angles of the triangles) is $450°$; so $a + b + c + d = 720° - 450° = 270°$. The answer is (C).

**Answer 18:**   $x + 2x + 20 + 3x - 20 = 180$, or $6x = 180$, so $x = 30$. $2x + 20 = 80$ and $3x - 20 = 70$. The largest angle is $80°$. The answer is (D).

**Answer 19:**   $2x + x + 60 = 180$; $x = 40°$. But $y = x = 40°$ (because $\ell_1 \parallel AB$). The answer is (A).

**Answer 20:**   $y$ cannot be determined. The answer is (E).

  The GRE occasionally asks a question for which there is no answer. However, I've never seen two in a row and I've seen thousands of similar questions.

**Answer 21:** $A = \dfrac{1}{2}bh = \dfrac{1}{2} \times 12 \times 4 = 24$. The answer is (B).

**Answer 22:** Use the distance formula to find sides $AB$ and $BC$. $p = AC + AB + BC$

$$= 12 + \sqrt{4^2 + 3^2} + \sqrt{(3-12)^2 + (4-0)}$$

$$= 12 + \sqrt{25} + \sqrt{97} = 17 + \sqrt{97}.$$

The answer is (A).

**Answer 23:** Do not include $BD$; $p = 5 \times 20 = 100$. The answer is (B).

**Answer 24:** Area $= s^2 + \dfrac{s^2\sqrt{3}}{4} = 20^2 + \dfrac{20^2\sqrt{3}}{4} = 400 + 100\sqrt{3}$. The answer is (C).

**Answer 25:** If the perimeter of $\triangle ABC$ is 1, and all the sides of $\triangle XYZ$ are half of those of $\triangle ABC$, so is the perimeter. The answer is (D).

**Answer 26:** If the sides of $\triangle XYZ$ are half of those of $\triangle ABC$, the area of $\triangle XYZ$ is $\left(\dfrac{1}{2}\right)^2 A = \dfrac{1}{4}$. The answer is (C).

**Answer 27:** If we draw lines parallel to $DE$ to divide the original rectangle into three congruent rectangles, and then divide each rectangle into two triangles, we see that each triangle is one-sixth of the rectangle. So the area of the rectangle is $6(10) = 60$. The answer is (C).

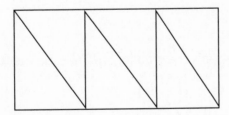

We'll have more of these types of exercises as part of Chapter 12, Circles.

Let's go on to good old Pythagoras.

# PYTHAGOREAN THEOREM

This is perhaps the most famous math theorem of all. Most theorems have one proof. A small fraction of these have two. This theorem, however, has more than a hundred, including three by past presidents of the United States. We've had some smart presidents who actually knew some math.

The Pythagorean Theorem simply states:

*In a right triangle, the hypotenuse squared is equal to the sum of the squares of the legs.*

In symbols, $c^2 = a^2 + b^2$.

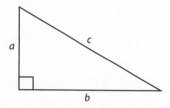

As a teacher, I must show you one proof.

*Proof:*

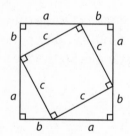

In this figure, the larger square equals the smaller square plus the four congruent triangles. In symbols, $(a + b)^2 = c^2 + 4\left(\frac{1}{2}ab\right)$.

Multiplying this equation out, we get $a^2 + 2ab + b^2 = c^2 + 2ab$. Then canceling $2ab$ from both sides, we get $c^2 = a^2 + b^2$. The proof is complete.

There are two basic problems the Pythagorean Theorem needs you to know how to do: finding the hypotenuse and finding one of the legs of the right triangle.

**Example 2:**   Solve for *x*:

**Solution:**   $x^2 = 7^2 + 5^2; x = \sqrt{74}.$

**Example 3:**   Solve for *x*:

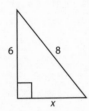

**Solution:**   $8^2 = 6^2 + x^2$, or $x^2 = 64 - 36 = 28$. So $x = \sqrt{28} = \sqrt{2 \times 2 \times 7} = 2\sqrt{7}.$

Notice that the hypotenuse squared is always by itself, whether it is a number or a letter.

## Pythagorean Triples

Because no calculator is allowed on the exam, it is a good idea to memorize some Pythagorean triples. These are the measures of sides of a triangle that are *always* right triangles. The hypotenuse is always listed third in the group.

The 3-4-5 group:        3-4-5, 6-8-10, 9-12-15, 12-16-20, 15-20-25

The 5-12-13 group:      5-12-13, 10-24-26

The rest:               8-15-17, 7-24-25, 20-21-29, 9-40-41, 11-60-61

## Special Right Triangles

You ought to know two other special right triangles, the isosceles right triangle (with angles 45°-45°-90°) and the 30°-60°-90° right triangle. The facts about these triangles can all be found by using the Pythagorean Theorem.

1.  The 45°-45°-90° isosceles right triangle:

    - The legs are equal.

    - To find a leg given the hypotenuse, divide by $\sqrt{2}$ $\left(\text{or multiply by } \dfrac{\sqrt{2}}{2}\right)$.

    - To find the hypotenuse given a leg, multiply by $\sqrt{2}$.

**Example 4:** Find *x* and *y* for this isosceles right triangle.

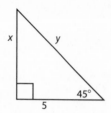

**Solution:** *x* = 5 (the legs are equal); $y = 5\sqrt{2}$.

**Example 5:** Find *x* and *y* for this isosceles right triangle.

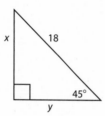

**Solution:** $x = y = \dfrac{18}{\sqrt{2}} = 18 \times \dfrac{\sqrt{2}}{2} = 9\sqrt{2}$.

2. The 30°-60°-90° right triangle.
   - If the shorter leg (opposite the 30° angle) is not given, get it first. It is always half the hypotenuse.
   - To find the short leg given the hypotenuse: divide by 2.
   - To find the hypotenuse given the short leg: multiply by 2.
   - To find the short leg given the long leg: divide by $\sqrt{3}$ $\left(\text{or multiply by } \dfrac{\sqrt{3}}{3}\right)$.
   - To find the long leg given the short leg: multiply by $\sqrt{3}$.

**Example 6:** Find *x* and *y* for this right triangle.

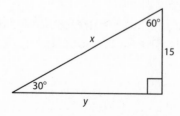

**Solution:** The short leg is given (15); *x* = 2(15) = 30; $y = 15\sqrt{3}$.

**Example 7:**  Find $x$ and $y$ for this right triangle.

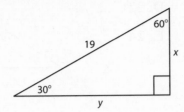

**Solution:**  $x = \dfrac{19}{2} = 9.5.\ y = 9.5\sqrt{3}.$

**Example 8:**  Find $x$ and $y$ for this right triangle.

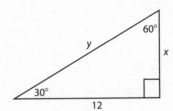

**Solution:**  $x = \dfrac{12}{\sqrt{3}} = 12\dfrac{\sqrt{3}}{3} = 4\sqrt{3}\ ; y = 2(4\sqrt{3}) = 8\sqrt{3}.$

**(Q)  Let's do a few exercises.**

**Exercise 28:**  Two sides of a right triangle are 3 and $\sqrt{5}$.

    I.   The third side is 2.

    II.  The third side is 4.

    III. The third side is $\sqrt{14}$.

    Which of the following choices is correct?

    **A.** Statement II is true      **D.** Statements I and III are true

    **B.** Statement III is true     **E.** Statements I, II, and III are true

    **C.** Statements I and II
       are true

**Exercise 29:**  The area of square $ABCD =$

    **A.** 50             **D.** 576

    **B.** 100           **E.** 625

    **C.** 225

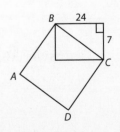

**Exercise 30:** $x =$

A. 16        D. 22

B. 18        E. 24

C. 20

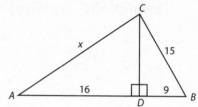

**Exercise 31:** $c^2 - b^2 =$

A. 72        D. 252

B. 144      E. 288

C. 216

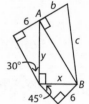

**Exercise 32:** $x =$

A. 1        D. 4

B. 2        E. 4.5

C. 3

**Exercise 33:** A 25-foot ladder is leaning on the floor. Its base is 15 feet from the wall. If the ladder is pushed until it is only 7 feet from the wall, how much farther up the wall is the ladder pushed?

A. 4 feet        D. 20 feet

B. 8 feet        E. 24 feet

C. 12 feet

 **Let's look at the answers.**

**Answer 28:** Try the Pythagorean Theorem with various combinations of 3, $\sqrt{5}$, and $x$ (the third side). The only ones that work are Statement I: $2^2 + \left(\sqrt{5}\right)^2 = 3^2$; and Statement III: $3^2 + \left(\sqrt{5}\right)^2 = \left(\sqrt{14}\right)^2$. The answer is (D).

**Answer 29:** We recognize the right triangle as a 7-24-25 triple, so side $BC = 25$. The area of the square is $(25)^2 = 625$. The answer is (E).

**Answer 30:** This is a 15-20-25 triple, so $x = 20$. The answer is (C).

**Answer 31:**    We see that $AB$ is the side of two triangles. By the Pythagorean Theorem, we get $c^2 - b^2 = x^2 + y^2 = \left(6\sqrt{2}\right)^2 + 12^2 = 72 + 144 = 216$. The answer is (C).

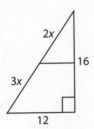

**Answer 32:**    This triangle is a 12-16-20 triple, so $3x + 2x = 5x = 20$, and $x = 4$. The answer is (D).

**Answer 33:**    The first figure is shows a 15-20-25 right triangle with the ladder 20 feet up the wall. The second figure is a 7-24-25 triple with the ladder 24 feet up the wall. The ladder is pushed another $24 - 20 = 4$ feet up the 4 wall. The answer is (A).

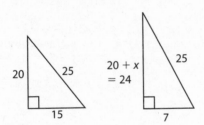

That's all for angles and triangles for the moment. We will see more when circles are discussed in Chapter 12. For now, though, let's look at rectangles and other polygons.

# CHAPTER 11: *Quadrilaterals and Other Polygons*

"*Mastering all shapes and sizes will enhance your journey.
We now deal with the rest of the polygons (closed figures with line-segment sides).*"

## QUADRILATERALS

### Parallelograms

A parallelogram is a quadrilateral (four-sided polygon) with parallel opposite sides.

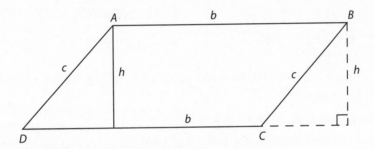

You should know the following properties about parallelograms:

* The opposite angles are equal. $\angle DAB = \angle BCD$ and $\angle ADC = \angle ABC$.

* The consecutive angles are supplementary. $\angle DAB + \angle ABC = \angle ABC + \angle BCD$ $= \angle BCD + \angle CDA = \angle CDA + \angle DAB = 180°$.

* The opposite sides are equal. $AB = CD$ and $AD = BC$.

* The diagonals bisect each other. $AE = EC$ and $DE = EB$.

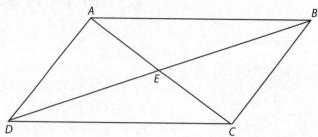

- Area = $A = bh$. This is a postulate (law taken to be true without proof) from which we get the area of all other figures with sides that are line segments.

- Perimeter = $p = 2b + 2c$

**Example 1:** For parallelogram *RSTU*, find the following if *RU* = 10:

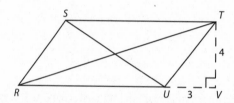

a. The area          c. Diagonal *RT*

b. The perimeter      d. Diagonal *SU*

**Solutions:**    a. $A = bh = (10)(4) = 40$ square units. The whole test should be this easy!

b. We have to find the length of $RS = TU$. $TU = 5$ because it is the hypotenuse of a 3-4-5 right triangle. So the perimeter is $p = 2(10) + 2(5) = 30$ units.

c. $RT = \sqrt{(RV)^2 + (TV)^2} = \sqrt{13^2 + 4^2} = \sqrt{185}$

d.

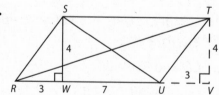

To find diagonal *SU*, draw the other altitude *SW* as pictured.

$SU = \sqrt{WU^2 + SW^2} = \sqrt{7^2 + 4^2} = \sqrt{65}$

**Example 2:**  For parallelogram *WXYZ* with altitudes *XM* and *YN*, find the following in terms of *a*, *b*, and *c*:

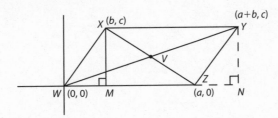

a.  The coordinates of point *M*

b.  The coordinates of point *N*

c.  The coordinates of point *V*

d.  The perimeter

e.  The area

**Solutions:**

a.  *M* has the same *x*-coordinate as point *X* and the same *y*-coordinate as point *W*, so the coordinates of *M* are $(b, 0)$.

b.  *N* has the same *x*-coordinate as point *Y* and the same *y*-coordinate as point *W*, so the coordinates of *N* are $(a + b, 0)$.

c.  *V* is halfway between *W* and *Y*, so use the formula for the midpoint between $Y(a + b, c)$ and $W(0,0)$: Midpoint $V = \left( \dfrac{a + b + 0}{2}, \dfrac{c + 0}{2} \right)$ $= \left( \dfrac{a + b}{2}, \dfrac{c}{2} \right)$.

d.  $WZ = XY$ is length *a*. By the distance formula, $WX = ZY$ $= \sqrt{(b - 0)^2 + (c - 0)^2} = \sqrt{b^2 + c^2}$. Therefore, the perimeter is $p = 2a + 2\sqrt{b^2 + c^2}$.

e.  Area $= A = $ base $\times$ height $= ac$.

**Example 3:**  For parallelogram *EFGH*, find the smaller angle.

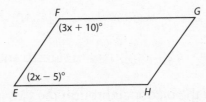

**Solution:**  Consecutive angles of a parallelogram are supplementary. Therefore, $(3x+10)° + (2x - 5)° = 180°$; $x = 35°$; so the smaller angle is $2(35°) - 5°$ $= 65°$. Be careful to give the answer the GRE wants. Two of the other choices would be 35° and 115°, for those who do not read carefully!!!

## Rhombus

A **rhombus** is an equilateral parallelogram.

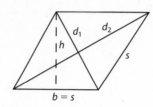

Thus, a rhombus has all of the properties of a parallelogram plus the following:

- The opposite angles are equal.
- All sides are equal.
- The diagonals are perpendicular to each other.
- Perimeter $= p = 4s$.
- Area $= A = bh = \dfrac{1}{2} \times d_1 \times d_2$, or, the area equals half the product of its diagonals.

**Example 4:**   For the given rhombus with side $s = 13$ and larger diagonal $BD = 24$, find the other diagonal and the area.

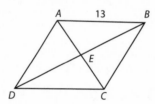

**Solutions:**   $AB = 13$ and $BD = 24$. Since the diagonals bisect each other, $BE = 12$.

The diagonals are perpendicular to each other, so $\triangle ABE$ is a 5-12-13

right triangle, and $AE = 5$. Therefore, the other diagonal $AC = 10$.

The area $= A = \dfrac{1}{2} \times d_1 \times d_2 = \dfrac{1}{2}(24)(10) = 120$ square units.

**Example 5:**   Find the area of a rhombus with side 10 and smaller interior angle of 60°.

**Solution:**   If you draw the diagonal through the two larger angles, you will have two congruent equilateral triangles. The area of this rhombus is twice the area of each triangle, or $2 \times \dfrac{s^2\sqrt{3}}{4}$. Since $s = 10$, the area is

$$A = 2 \times \frac{10^2\sqrt{3}}{4} = 50\sqrt{3} \text{ square units.}$$

Now let's go on to more familiar territory.

## Rectangle

A **rectangle** is a parallelogram with right angles. Therefore, it has all of the properties of a parallelogram plus the following:

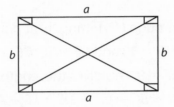

*   All angles are 90°.
*   Diagonals are equal (but *not* perpendicular).
*   Perimeter $= p = 2b + 2h$
*   Area $= A = bh$

The easier the shape, the more likely the GRE will have a problem or problems about it.

**Example 6:**   One base is 8; one diagonal is 9. Find all the sides and the other diagonal. Find the perimeter an area.

**Solution:**   The top base and bottom base are both 8. Both diagonals are 9. The other two sides are each $\sqrt{9^2 - 8^2} = \sqrt{17}$. So the perimeter is $p = 16 + 2\sqrt{17}$ units; and the area is $A = 8\sqrt{17}$ square units.

**Example 7:**   $AB = 10$, $BC = 8$, $EF = 6$, and $FG = 3$. Find the area of the shaded region of the figure.

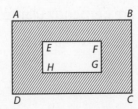

**Solution:**     The area of the shaded region is the area of the outside rectangle minus the area of the inside one. $A = (10)(8) - (6)(3) = 62$ square units.

**Example 8:**     In polygon $ABCDEF$, $BC = 30$, $AF = 18$, $AB = 20$, and $CD = 11$. Find the perimeter and area of the polygon.

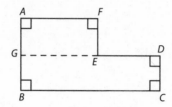

**Solution:**     Draw a line through $DE$, hitting $AB$ at point $G$. Then $AF = GE$ and $BC = GD$. Since $DG = 30$ and $GE = 18$, $DE = 12$. $AB = CD + EF$. $AB = 20$ and $CD = 11$, so $EF = 9$. This gives the lengths of all the sides. The perimeter thus is $p = AB + BC + CD + DE + EF + AF = 30 + 20 + 11 + 12 + 9 + 18 = 100$ units.

The area of rectangle $BCDG$ is $BC \times CD = (30)(11) = 330$. The area of rectangle $AFEG$ is $AF \times FE = (18)(9) = 162$. Therefore, the total area is $330 + 162 = 492$ square units. There are other ways to find this area, as you might be able to see.

## Square

A **square** is a rectangle with equal sides, or it can be thought of as a rhombus with four equal $90°$ angles. Therefore, it has all of the properties of a rectangle and a rhombus:

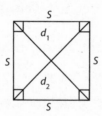

- All sides are equal.
- All angles are $90°$.
- Both diagonals bisect each other, are perpendicular to each other, and are equal.
- Each diagonal $d = d_1 = d_2 = s\sqrt{2}$, where $s = $ a side.

- Perimeter $= p = 4s$

- Area $= A = \dfrac{d^2}{2} = s^2$

**Q** **Let's do some exercises.**

**Exercise 1:** The areas of the rectangle and triangle are the same. If $\dfrac{LW}{4} = 20$, then $bh =$

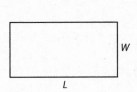
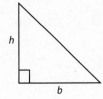

A. 20           D. 160

B. 40           E. 640

C. 80

**Exercise 2:** The area of this square is

A. $\dfrac{1}{4}$           D. $2\dfrac{1}{4}$

B. $\dfrac{1}{2}$           E. 3

C. $1\dfrac{1}{2}$

**Exercise 3:** The area of square C is 36; the area of square B is 25. The area of square A is

A. 61           D. 100

B. 121           E. $61^2$

C. 900

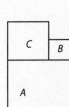

The figure is a square surmounted by an equilateral triangle. (I've always wanted to write that word.) $CE = 10$. Use this figure for Exercises 4 and 5.

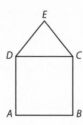

**Exercise 4:** The perimeter of the figure is

A. 50                 D. 1200

B. 60                 E. 2400

C. 600

**Exercise 5:** The area of the figure is

A. 150              D. $2500\sqrt{3}$

B. $25(4 + \sqrt{3})$      E. 7500

C. $125\sqrt{3}$

**(A)** **Let's look at the answers.**

**Answer 1:** $\dfrac{LW}{4} = 20$; so the area of the rectangle is $LW = 80$. So the area of the triangle is $\dfrac{1}{2}bh = 80$, and $bh = 160$. The answer is (D).

**Answer 2:** Since it is a square, $5x - 1 = x + 1$, so $x = \dfrac{1}{2}$. By substitution, one side of the square is $\dfrac{1}{2} + 1 = 1\dfrac{1}{2}$. Then $A = \left(1\dfrac{1}{2}\right)^2 = 2\dfrac{1}{4}$. The answer is (D).

**Answer 3:** The side of square $C$ must be 6, and the side of square $B$ must be 5. Therefore, the side of square $A$ is 11, and the area of square $A$ is $11^2 = 121$. The answer is (B).

**Answer 4:**    The perimeter is $5(10) = 50$. Note that $CD$ is not part of the perimeter. The answer is (A).

**Answer 5:**    $A = s^2 + \dfrac{s^2\sqrt{3}}{4} = 10^2 + \dfrac{10^2\sqrt{3}}{4} = 100 + 25\sqrt{3} = 25(4 + \sqrt{3})$. Note that

we factor out this problem since the answer choices are factored out.

The answer is (B).

# TRAPEZOID

A **trapezoid** is a quadrilateral with exactly one pair of parallel sides.

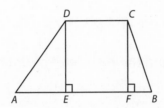

Because a trapezoid is *not* a type of parallelogram, it has its own unique set of properties, as follows:

*   The parallel sides, *AB* and *CD*, are called **bases.**

*   The heights, *DE* and *CF*, are equal.

*   The legs, *AD* and *BC*, may or may not be equal.

*   The diagonals, *AC* and *BD*, may or may not be equal.

*   Perimeter $= p = AB + BC + CD + AD$

*   Area $= A = \dfrac{1}{2}h(b_1 + b_2)$, where $b_1$ and $b_2$ are the bases.

**Note**   *If we draw one of the diagonals, we see that a trapezoid is the sum of two triangles. Factoring out $\dfrac{1}{2}h$, we get the formula for the area of the trapezoid.*

If the legs are equal, the trapezoid is called an **isosceles trapezoid**, shown below.

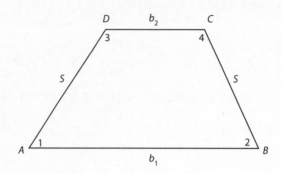

An isosceles trapezoid has these additional properties:

•    Perimeter $= p = b_1 + b_2 + 2s$

•    The diagonals are equal, $AC = BD$.

•    The base angles are equal, $\angle 1 = \angle 2$ and $\angle 3 = \angle 4$

      **Example 9:**    Find the area and the perimeter of Figure *ABCD*.

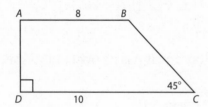

      **Solution:**    Draw the other height, *BG*, as shown.

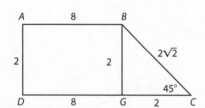

      $DG = 8$; $CG = 2$; since $\triangle BGC$ is an isosceles right triangle, the height

      *BG* (and *AD*) $= 2$. *BC*, the hypotenuse of the isosceles right triangle,

      is therefore $2\sqrt{2}$. Therefore, the perimeter is $p = 10 + 2 + 8 + $

      $2\sqrt{2} = 20 + 2\sqrt{2}$, and the area is $A = \dfrac{1}{2}h(b_1 + b_2) = \dfrac{1}{2}(2)(8 + 10) = 18$.

**Example 10:**   Given trapezoid *ORST*, with $RS \parallel OT$, find the coordinates of point *S*. Find the perimeter and the area of trapezoid *ORST*.

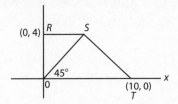

**Solution:**   Since $\triangle ORS$ is a 45°-45°-90° triangle, $OR = RS = 4$, so *S* is the point

(4, 4). The length of $OT = 10$. By the distance formula, the length of

$ST = \sqrt{(10-4)^2 + (0-4)^2} = \sqrt{52} = 2\sqrt{13}$. Therefore, the perimeter is

$p = 10 + 4 + 4 + 2\sqrt{13}$, or, to be fancy, $2(9 + \sqrt{13})$.

$Area = \frac{1}{2} h(b_1 + b_2) = \frac{1}{2}(4)(10 + 4) = 28$. In a multiple-choice question,

the GRE would ask about either the area or perimeter, but not both. But

sometimes the GRE is fancy, like here.

**Example 11:**   Find the area of isosceles trapezoid *EFGH*.

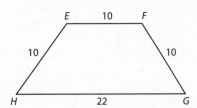

**Solution:**   Draw in the two heights for the trapezoid.

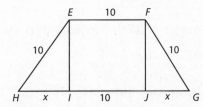

The two bases of the triangles formed are equal since it is an isosceles

triangle. From the figure, $2x + 10 = 22$, so $x = 6$. Each of the triangles

is a 6-8-10 Pythagorean triple, so the height of the trapezoid is 8.

Therefore, $A = \frac{1}{2}(8)(10 + 22) = 128$.

## POLYGONS

Let's talk about polygons in general. Most of the time we deal with **regular** polygons. A regular polygon has all sides equal and all angles equal. A square and an equilateral triangle are examples of regular polygons we have already discussed.

Any *n*-sided polygon has the following properties.

- The sum of all the interior angles is $(n - 2)180°$.

- The sum of all exterior angles always equals 360°.

- The number of diagonals is $\dfrac{n(n - 3)}{2}$, where n ≥ 3.

In addition, if the polygon is regular, it has the following additional properties:

- One exterior angle $= \dfrac{360°}{n}$.

- An interior angle plus its exterior angle always add to 180°.

- An interior angle $= \dfrac{(n - 2)180°}{n}$

Polygons are named for the number of sides they have.

A **pentagon** is a 5-sided polygon.

A **hexagon** is a 6-sided polygon.

A **heptagon** is a 7-sided polygon.

An **octagon** is an 8-sided polygon.

A **nonagon** is a 9-sided polygon.

A **decagon** is a 10-sided polygon.

A **dodecagon** is a 12-sided polygon.

An **n-gon** is an *n*-sided polygon.

**Example 12:** An octagon has a perimeter of 27. If 5 is added to each sided, what is the perimeter of the new octagon?

**Solution:** It doesn't matter how long each side is! If 5 is added to each of 8 sides, 40 is added to the perimeter. The new perimeter is $27 + 40 = 67$.

**Example 13:** The side of a regular hexagon is 4. Find its area.

**Solution:** A regular hexagon is made up of six equilateral triangles. The side of each triangle is 4, and the area is $A = 6\dfrac{s^2\sqrt{3}}{4} = 6\dfrac{4^2\sqrt{3}}{4} = 24\sqrt{3}$.

**Example 14:** The sum of the interior angles of a regular polygon is 720°. Find the number of sides, the number of degrees in one exterior angle, and the number of degrees in one interior angle.

**Solution:** $(n - 2)(180) = 720$. Divide each side by 180 to simplify: $n - 2 = 4$, so $n = 6$ sides.

One exterior angle $= \dfrac{360°}{6} = 60°$. An interior angle is supplemental to its external angle, by definition, so $180° - 60° = 120°$ for each interior angle.

We'll get more GRE-looking questions at the end of the chapter on circles, which is next.

# CHAPTER 12: *Circles*

"*Although sometimes it seems you are going in circles, you are really heading toward your goal.*"

**Circles** are a favorite topic of the GRE. Circles allow for many short questions that can be combined with the other geometric chapters. Let's get started.

## PARTS OF A CIRCLE

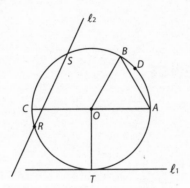

We all know what a circle looks like, but maybe we're not familiar with its "parts."

*O* is the **center** of the circle. A circle is often named by its center, so this is circle *O*.

*OA, OT, OC,* and *OB* are **radii** (singular: radius); a radius is a line segment from the center to the **circumference**, or edge, of the circle.

**Note** *All radii (r) of a circle are equal. This is a postulate or axiom, a law taken to be true without proof. It is probably a good idea to tell you there are no proofs on the GRE, as there were when you took geometry.*

*AC* is the **diameter**, *d*, the distance from one side of the circle through the center to the other side; $d = 2r$ and $r = \dfrac{d}{2}$.

$\ell_1$ is a **tangent**, a line that touches a circle in one and only one point

$T$ is a **point of tangency**, the point where a tangent touches the circle. The radius to the point of tangency ($OT$) is always perpendicular to the tangent, so $OT \perp \ell_1$.

$\ell_2$ is a **secant**, a line that passes through a circle in two places.

$RS$ is a **chord**, a line segment that has each end on the circumference of the circle. The diameter is the longest chord in a circle.

$OADBO$ is a **sector** (a pie-shaped part of a circle). There are a number of sectors in this figure; others include $BOCSB$ and $OATRCSBO$. We will see these again soon.

An **arc** is any distance along the circumference of a circle.

  Arc $ADB$ is a **minor arc** because it is less than half a circle.

  Arc $BDATRC$ is a **major arc** because it is more than half a circle.

  Arc $ATRC$ is a **semicircle** because it is exactly half a circle

Whew! Enough! However, we do need some more facts about circles.

The following are mostly theorems, proven laws. Again, there are no proofs on the GRE, but you need to be aware of these facts.

## AREA AND CIRCUMFERENCE

Area of a circle:

$$A = \pi r^2$$

Circumference (perimeter of a circle):

$$C = 2\pi r \text{ or } \pi d.$$

## SECTORS

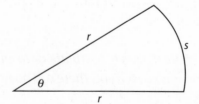

Area of a sector:

$$A = \frac{\theta}{360°}\pi r^2,$$

where $\theta$ (theta) is the angle of the sector in degrees.

Arc length of a sector:

$$s = \frac{\theta}{360°} \times 2\pi r$$

Perimeter of a sector:

$$p = s + 2r,$$

where $s$ is the arc length

**Example 1:**  Find the area and perimeter of a 60° sector of a circle of diameter 12.

**Solution:**

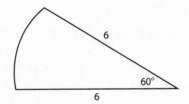

If the diameter is 12, the radius is 6. The sector is pictured here. Its area is $A = \dfrac{60°}{360°} \times \pi 6^2 = 6\pi$ square units. Although you should know that pi ($\pi$) is about 3.14, I've never seen a problem for which you had to multiply 6 times 3.14. The answer is left in terms of $\pi$. The perimeter of the sector is $s = 2(6) + \dfrac{60°}{360°} \times 2\pi(6) = 12 + 2\pi$ units.

**Ⓠ  Let's do some exercises.**

For Exercises 1 through 5, refer to the following circle. *O* is the center of the circle.

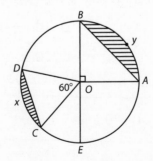

**Exercise 1:**    If the area of $\triangle AOB$ is 25, the area of circle $O$ is

    **A.** $12.5\pi$              **D.** $100\pi$

    **B.** $25\pi$               **E.** $200\pi$

    **C.** $50\pi$

**Exercise 2:**    If $OA = 8$, the area of the shaded region $BAYB$ is

    **A.** $16(\pi - 2)$        **D.** $64(\pi - 1)$

    **B.** $16(\pi - 1)$        **E.** $32(\pi - 2)$

    **C.** $8(2\pi - 1)$

**Exercise 3:**    If $CD = 10$, the perimeter of sector $DOCXD$ is

    **A.** $30 + \dfrac{10\pi}{3}$        **D.** $20 + \dfrac{20\pi}{3}$

    **B.** $30 + \dfrac{20\pi}{3}$        **E.** $30 + 30\pi$

    **C.** $20 + \dfrac{10\pi}{3}$

**Exercise 4:**    If $OC = 2$, the area of the shaded portion $DCXD$ is

    **A.** $\pi - \sqrt{3}$        **D.** $\dfrac{2\pi - 3\sqrt{3}}{3}$

    **B.** $2\pi - \sqrt{3}$        **E.** $\dfrac{8\pi - 3\sqrt{3}}{3}$

    **C.** $4\pi - \sqrt{3}$

**Exercise 5:**    If the area of $\triangle COD$ is $25\sqrt{3}$, the perimeter of semicircle $EOBDXCE$ is

    **A.** $10\pi$              **D.** $10(2\pi + 1)$

    **B.** $10(\pi + 1)$        **E.** $20(\pi + 1)$

    **C.** $10(\pi + 2)$

I guess you get the idea already.

**Let's look at the answers.**

**Answer 1:**     $A = \frac{1}{2}(r)(r) = \frac{1}{2}r^2$, so $r^2 = 50$. The area of the circle is thus $\pi r^2 = 50\pi$. The answer is (C). Notice that once you have a value for $r^2$, you don't have to find $r$ to do this problem.

**Answer 2:**     The area of region *BAYB* is the area of one-fourth of a circle minus the area of $\triangle AOB$. So the area is $A = \frac{1}{4}\pi 8^2 - \frac{1}{2}(8)(8) = 16\pi - 32 = 16(\pi - 2)$. The answer is (A).

**Answer 3:**     The perimeter of sector *DOCXD* $= 2r + s$, where $s$ is the length of arc *CXD*. $\triangle COD$ is equilateral, so $CD = CO = DO = r = 10$. $s = \frac{60°}{360°}2\pi(10) = \frac{10\pi}{3}$. So the perimeter of sector *CODXD* is $p = 20 + \frac{10\pi}{3}$. The answer is (C).

**Answer 4:**     The area of region *DCXD* is the area of sector *ODXCO* minus the area of $\triangle DOC$, when $OC = 2$. So the area is $A = \frac{60°}{360°}\pi 2^2 - \frac{2^2\sqrt{3}}{4} = \frac{2\pi}{3} - \sqrt{3} = \frac{2\pi - 3\sqrt{3}}{3}$. The answer is (D).

**Answer 5:**     We must first find the radius. The area of equilateral $\triangle COD = \frac{s^2\sqrt{3}}{4} = 25\sqrt{3}$. So $s^2 = 100$, and $s = r = 10$. The perimeter of the semicircle is $\frac{1}{2}(2\pi r) + 2r = \pi r + 2r = 10\pi + 20 = 10(\pi + 2)$. The answer is (C).

There are a few more things we need to know. When we talked about two intersecting lines earlier, we saw that *CE* might equal *ED*; however, if the description of the figure doesn't say so, you cannot assume it. Also, *ED* might be perpendicular to *CE*, but if it doesn't say so, you cannot assume it, either. In fact, we can say *CD* **bisects** *AB* at *E* only if we know that *AE* = *EB* or *E* is the midpoint of *AB*.

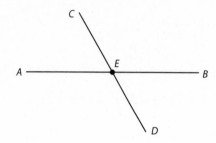

Now we consider two intersecting lines in a circle, however, such as chord *AB* and radius *CO* in circle *O*.

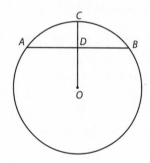

If one of the following facts is true, all are true:

1.  *OD* ⊥ *AB*

2.  *CDO* bisects *AB*

3.  *CO* bisects $\overset{\frown}{ACB}$ (read "arc *ACB*")

**Ⓠ** **Let's do some more exercises.**

For Exercises 6 and 7, use this figure, which is a triangle-semicircle shape.

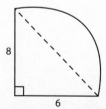

**Exercise 6:**   The perimeter of this figure is

A. $14 + 5\pi$            D. $24 + 10\pi$

B. $14 + 10\pi$           E. $12 + 10\pi$

C. $24 + 5\pi$

**Exercise 7:**   The area of the figure is

A. $24 + \dfrac{25\pi}{2}$        D. $48 + 25\pi$

B. $24 + 25\pi$           E. $48 + 50\pi$

C. $24 + 50\pi$

**Exercise 8:**   A circle is **inscribed** in (inside and touching) figure *MNPQ*, which has all right angles. Diameter $AB = 10$. The area of the shaded portion is

A. $100 - 12.5\pi$        D. $40 - 5\pi$

B. $100 - 25\pi$          E. $100 - 100\pi$

C. $40 - 10\pi$

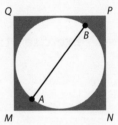

**Exercise 9:**   If $AB = 10$, the area of the shaded portion in the figure is

A. $100 - 12.5\pi$        D. $40 - 5\pi$

B. $100 - 25\pi$          E. $100 - 100\pi$

C. $40 - 10\pi$

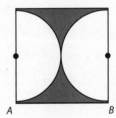

For Exercises 10 and 11, use this figure. The perimeter of the 16 semicircles is 32π.

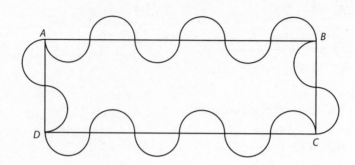

**Exercise 10:**   The area of rectangle *ABCD* is

A. 64                          D. 16π

B. 128                       E.  Cannot be determined

C. 192

**Exercise 11:**   The area inside the region formed by the semicircular curves from *A* to *B* to *C* to *D* and back to *A* is

A. 64                          D. 16π

B. 128                       E.  Are you for real??!!

C. 192

**Exercise 12:**   In the figure, $EF = CD = 12$, *B* is the midpoint of *OD*, and *A* is the midpoint of *CO*. The area of the shaded portion is

A. $36(4\sqrt{3} - \pi)$            D. $72(3\sqrt{3} - \pi)$

B. $6(6\sqrt{3} - \pi)$             E. $36(6\sqrt{3} - \pi)$

C. $144(\pi - 3)$

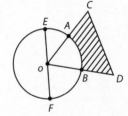

For Exercises 13 and 14, use this figure.

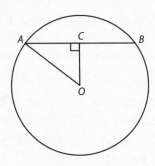

**Exercise 13:** If the diameter $= 20$, $OC \perp AB$, and $\angle A = 30°$, $AB =$

A. 10                    D. $10\sqrt{3}$

B. 5                     E. $5\sqrt{2}$

C. $5\sqrt{3}$

**Exercise 14:** If $OC$ bisects $AB$, $AB = 16$, and $OC = 6$, the area of circle $O$ is

A. $10\pi$               D. $100\pi$

B. $20\pi$               E. $400\pi$

C. $40\pi$

 **Let's look at the answers.**

**Answer 6:** The figure is a 6-8-10 Pythagorean triple, but 10 is not part of the perimeter. $p = 6 + 8 + \frac{1}{2}2\pi(5) = 14 + 5\pi$. The answer is (A).

**Answer 7:** $A = \frac{1}{2}bh + \frac{1}{2}\pi r^2 = \frac{1}{2}6 \times 8 + \frac{1}{2}\pi 5^2 = 24 + \frac{25\pi}{2}$. The answer is (A).

**Answer 8:** The area is the area of the square minus the area of the circle. $A = s^2 - \pi r^2 = 10^2 - \pi 5^2 = 100 - 25\pi$. The answer is (B).

**Answer 9:** Answer 8 and Answer 9 are exactly the same problems. The answer is (B). In Answer 8, you could also say the square **circumscribes** the circle.

**Answer 10:**   Each semicircle has arc length $\dfrac{180°}{360°}\pi d$, and there are 16 semicircles, so

$16\left(\dfrac{1}{2}\pi d\right) = 32\pi$, or $8\pi d = 32\pi$, so $d = 4$. The rectangle's dimensions

are thus 8 and 24. The area is $A = b \times h = 8(24) = 192$. The answer is (C).

**Answer 11:**   Believe it or not, Exercise 11 is exactly the same as Exercise 10! The answer is (C). You can think of the areas of the "outer" semicircles as canceling out the areas of the "inner" semicircles, and you are left with only the area of rectangle *ABCD*.

**Answer 12:**   The information is enough to tell us the triangle is equilateral and $\angle AOB$

$= 60°$. The shaded area is the area of $\triangle COD$ minus the area of sector

$OABO$. Thus, $A = \dfrac{s^2\sqrt{3}}{4} - \dfrac{1}{6}\pi r^2 = \dfrac{12^2\sqrt{3}}{4} - \dfrac{1}{6}\pi 6^2$.

The answer is (B).

**Answer 13:**   *AO*, the radius, is 10; *CO*, the side opposite the 30° angle, is 5; and *AC*, the side opposite the 60° angle, is $5\sqrt{3}$. $AB = 2(AC) = 2(5\sqrt{3}) = 10\sqrt{3}$. The answer is (D).

**Answer 14:**   To find the area of the circle, we need to find the radius *OA*. We know *AC* is 8 and *OC* is 6. We have a 6-8-10 right triangle, so $AO = r = 10$. The area is $\pi(10)^2 = 100\pi$. The answer is (D).

Okay. Now let's go from two dimensions to three dimensions.

# CHAPTER 13: *Three-Dimensional Figures*

*"Many dimensions in your trip will add to your ultimate success."*

**This** chapter is relatively short. There are only a few figures we need to know. Since these are three-dimensional figures, we discuss their volumes and surface areas (areas of all of the sides). The diagonal is the distance from one corner internally to an opposite corner.

## BOX

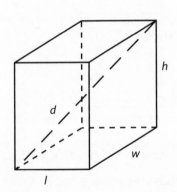

This figure is also known as a **rectangular solid**, and if that isn't a mouthful enough, its correct name is a **rectangular parallelepiped**. But essentially, it's a **box**.

- Volume $= V = \ell wh$

- Surface area $= SA = 2\ell w + 2\ell h + 2wh$

- Diagonal $= d = \sqrt{\ell^2 + w^2 + h^2}$, known as the 3-D Pythagorean Theorem

**Example 1:**    For the given figure, find $V$, $SA$, and $d$.

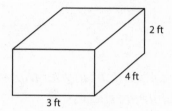

**Solution:**    $V = \ell wh = (3)(4)(2) = 24$ cubic feet;

$SA = 2\ell w + 2\ell h + 2wh = 2(3)(4) + 2(3)(2) + 2(4)(2) = 52$ square feet;

$d = \sqrt{\ell^2 + w^2 + h^2} = \sqrt{3^2 + 4^2 + 2^2} = \sqrt{29} \approx 5.4$ feet

# CUBE

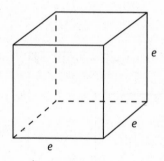

A **cube** is a box for which all of the faces, or sides, are equal squares.

•    $V = e^3$ (read, "$e$ cubed"). Cubing comes from a cube!

•    $SA = 6e^2$

•    $d = e\sqrt{3}$

•    A cube has 6 faces, 8 vertices, and 12 edges.

**Example 2:**    For a cube with an edge of 10 meters, find $V$, $SA$, and $d$.

**Solution:**    $V = 10^3 = 1{,}000$ cubic meters; $SA = 6e^2 = 6(10)^2 = 600$ square meters;

$d = e\sqrt{3} = 10\sqrt{3} \approx 17.32$ meters

# CYLINDER

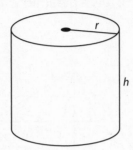

A cylinder is shaped like a can. The curved surface is considered as a side, and the top and bottom are equal circles.

- $V = \pi r^2 h$

- $SA = \text{top} + \text{bottom} + \text{curved surface} = 2\pi r^2 + 2\pi rh$

Once a neighbor of mine wanted to find the area of the curved part of a cylinder. He wasn't interested in why; just the answer. Of course, being a teacher I had to explain it to him. I told him that if you cut a label off a soup can and unwrap it, the figure is a rectangle; neglecting the rim, the height is the height of the can and the width is the circumference of the circle. Multiply this height and width, and the answer is $2\pi r \times h$. He waited patiently and then soon moved. Just kidding!

In general, the volume of any figure for which the top is the same as the bottom is $V = Bh$, where $B$ is the area of the base. If the figure comes to a point, the volume is $\left(\dfrac{1}{3}\right)Bh$. The surface area is found by adding up all the sides.

**Example 3:**    Find $V$ and $SA$ for a cylinder of height 10 yards and diameters of 8 yards.

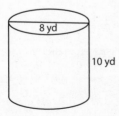

**Solution:**    We see that since $d = 8$, $r = 4$. Then $V = \pi r^2 h = \pi(4^2 \times 10) = 160\pi$ cubic yards; $SA = 2\pi r^2 + 2\pi rh = 2\pi 4^2 + 2\pi(4)(10) = 112\pi$ square yards.

(Q)   **Let's do some exercises.**

Use this figure for Exercises 1 through 3. It is a pyramid with a square base. $WX = 8$, $BV = 3$, and $B$ is in the middle of the base.

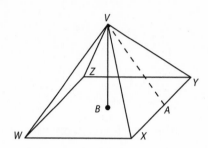

**Exercise 1:**   The volume of the pyramid is

A. 192            D. 32

B. 96             E. 16

C. 64

**Exercise 2:**   The surface area of the pyramid is

A. 72             D. 224

B. 112            E. 448

C. 144

**Exercise 3:**   $VY =$

A. 6              D. 9

B. $\sqrt{41}$    E. $\sqrt{89}$

C. 7

**Exercise 4:**   In the given rectangular solid, the perimeter of $\triangle ABC =$

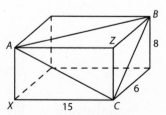

A. $\sqrt{325} = 5\sqrt{13}$   D. 37

B. 30             E. 41

C. $27 + \sqrt{261}$

**Exercise 5:** The volume of the cylinder shown is:

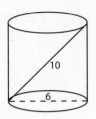

A. $640\pi$        D. $144\pi$

B. $320\pi$        E. $72\pi$

C. $288\pi$

**Exercise 6:** *ABKL* is the face of a cube with *AB* = 10, and box *BCFG* has a square front with *BC* = 6.

The surface area that can be viewed in this configuration is

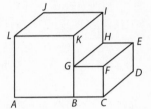

A. 300        D. 400

B. 356        E. 1360

C. 396

**Exercise 7:** A cylinder has volume *V*. If we triple its radius, by what factor should we multiply the height in order that the volume stays the same?

A. $\dfrac{1}{9}$        D. 3

B. $\dfrac{1}{3}$        E. 9

C. 1

 **Let's look at the answers.**

**Answer 1:** $V = \left(\dfrac{1}{3}\right)Bh = \dfrac{1}{3}s^2h = \dfrac{1}{3}(8^2)(3) = 64$. The answer is (C).

**Answer 2:** $SA = s^2 + 4\left(\dfrac{1}{2}bh\right)$. $AB = \left(\dfrac{1}{2}\right)WX = 4$; $\triangle ABV$ is a 3-4-5 right triangle with $AB = 4$ and $BV = 3$, so $AV = 5$. $AV$ is the height of each triangular side, $h$, and $b = XY = 8$. So $SA = 8^2 + 2(8)(5) = 144$. The answer is (C).

**Answer 3:** $\triangle AVY$ is a right triangle with right angle at $A$. $AY = 4$ and $AV = 5$, so $VY = \sqrt{4^2 + 5^2} = \sqrt{41}$. The answer is (B).

**Answer 4:** In the given figure, we have to use the 2-D Pythagorean Theorem three times to find the sides of $\triangle ABC$. $\triangle BCY$ is a 6-8-10 triple, so $BC = 10$, and $\triangle ACX$ is a 8-15-17 triple, so $AC = 17$. For $\triangle ABZ$, we actually have to calculate the missing side $AB = \sqrt{6^2 + 15^2} = \sqrt{261}$. So the perimeter is $10 + 17 + \sqrt{261}$. The answer is (C).

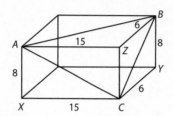

**Answer 5:** The diameter of the base is 6, and again we have a Pythagorean triple; so $h = 8$. The volume is $\pi(3^2)(8) = 72\pi$. The answer is (E).

**Answer 6:** The areas are: $ABKL = 100$; $IJLK = 100$; $BCFG = 36$; $CDEF = 60$; $EFGH = 60$; $GHIK = 40$. The total is 396. The answer is (C).

**Answer 7:** The volume $V = \pi r^2 h$. For simplicity, let $r = 1$ and $h = 1$. So $V = \pi$. If we triple the radius $V = \pi(3)^2 h$. For the original volume to still be $\pi$, $9h = 1$ or $h = \dfrac{1}{9}$. The answer is (A).

Let's go to the last regular chapter of the book, not quite so short, but not too long.

"*At this point, your probability of success has greatly increased. This chapter is a combination of related topics. Let's start with measures of central tendency.*"

## CENTRAL TENDENCY

**People** say you can prove anything with statistics. You need to know what you are taking statistics of, how many in the group, and many other variables. Even then, depending on the "spin" you want, you can choose among three measures to describe the data and prove your point. These measures of central tendency are ways to find a "typical" value. The measures of central tendency, introduced in Chapter 1, are:

**Mean:** Add up the number of terms and divide the sum by the number of terms; that's the way your grades are usually determined in school.

**Median:** The middle term when the numbers are put in order from smallest to largest (or the other way around); for an odd number of terms, it is the middle term; for an even number, it's the mean of the middle two numbers.

**Mode:** The most common term; there can be one mode, two modes (bimodal), or any number of modes.

**Example 1:** For the data consisting of the numbers 5, 6, 8, 9, 12, 12, 18,

The mean is $\dfrac{5 + 6 + 8 + 9 + 12 + 12 + 18}{7} = \dfrac{70}{7} = 10$.

The median is 9. There are three numbers above it and three numbers below it.

The mode is 12. It is the most common number, appearing twice.

Now can you see how you can prove anything with statistics?

**Ⓠ Let's do some exercises.**

For Exercises 1–3, use the following numbers:

$$8, 10, 10, 16, 16, 18$$

**Exercise 1:** The mean is

A. 8

B. 10

C. 13

D. 16

E. There are two of them

**Exercise 2:** The median is

A. 8

B. 10

C. 13

D. 16

E. There are two of them

**Exercise 3:** The mode is

A. 8

B. 10

C. 13

D. 13

E. There are two of them

**Ⓐ Let's look at the answers.**

**Answer 1:** $\dfrac{8 + 10 + 10 + 16 + 16 + 18}{6} = 13$. The answer is (C).

**Answer 2:** There are an even number of numbers, so we have to take the average of the middle two: $\dfrac{10 + 16}{2} = 13$. The answer is (C).

**Answer 3:** It's bimodal; the modes are 10 and 16, each appearing twice. The answer is (E).

Sometimes statistics are given in frequency distribution tables, such as this one showing the grades Sandy received on 10 English quizzes.

**Example 2:** Find the measures of central tendency of Sandy's quiz scores.

| Grade | Number |
|---|---|
| 100 | 4 |
| 98 | 3 |
| 95 | 2 |
| 86 | 1 |
| Total | 10 |

**Solution:** The mean is the longest measure to compute:

$$\frac{4 \times 100 + 3 \times 98 + 2 \times 9 + 86}{10} = 97.$$

The median is determined by putting all of the numbers in order, so we have 100, 100, 100, 100, 98, 98, 98, 95, 86. The middle terms are 98 and 98, so the median is 98.

The mode is 100 since that is the most common score; there are four of them.

# STANDARD DEVIATION

Look at these two sets of numbers:

Set $A$: {16, 18, 18, 19, 22, 23, 24}

Set $B$: {2, 18, 18, 19, 25, 28, 30}

If we find the median for each set, it is 19; if we find the mean for each set, it is 20; if we find the mode for each set, it is 18. The measures of central tendency are the same for both sets. However, there is something different about each set. In set $A$, all the numbers are relatively close to the mean. In set $B$, that is not true. We can measure the spread of the data by finding the **standard deviation.** Here are the steps to calculate it:

1. Find the mean of the set.
2. For each number, subtract the mean and square the result.
3. Add these squares together and divide by the number of elements in the set.
4. Take the square root of this result. That is the standard deviation.

The standard deviation of set *A* is:

$$\sqrt{\frac{(16-20)^2 + (18-20)^2 + (18-20)^2 + (19-20)^2 + (22-20)^2 + (23-20)^2 + (24-20)^2}{7}}$$

$$= 2.78$$

The standard deviation of set *B* is:

$$\sqrt{\frac{(2-20)^2 + (18-20)^2 + (18-20)^2 + (19-20)^2 + (25-20)^2 + (28-20)^2 + (30-20)^2}{7}}$$

$$= 8.64$$

By comparing these two results, we have proof that the numbers in set *B* are more spread out, or dispersed, than those in set *A*. The standard deviation is a useful measure, especially in relation to the normal or bell-shaped curve. For example, by using multiples of the standard deviation (there are published tables for this), a manufacturer can determine how many items to produce. Suppose the manufacturer wanted to produce 100,000 pairs of a particular shoe. The standard deviation will tell how many of each size to produce. It also says that if you are a man wearing size 15 or a woman wearing size 12, you must go to a specialty store. If you are a man wearing size 5 or a woman wearing size 3, most of your shoes are children's shoes. The statistics tell you it that it doesn't pay to make many shoes, if any, in those sizes.

This topic will be on the GRE exam. In all honesty, they couldn't ask the question this way because you would need a calculator for almost every example. However, you should be familiar with the vocabulary presented here.

## COUNTING

The **basic law of counting** says: "If you can do something in *p* ways, and a second thing in *q* ways, and a third thing in *r* ways, and so on, the total number of ways you can do the first thing, then the second thing, then the third thing, etc., is $p \times q \times r \times \ldots$

**Example 3:**   If you have a lunch choice of 5 sandwiches, 4 desserts, and 3 drinks, and you can have one of each, how many different meals could you choose?

**Solution:**   You can choose from (5)(4)(3) = 60 different meals

## Arrangements

Let *n*(*A*) be the number of elements in set *A*. In how many ways can these elements be arranged? The answer is that the first has *n* choices, the second has (*n* − 1) choices (since one is already used), the third has (*n* − 2) choices, all the way down to the last element, which has only one choice. In general, if there are *n* choices, the number of ways to choose is *n*! (*n* **factorial**) = $n(n-1)(n-2) \times \ldots (3)(2)(1)$.

**Example 4:**     How many ways can five people line up?

**Solution:**     This is just $5 \times 4 \times 3 \times 2 \times 1 = 120$.

**Example 5:**     How many ways can 5 people sit in a circle?

**Solution:**     It would appear to be the same question as Example 4, but it's not. If you draw the picture, each of 5 positions would be the same. The answer is $(5)(4)(3)(2)(1) \div 5 = (4)(3)(2)(1) = 24$. So $n$ people can sit in a circle in $(n - 1)!$ ways.

## Permutations

**Permutations** are essentially the law of counting without repeating, but order counts.

**Example 6:**     How many ways can 7 people occupy 3 seats on a bench?

**Solution:**     Any one of 7 people can be in the first seat, then any one of 6 people can be in the second seat, and any one of 5 people can be in the third seat. The total number would be $(7)(6)(5) = 210$ ways. There are many notations for permutations. One notation for this example would be $P(7, 3)$.

## Combinations

**Combinations** are essentially the law of counting, with no repetition, and order doesn't count.

**Example 7:**     How many sets of three different letters can be made from eight different letters?

**Solution:**     Since order doesn't count, unlike with permutations, *AB* is the same as *BA*. So we can take the number of permutations, but we have to divide by the number of duplicates. It turns out that the duplicates for 3 letters is $3 \times 2 \times 1 = 6$. So we would have $\dfrac{8 \times 7 \times 6}{3 \times 2 \times 1} = 56$. Again, there are many notations for combinations. One notation for this example is $C(8, 3)$.

## Avoiding Duplicates

When we count how many ways to do A or B, we should be careful not to count any item twice. We must subtract out any items that include both A and B:

$$N(A \text{ or } B) = N(A) + N(B) - N(A \text{ and } B)$$

**Example 8:**   Thirty students take French or German. If 20 took French and 18 took German, and if each student took at least one language, how many took both French and German?

**Solution:**   $N(A \text{ or } B) = N(A) + N(B) - N(A \text{ and } B)$, or $30 = 20 + 18 - x$, so $x = 8$ took both languages.

**Example 9:**   Forty students take Chinese or Japanese. If 9 take both and 20 take Japanese, how many students take Chinese?

**Solution:**   $N(C \text{ or } J) = N(C) + N(J) - N(\text{both})$, or $40 = x + 20 - 9$, so $x = 29$ take Chinese.

Ⓠ   **Let's do some exercises.**

For Exercises 4–8, use the set {e, f, g, h, i}. A word is considered to be any group of letters together; for example, *hhg* is a three-letter word.

**Exercise 4:**   From this set, the number of three-letter word is:

A. 6                    D. 60

B. 27                   E. 125

C. 30

**Exercise 5:**   How many three-letter permutations are there in this set?

A. 6                    D. 60

B. 27                   E. 125

C. 30

**Exercise 6:** How many three-letter words starting with a vowel and ending in a consonant can be made from this set?

A. 6                  D. 60

B. 27                 E. 125

C. 30

**Exercise 7:** How many three-letter words with the second and third letters the same can be made from this set?

A. 5                  D. 60

B. 20                 E. 125

C. 25

**Exercise 8:** How many three-letter permutations with the first and last letters *not* vowels can be made from this set?

A. 18                 D. 45

B. 27                 E. 125

C. 30

**Exercise 9:** Fifty students take Spanish or Portuguese. If 20 take both and 40 take Spanish, the number of students taking *only* Portuguese is

A. 0                  D. 20

B. 5                  E. 30

C. 10

 **Let's look at the answers.**

**Answer 4:** $(5)(5)(5) = 125$. The answer is (E).

**Answer 5:** $(5)(4)(3) = 60$. The answer is (D).

**Answer 6:** The first letter has 2 choices, the second can be any (5), and the third has 3 choices, so $(2)(5)(3) = 30$. The answer is (C).

**Answer 7:** There are 5 choices for the first two letters, but there is only 1 choice for the third letter since it must be the same as the second, so $(5)(5)(1) = 25$. The answer is (C).

**Answer 8:** There are 3 choices for the first letter, but only 2 choices for the last letter since it can't be a vowel and must be different than the first letter. There are 3 choices for the middle letter since two letters have already been used; so the answer is (3)(3)(2) = 18. The answer is (A). These questions must be read very carefully!

**Answer 9:** This is not quite the same. $N(S \text{ or } P) = N(S) + N(P) - N(\text{both})$; $50 = 40 + x - 20$; $x = 30$, but that is not the answer. If 30 take Portuguese and 20 take both, then 10 take only Portuguese. The answer is (C).

## PROBABILITY

The probability of an event is the number of "good" outcomes divided by the total number of outcomes possible, or $Pr(\text{success}) = \dfrac{\text{good outcomes}}{\text{total outcomes}}$.

**Example 10:** Consider the following sets: {26 letter English alphabet}; vowels = {a, e, i, o, u}; consonants = {the rest of the letters}. What are the probabilities of choosing a vowel? a consonant? any letter? $\pi$?

**Solution:** $Pr(\text{vowel}) = \dfrac{5}{26}$; $Pr(\text{consonant}) = \dfrac{21}{26}$; $Pr(\text{letter}) = \dfrac{26}{26} = 1$; $Pr(\pi) = \dfrac{0}{26} = 0$.

Probability follows the same rule about avoiding duplicates as discussed in the previous section.

$$Pr(A \text{ or } B) = Pr(A) + Pr(B) - Pr(A \text{ and } B)$$

**Example 11:** What is the probability that a spade or an ace is pulled from a 52-card deck?

**Solution:** $Pr(\text{Spade or ace}) = Pr(\text{Spade}) + Pr(\text{Ace}) - Pr(\text{Spade ace}) =$

$$\dfrac{13}{52} + \dfrac{4}{52} - \dfrac{1}{52} = \dfrac{16}{52} = \dfrac{4}{13}.$$

As weird as it sounds, whenever I taught this in a class, I never failed to have at least two students who didn't know what a deck of cards was, and I taught in New York City!

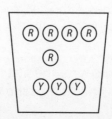

Use this figure for Examples 12 and 13. In the jar are 5 red balls and 3 yellow balls.

**Example 12:** What is the probability that two yellow balls are picked, with replacement?

**Solution:** $Pr(\text{2 yellow balls, with replacement}) = \left(\dfrac{3}{8}\right)\left(\dfrac{3}{8}\right) = \dfrac{9}{64}$

**Example 13:** What is the probability of picking two yellow balls, without replacement?

**Solution:** $Pr(\text{2 yellow balls, no replacement}) = \left(\dfrac{3}{8}\right)\left(\dfrac{2}{7}\right) = \dfrac{3}{28}$

## CHARTS AND GRAPHS

A significant part of the GRE consists of charts and graphs. In all likelihood, out of 60 questions, there will be 10 such questions: two graphs and chart problems, with five questions each. Here is one problem having one pie chart and one bar graph. There will be more such exercises in the practice tests in Chapters 16 through 18.

The arithmetic on the actual GRE could be less or more, nicer or messier, than the following exercises. It depends on the edition of test you actually take.

**Ⓠ** **Let's do some exercises.**

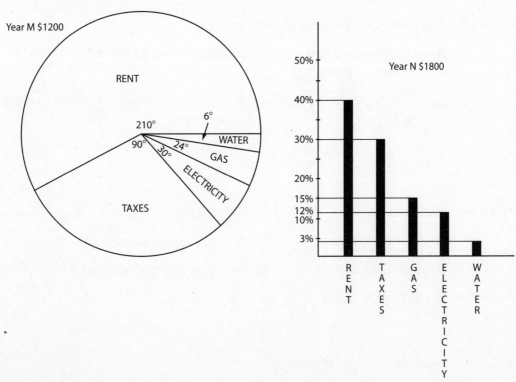

Some of the major expenses of the apartment of Mr. and Mrs. Smith in Smallville, USA, are shown in this pie chart and bar graph. The pie chart is for year *M* with a $1200 budget, and the bar graph is for year *N*, some years later, with an $1800 budget. Use these data for Exercises 10 through 14.

**Exercise 10:**   The smallest percentage increase from year *M* to year *N* is for

         **A.** Rent                 **D.** Gas

         **B.** Taxes              **E.** Water

         **C.** Electricity

**Exercise 11:**   The largest percentage increase from year *M* to year *N* is for

         **A.** Rent                 **D.** Gas

         **B.** Taxes              **E.** Water

         **C.** Electricity

**Exercise 12:**   The change in rent from year *M* to year *N* was

         **A.** −$80             **D.** +$100

         **B.** none             **E.** +$190

         **C.** +$20

**Exercise 13:**   The two closest monetary amounts are

         **A.** Rent in year *M* and       **D.** Taxes in year *M* and Gas in year *N*
            the Rent in year *N*

         **B.** Electricity in year *M* and     **E.** Electricity in year *M* and Electricity
            Gas in year *N*                       in year *N*

         **C.** Water in year *M* and
            Water in year *N*

**Exercise 14:**   Which expenses exceeded the percentage increase in the total budget?

         **A.** All the expenses       **D.** All except Water and Rent

         **B.** All except Rent          **E.** All except Rent and Taxes

         **C.** All except Water

These exercises are easier to answer if we exactly calculate all of the money answers and put the items next to each other in a table:

|  | Year *M* | Year *N* |
|---|---|---|
| Rent | $\frac{210}{360} \times \$1200 = \frac{7}{12} \times \$1200 =$ | $.40 \times \$1800 =$ |
|  | $700 | $720 |
| Taxes | $300 | $540 |
| Electricity | $100 | $216 |
| Gas | $80 | $270 |
| Water | $20 | $54 |

 **Let's look at the answers.**

**Answer 10:** Rent increased by only $20 (due perhaps to rent control or family member owner); the percentage increase is the smallest increase $(= \frac{20}{700} \times 100)$. You don't actually have to calculate the exact percentage. You only have to note the percentage increase is obviously much smaller than the percentage increase of any other item. The answer is (A).

**Answer 11:** The percentage increase for gas is $\frac{190}{80} \times 100\%$, or more than a 200% increase. The answer is (D).

**Answer 12:** $720 − $700 = $20. The answer is (C).

**Answer 13:** The rents in year *M* and year *N* are only $20 apart. No other choices are this close. The answer is (A).

**Answer 14:** The total increase from year *M* to year *N* is 50%; taxes almost doubled; electricity more than doubled; gas more than tripled, and water almost tripled. The answer is (B).

Now we are ready for the practice tests.

*"Once you have mastered your skills, it is necessary to understand what you are up against."*

## PAPER-AND-PENCIL GRE

**Now** that you have learned the math skills, you need to take the actual test. However, there are two kinds of GRE you might take. The first is like the next three chapter practice tests. The low score on the math GRE is 200 and the high score is 800. The average score is 575. To repeat, you cannot use calculators, and formulas are not given.

Wrong answers have no additional deductions. To maximize your score, you should answer every question, even if you have no idea of the correct answer. By this time, you should have determined the best way to take this test. You know every section is timed. You must try to do the questions as quickly as possible. If time permits, go back to the questions you left out and/or have missed. My own rule is never to change a question unless you are 100% sure that your change is correct. The last time I took a test, I changed two answers. For one, I was 100% sure I was right, and the change was correct. The second one I wasn't sure about, and I went from a right answer to a wrong answer.

## COMPUTER-ADAPTIVE TEST

For the second type of test, known as the CAT, which is taken on a computer, the computer "adapts" to your performance (except on the essay section). The computer starts with average questions. If you get them correct, the questions get harder. If you get them wrong, the questions get easier. You should therefore take the time to make sure you get the answer correctly. Once a question is gone, it is gone forever. You cannot go back. The harder the questions, the higher your score will be. If the questions seem to get harder and harder, that means you are doing well. You must answer all questions. There is an additional penalty for unanswered questions. So you must guess intelligently. You will eventually reach a level where you get about the same number right as wrong. That will be your score.

The GRE just added (while I was writing this book, in fact) a new type of problem for those taking computer-based tests. It includes a format that I have not seen on any GRE exam. Essentially, these new questions are fill-ins. You must get your answer without being given a selection of choices. The format is a single-answer box that you fill in by using the computer keyboard. Also added were questions on function. Specific directions, sample questions, and functions are included in Chapter 19.

In the CAT math section, there will be one quantitative section of 28 questions to be taken in 45 minutes. About 14 of the questions will be comparisons and 14 will be solving problems. About 7 of the problem-solving problems will be on charts and graphs.

Before you consider which test you should take, you should practice on the three test chapters that follow in this book plus the last chapter, which contains the new type of questions to be included in the computer-based test. Based on what I've seen, they are an accurate depiction of previous math GRE tests, both in difficulty and kinds of questions. Good luck!

"*For total success, you must practice your skills.* "

## Part 1A

**Directions:** Each of the Questions 1–15 consists of two quantities, one in Column A and one in Column B. You are to compare the two quantities and choose:

**A** if the quantity in Column A is greater;

**B** if the quantity in Column B is greater;

**C** if the two quantities are equal;

**D** if the relationship cannot be determined from the information given

**Note** *Since there are only four choices, NEVER MARK (E).*

|  | **Column A** | **Column B** |
|---|---|---|
| 1. | $6(4 - 6)$ | $4(6 - 4)$ |
| 2. | $(x + y)^2$ | $x^2 + y^2$ |
| 3. | $x$ | $80°$ |

(Triangle for question 3: apex angle $20°$, two equal sides labeled $20$ and $20$, bottom left angle labeled $x$)

| 4. | $(343)(78)$ | $(342)(79)$ |
| 5. | $22\%$ of $68$ | $68\%$ of $22$ |

6.

Side of a square with area 25 square feet

Side of a square with perimeter 20 feet

7. $a^2 = 16; b^2 = 36$

$a$

$b$

8. $xyz = 0, x \neq 0$

$y$

$z$

9. $2x - 5 = 10$

$(2x - 7)^2$

64

10.

$\dfrac{\sqrt{48}}{\sqrt{6}}$

$\dfrac{\sqrt{88}}{\sqrt{11}}$

11. $7x + 9y = 53$
    $5x + 7y = 19$

$x + y$

17

12.

$c°$

$(180° - c°)$

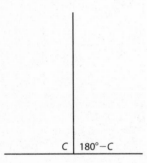

$C$ | $180° - C$

13.

$\dfrac{2^{102} - 2^{101}}{2}$

$2^{100}$

14. $y = mx + b$

$m$

$\dfrac{b}{a}$

(o, b)

(a, o)

15. $m > 100$ and $n > 100$

$\dfrac{1}{\frac{1}{m} + \frac{1}{n}}$

$\dfrac{1}{m} + \dfrac{1}{n}$

## Part 1B

**Directions:** Each of the Questions 16–30 has five choices. For each of these questions, select the best of the answer choices given.

16. John starts to read at the top of page 222 and ends reading at the bottom of page 358. The number of pages he has read is

   A. 135          D. 138

   B. 136          E. 580

   C. 137

17. Let $a \blacksquare b = ab^2 - b$. $-5 \blacksquare 3 =$

   A. 222          D. $-35$

   B. $-5$          E. $-48$

   C. $-30$

18. If $3x + 5$ is an odd integer, the sum of the next two consecutive odd integers is:

   A. $6x + 13$          D. $6x + 16$

   B. $6x + 14$          E. $6x + 20$

   C. $6x + 15$

19. If $x$ pounds of fruit cost $c$ cents, how many pounds of fruit can you buy for $d$ dollars?

   A. $\dfrac{100dx}{c}$          D. $\dfrac{cx}{100d}$

   B. $100cdx$          E. $\dfrac{1}{100cdx}$

   C. $\dfrac{100c}{xd}$

20. $x + y = 12; \left(x + \dfrac{y}{3}\right) + \left(y + \dfrac{x}{3}\right) =$

   A. 4          D. 16

   B. 8          E. 20

   C. 12

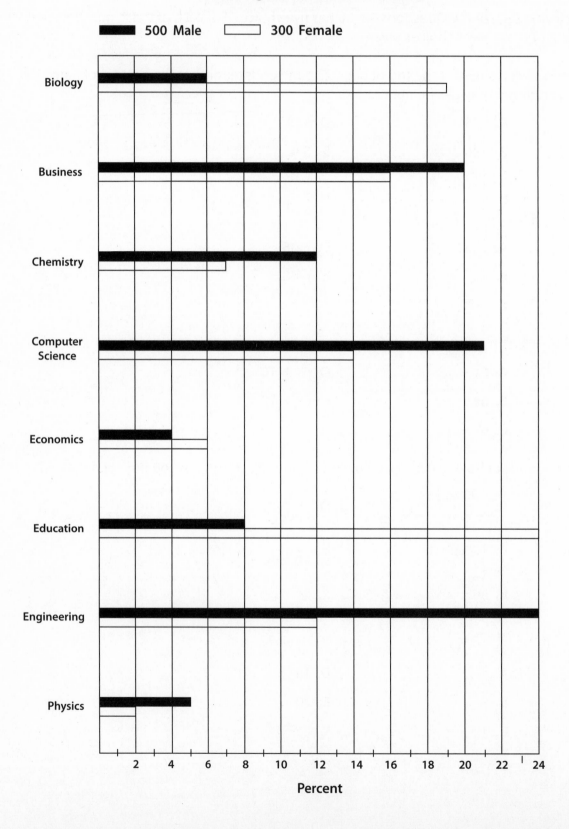

## Percent of male and female faculty population at college in math-related fields

■ 500 Male  □ 300 Female

*Percent*

**Questions 21–25 refer to the preceding chart.**

21. In how many fields is the female faculty more than 7% of the faculty?

    **A.** 1        **D.** 4

    **B.** 2        **E.** 5

    **C.** 3

22. How many more of the men than the women faculty are in computer science?

    **A.** 40        **D.** 77

    **B.** 57        **E.** 105

    **C.** 63

23. In what field are the men on the faculty approximately equal to the women in the faculty?

    **A.** Biology        **D.** Education

    **B.** Business        **E.** Physics

    **C.** Economics

24. If 450 students are in physics, the ratio of students to physics faculty is closest to

    **A.** 9 to 1        **D.** 18 to 1

    **B.** 12 to 1        **E.** 22 to 1

    **C.** 15 to 1

25. If the male numbers in the biology department increased by 80%, the total male biology faculty would be:

    **A.** 24        **D.** 54

    **B.** 30        **E.** 74

    **C.** 44

26. The perimeter of $\triangle ABC$ is

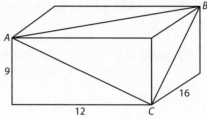

     **A.** $\sqrt{481}$           **D.** 53

     **B.** 37              **E.** 1728

     **C.** $35 + \sqrt{337}$

27. The fewest number of trees with six rows with four in each row is

     **A.** 24            **D.** 16

     **B.** 23            **E.** 12

     **C.** 20

28. $\dfrac{1}{a + \dfrac{1}{b + \frac{1}{c}}} =$

     **A.** $\dfrac{bc + 1}{abc + a + c}$      **D.** $\dfrac{abc + 1}{abc + a + b + c}$

     **B.** $\dfrac{ab + 1}{abc + b + c}$      **E.** $\dfrac{abc + a + c}{abc + 1}$

     **C.** $\dfrac{ac + 1}{abc + b + c}$

29. $\sqrt{x - 3} = 5.$      $x =$

     **A.** 8             **D.** 64

     **B.** 25            **E.** 628

     **C.** 28

30. All of the following are factors of 30,000 EXCEPT

     **A.** 8             **D.** 18

     **B.** 15           **E.** 150

     **C.** 16

## Part 2A

**Directions:** Each of the Questions 1–15 consists of two quantities, one in Column A and one in Column B. You are to compare the two quantities and choose:

**A** if the quantity in Column A is greater;

**B** if the quantity in Column B is greater;

**C** if the two quantities are equal;

**D** if the relationship cannot be determined from the information given

**Note** *Since there are only four choices, NEVER MARK (E).*

| | **Column A** | **Column B** |
|---|---|---|
| 1. | $x$ | $y$ |
| 2. | $(x - y)^2$ | $x^2 + y^2$ |
| 3. | largest prime factor of 98 | largest prime factor of 100 |
| 4. $-110 < x < -101$ | $2x$ | $\dfrac{1}{x}$ |
| 5. | $\dfrac{567 \times 34 \times 5 \times 6 \times 7}{8 \times 9}$ | $\dfrac{7 \times 8 \times 9 \times 34 \times 567}{5 \times 6}$ |
| 6. | Radius of a circle with area $4\pi$ | Radius of a circle with circumference $4\pi$ |
| 7. | $4(2x + 2y)$ | $2(4y + 4x)$ |
| 8. | $(-5)^6$ | $(-6)^5$ |
| 9. | $50°$ | $(2x - 200)°$ |

10.  $-1 < x < 0$                   $x^4$                           $(3x)^3$

11.

| | Rate | Distance |
|---|---|---|
| Car A | 60mph | 1mile |
| Car B | 50mph | 1mile |

time of car A                time of car B

12.  $x^4 = y^4$                     $x$                             $y$

13.  $b > 4$                         $\sqrt{b^2 + 4}$                $b + 2$

14.                                  Ratio of two inches            $\dfrac{2}{5}$
                                     to five feet

15.  $WXYZ$ is a square             $9m^2$                          $16n^2$

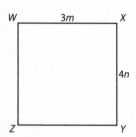

# Part 2B

**Directions:** Each of the Questions 16–30 has five choices. For each of these questions, select the best of the answer choices given.

16.  The largest side is

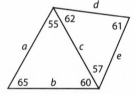

    **A.** $a$             **D.** $d$

    **B.** $b$             **E.** $e$

    **C.** $c$

17.  $3(2x - 1) + 4 = 2x; x =$

    **A.** $-\dfrac{1}{8}$           **D.** $\dfrac{1}{4}$

    **B.** $-\dfrac{1}{4}$           **E.** $\dfrac{1}{2}$

    **C.** $-\dfrac{1}{2}$

18. In a small class, every girl sees that there are an equal number of boys and girls, and each boy sees there are twice as many girls as boys, not counting himself or herself. How many children are in the class?

    **A.** 3 boys and 3 girls      **D.** 4 boys and 6 girls

    **B.** 3 boys and 4 girls      **E.** 2 boys and 3 girls

    **C.** 3 girls and 4 boys

19. John is 16 years old and his father is 50. In how many years will John be half as old as his father?

    **A.** 10      **D.** 18

    **B.** 12      **E.** It can't happen

    **C.** 16

20. If 3 bligs = 5 bloogs, and 7 bloogs = 8 blugs, the ratio of bligs to blugs =

    **A.** $\dfrac{21}{40}$      **D.** $\dfrac{8}{105}$

    **B.** $\dfrac{40}{21}$      **E.** $\dfrac{21}{13}$

    **C.** $\dfrac{105}{8}$

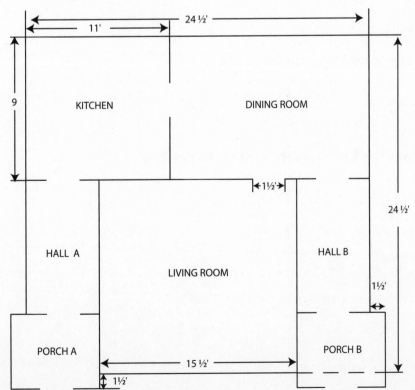

Questions 21–25 refer to the above floor plan. All rooms are rectangles with these conditions: (1) both halls are the same size; (2) both porches are the same size; and (3) each porch is a square.

21. The area of the dining room is

    A. 42                    D. 126

    B. 45                    E. 222.5

    C. 121.5

22. If the ceilings and walls of the living room are painted, how many square feet of paint are needed?

    A. 240.25                D. 960.5

    B. 702.25                E. Not enough information

    C. 720.25

23. The perimeter of one porch is

    A. 16                    D. 24

    B. 18                    E. 32

    C. 20.25

24. The length of one hall is

    A. 9.5                   D. 14

    B. 11                    E. 15.5

    C. 12.5

25. The ratio of the area of the kitchen to the area of the porch is

    A. $\dfrac{4}{11}$        D. $\dfrac{11}{8}$

    B. $\dfrac{8}{11}$        E. $\dfrac{11}{4}$

    C. 1

26. $\dfrac{\left(5x^4\right)^2 x^3}{5x^4}$

      **A.** $x^3$                 **D.** $5x^7$

      **B.** $5x^3$             **E.** $x^{15}$

      **C.** $x^7$

27. Given the numbers 2, 2, 5, 7, 9, 17: The sum of the mean, median, and mode is

      **A.** 13               **D.** 16

      **B.** 14               **E.** Cannot be determined from the information given

      **C.** 15

28. All 35 students at a school take at least Spanish or French. If 25 take Spanish and 10 take both, how many students take only French?

      **A.** 5               **D.** 20

      **B.** 10               **E.** 25

      **C.** 15

29. $x^6 = m$ and $x^5 = \dfrac{n}{2}$. In terms of $m$ and $n$, $x =$

      **A.** $2mn$              **D.** $\dfrac{2m}{n}$

      **B.** $\dfrac{2}{mn}$          **E.** $\dfrac{2n}{m}$

      **C.** $\dfrac{mn}{2}$

30. A sixty-dollar radio is discounted 25% and then another 10%. If the state has a 4% sales tax, the final cost would be

      **A.** $41.06         **D.** $44.24

      **B.** $42.12         **E.** $45.30

      **C.** $43.18

# ANSWERS

## Part 1A

1. **(B)**   B is positive and A is negative.

2. **(D)**   $(x + y)^2 = x^2 + 2xy + y^2$ (you should know this). Since we don't know if $2xy$ is positive, negative or zero, the answer is (D).

3. **(C)**   Each base angle is $x$; $2x + 20 = 180$; $x = 80$.

4. **(B)**   $(343)(78) = (342 + 1)78 = 342(78) + 1(78)$; $(342)(79) = 342(78 + 1) = 342(78) + 342(1)$.

5. **(C)**

6. **(C)**   The side of each square would be 5.

7. **(D)**   $a = \pm 4$; $b = \pm 6$.

8. **(D)**   Either $y$ or $z = 0$, and the other can be anything, positive or negative.

9. **(C)**   If $2x - 5 = 10$, then $2x - 7 = 2x - 5 - 2 = 10 - 2 = 8$, and $8^2 = 64$.

10. **(C)**   Reducing, each side $= \sqrt{8}$.

11. **(C)**   Subtracting, we get $2x + 2y = 34$ or $x + y = 17$.

12. **(D)**   It doesn't say the lines are perpendicular; you cannot assume they are.

13. **(C)**   Factoring the top of A, we get $2^{101}(2 - 1)$ or $2^{101}$, and $\dfrac{2^{101}}{2} = 2^{100}$.

14. **(B)**   The slope $m = \dfrac{b - 0}{0 - a} = -\dfrac{b}{a}$.

15. **(A)**   $A > 1$ and $B < 1$.

## Part 1B

16. **(C)**   You must count the first page also. $358 - 222 + 1 = 137$.

17. **(E)**   $(-5)3^2 - 3 = -45 - 3 = -48$.

18. **(D)** $(3x + 7) + (3x + 9) = 6x + 16$.

19. **(A)** Use the proportion $\dfrac{x}{c} = \dfrac{?}{100d}$.

20. **(D)** Rearranging, we get $(x + y) + \dfrac{1}{3}(x + y) = 12 + \dfrac{12}{3} = 16$.

21. **(B)** The faculty has 800 members. 7% of 800 is 56. Education and biology are the only departments with more than 56 female members (or more than 18.7% of the females).

22. **(C)** 21% of 500 is 105; 14% of 300 is 42; $105 - 42 = 63$.

23. **(C)** The percentage of women must be close to $\dfrac{5}{3} \times$ the percentage of men. This is true only for economics.

24. **(C)** 5% of 500 = 25 male faculty, and 2% of 300 = 6 female faculty. The total faculty is 31. $\dfrac{450}{31} \approx \dfrac{15}{1}$.

25. **(D)** 6% of 500 = 30. Then $30 + .8(30) = 30 + 24 = 54$.

26. **(C)** $AC = 15$ (9-12-15 triple); $AB = 20$ (12-16-20 triple); $BC = \sqrt{9^2 + 16^2} = \sqrt{337}$.

27. **(E)** See this figure!

28. **(A)** $\dfrac{1}{a + \dfrac{1}{b + \frac{1}{c}}} = \dfrac{1}{a + \dfrac{1}{\frac{bc+1}{c}}} = \dfrac{1}{a + \dfrac{c}{bc+1}} = \dfrac{1}{\frac{abc+a+c}{bc+1}} = \dfrac{bc+1}{abc+a+c}$.

29. **(C)** Squaring, we get $x - 3 = 25$.

30. **(D)** $18 = 2(9)$ and 9 is not a factor of 30,000.

## Part 2A

1.  **(A)**  Missing angle in the triangle is 65°. $y = 180° - 70°$; $x = 180° - 65°$.

2.  **(D)**  Multiplying out, we don't know if $-2xy$ is positive, negative, or 0.

3.  **(A)**  (7 versus 5.)

4.  **(B)**  It's much closer to 0.

5.  **(B)**  Canceling out the same terms from both expressions, we get $\dfrac{5 \times 6 \times 7}{8 \times 9}$ and $\dfrac{7 \times 8 \times 9}{5 \times 6}$.

6.  **(C)**  $r = 2$ in each case.

7.  **(C)**

8.  **(A)**  A positive is always bigger than a negative.

9.  **(B)**  $x = 130°$; $(2x - 200)° = 60°$.

10. **(A)**  A positive is always bigger than a negative.

11. **(B)**  Car A takes less time (and thus is faster), the smaller number!

12. **(D)**  $x = \pm y$.

13. **(B)**  Square both and compare $b^2 + 4$ to $(b + 2)^2 = b^2 + 4b + 4$.

14. **(B)**  Both must be in the same measurement, inches. Column A has a value of $\dfrac{2}{60} = \dfrac{1}{30}$

15. **(C)**  Since it's a square, $3m = 4n$.

## Part 2B

16. **(E)**  In the left triangle, $c$ is bigger; in the right triangle, $e$ is bigger; but both $c$ and $e$ are in the same triangle; so $e$ must be the biggest.

17. **(B)**  $6x - 3 + 4 = 2x$; $4x = -1$.

18. **(B)**  Check each answer choice. Just plug in the numbers!

19. **(D)**  $\dfrac{16 + x}{50 + x} = \dfrac{1}{2}$; then $32 + 2x = 50 + x$.

20. **(B)** 3 bligs = 5 bloogs, and 8 blugs = 7 bloogs. Dividing equals into equals, we get $\dfrac{3 \text{ bligs}}{8 \text{ blugs}} = \dfrac{5 \text{ bloogs}}{7 \text{ bloogs}}$. The bloogs cancel. Multiplying both sides by $\dfrac{8}{3}$, we get $\dfrac{40}{21}$.

21. **(C)** $13.5 \times 9 = 121.5$.

22. **(E)** We don't know how high the walls are.

23. **(D)** Let $x$ = the side of a porch. Then $2x + 15.5 - 3 = 24.5$; $2x = 12$; $x = 6$. The perimeter is 24.

24. **(B)** $24.5 - 9 - 4.5 = 11$.

25. **(E)** $\dfrac{99}{36} = \dfrac{11}{4}$.

26. **(D)** $\dfrac{25x^8(x^3)}{5x^4} = 5x^7$

27. **(C)** $7 + 6 + 2 = 15$.

28. **(B)** $N(\text{F or S}) = N(\text{F}) + N(\text{S}) - N(\text{both})$. $35 = x + 25 - 10$; $x = 20$. However, 20 students take French and 10 of these take both French and Spanish, so 10 take only French.

29. **(D)** Dividing the second equation into the first, we get $x = \dfrac{m}{\left(\frac{n}{2}\right)} = \dfrac{2m}{n}$.

30. **(B)** $60 \times .75 = \$45.00$, and $\$45 \times .90 = \$40.50$. Then $\$40.50 \times .04 = \$1.62$. Finally, $\$40.50 + \$1.62 = \$42.12$.

*"Be patient, more practice may be needed for success."*

## Part 1A

**Directions:** Each of the Questions 1–15 consists of two quantities, one in Column A and one in Column B. You are to compare the two quantities and choose:

**A** if the quantity in Column A is greater;

**B** if the quantity in Column B is greater;

**C** if the two quantities are equal;

**D** if the relationship cannot be determined from the information given

**Note** *Since there are only four choices, NEVER MARK (E).*

| <u>Column A</u> | <u>Column B</u> |
|---|---|
| | |

1.  $3\{3 + 3[3 + 3(3 \times 3)]\}$     333

A(m, n)

B(q, r)

For Questions 2 and 3, use the preceding figure, where (0,0) is the midpoint of line segment *AB*.

|  | **Column A** | **Column B** |
|---|---|---|
| 2. | $m$ | $-q$ |
| 3. | $n$ | $-r$ |
| 4. | $(x + 1)(x - 1)$ | $x^2$ |
| 5. $3 < m < 6$ | $\left(\dfrac{m}{8}\right)^2$ | $\left(\dfrac{m}{.08}\right)^2$ |

For Questions 6 and 7: $p < q < r$

| 6. | $pq$ | $qr$ |
|---|---|---|
| 7. | $q^2$ | $r^2$ |

For Questions 8 and 9: Circle *A* has radius *x*; Circle *B* has radius *2x*

| 8. | Twice the circumference of circle *A* | Circumference of circle *B* |
|---|---|---|
| 9. | Twice the area of circle *A* | Area of circle *B* |
| 10. $m < 0$ | $m - 1$ | $1 - m$ |
| 11. | $\sqrt{100 + 81}$ | $19$ |
| 12. $43 < x < y < 957$ | $\dfrac{x}{y}$ | $\dfrac{y}{x}$ |
| 13. | $-7^6$ | $(-7)^6$ |
| 14. | $.6250$ | $\dfrac{5}{8}$ |
| 15. $m, n > 5$ | $\dfrac{m}{n}$ | $\dfrac{m + 1}{n + 1}$ |

## Part 1B

**Directions:** Each of the Questions 16–30 has five choices. For each of these questions, select the best of the answer choices given.

16. $\angle BOA = 90°$, $\angle AOC = 60°$. Let $S =$ Area of $\triangle AOB +$ Area of $\triangle AOC$.
    If $OA = 2$, then which of the following is correct?

    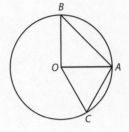

    **A.** $1 < S < 2$          **D.** $4 < S < 5$

    **B.** $2 < S < 3$          **E.** $S > 5$

    **C.** $3 < S < 4$

17. $a$ and $b$ are positive odd integers and $b > 4$:

    I   $a^{b+1}$

    II  $ab + a + b$

    III $(a - 2)^{b-4}$

    Which of the following statements is always odd?

    **A.** None          **D.** II and III only

    **B.** I and II only          **E.** I, II, and III

    **C.** I and III only

18. $m$ years in the future, Jack will be $n$ years old. $p$ years in the future, Jack will be how old?

    **A.** $p + n + m$          **D.** $p + n - m$

    **B.** $p - n + m$          **E.** $n - m - p$

    **C.** $p - n - m$

19. If $y$ is four less than the square root of $x$ and $x, y > 10$, write $x$ in terms of $y$.

    **A.** $x = 4 + y^2$          **D.** $x = (y - 4)^2$

    **B.** $x = 4 - y^2$          **E.** $x = (y + 4)^2$

    **C.** $x = y^2 - 4$

20. If $-1 < x < 0$, which of the following is arranged in order, smallest to largest?

    **A.** $x^3 < x^4 < x^5$          **D.** $x^5 < x^3 < x^4$

    **B.** $x^5 < x^4 < x^3$          **E.** $x^3 < x^5 < x^4$

    **C.** $x^4 < x^3 < x^5$

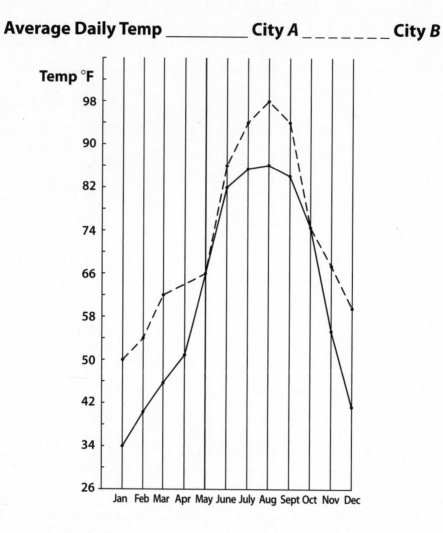

**Average Daily Temp** _____ **City A** _ _ _ _ _ _ _ **City B**

Questions 21–25 refer to the line graph shown here.

21. The month of greatest temperature difference occurs in

    **A.** January            **D.** August

    **B.** February          **E.** December

    **C.** March

22. The average (mean) difference in temperature in the months between the months where the temperatures are the same is about

    **A.** $5\frac{2}{3}°$           **D.** $14°$

    **B.** $6.8°$            **E.** $32°$

    **C.** $8.5°$

23. The percentage increase in temperature in January from city *A* to city *B* is closest to

      **A.** 16               **D.** 53

      **B.** 32               **E.** 64

      **C.** 47

24. The percentage decrease in temperature in December from city *B* to city *A* is

      **A.** 20               **D.** 40

      **B.** 25               **E.** 50

      **C.** $33\frac{1}{3}$

25. At 60° F, you need a 15 SPF sunscreen to protect yourself. For each 5° increase, you need to increase the SPF by 3. In August in city *B*, what SPF is needed, to the nearest integer?

      **A.** 30               **D.** 40

      **B.** 35               **E.** 42

      **C.** 38

26. In a large lecture hall, the ratio of men to women is 2:3. If there are 365 in the lecture hall, the number of women is

      **A.** 73               **D.** 155

      **B.** 105              **E.** 219

      **C.** 126

27. A circle has area 1. Its diameter is

      **A.** $\dfrac{1}{\pi}$               **D.** $\dfrac{2}{\sqrt{\pi}}$

      **B.** $\dfrac{2}{\pi}$               **E.** $\pi$

      **C.** $\dfrac{1}{\sqrt{\pi}}$

28. The surface area of this box is

    **A.** $30x^3$              **D.** $60x^3$

    **B.** $31x^2$              **E.** $62x^2$

    **C.** $50x^2$

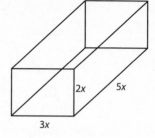

29. If $\dfrac{x}{2} + \dfrac{x}{3} = 1$, $x =$

    **A.** $\dfrac{2}{3}$              **D.** $\dfrac{9}{4}$

    **B.** $\dfrac{3}{2}$              **E.** $\dfrac{11}{10}$

    **C.** $\dfrac{6}{5}$

30. $2^n + 2^n =$

    **A.** $2^{n+1}$              **D.** $4^n$

    **B.** $2^{n+2}$              **E.** $2^{n^2}$

    **C.** $2^{n+3}$

## Part 2A

**Directions:** Each of the Questions 1–15 consists of two quantities, one in Column A and one in Column B. You are to compare the two quantities and choose:

**A** if the quantity in Column A is greater;

**B** if the quantity in Column B is greater;

**C** if the two quantities are equal;

**D** if the relationship cannot be determined from the information given

**Note** *Since there are only four choices,* NEVER MARK (E).

|     |  | **Column A** | **Column B** |
|-----|--|--------------|--------------|
| 1.  |  | .5% | $\dfrac{1}{20}$ |
| 2.  | $M$ is the mean of $5 + x + 7$ | $M$ | $\dfrac{(5 + x + M + 7)}{4}$ |
| 3.  |  | 3% of 4% of 2 | 2% of 3% of 4 |
| 4.  | Line 1: $y = mx + b$<br>Line 2: $y = \dfrac{-1}{m}x + b$ | slope of line 1 | slope of line 2 |
| 5.  | $y > x > N > 2$ and $N = y - x$ | $N^2$ | $y^2 + x^2$ |
| 6.  | $1^m = 1^n$ | $m$ | $n$ |
| 7.  | $m$ and $n =$ either 50 or 60: $0^{m-n} = 0$ | $m$ | $n$ |
| 8.  | $2^{m-n} = 2$ | $m$ | $n$ |
| 9.  | $a \otimes b = b^2 - ab;\ 2 \otimes y = -1$ | $y$ | $1$ |
| 10. |  | $.1\pi$ | $\sqrt{.81}$ |

**For Questions 11–13, refer to the following inequality: $-15 < x < -11$**

|     | **Column A** | **Column B** |
|-----|--------------|--------------|
| 11. | $\dfrac{1}{x^4}$ | $\dfrac{1}{x^2}$ |
| 12. | $\dfrac{1}{x^4}$ | $\dfrac{1}{x^3}$ |
| 13. | $\dfrac{1}{x^5}$ | $\dfrac{1}{x^3}$ |

14. 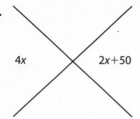  $x$                    25°

15. 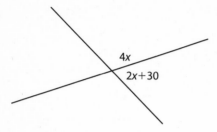  $x$                    25°

## Part 2B

**Directions:** Each of the Questions 16-30 has five choices. For each of these questions, select the best of the answer choices given.

16.  $\dfrac{x - b}{bx} = 2; x =$

  A. $3b$                    D. $\dfrac{1 - 2b}{b}$

  B. $2b^2 - b$              E. $\dfrac{2b - 1}{b}$

  C. $\dfrac{b}{1 - 2b}$

17.  42% of 37 is 21% of $x$; $x =$

  A. 18.5                    D. 74

  B. 37                      E. 1850

  C. 55.5

18. The area of the rectangle equals the area of the triangle, and $mn = 170$. $pq =$

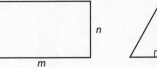 

    A. 85

    B. 170

    C. 255

    D. 340

    E. 680

19. $(5ab^3)^3 =$

    A. $15ab^6$

    B. $75a^3b^6$

    C. $125ab^9$

    D. $125a^3b^9$

    E. $125a^3b^{27}$

20. The angles of a triangle are in the ratio 5:6:7. The largest angle of the triangle is

    A. $10°$

    B. $50°$

    C. $60°$

    D. $70°$

    E. $80°$

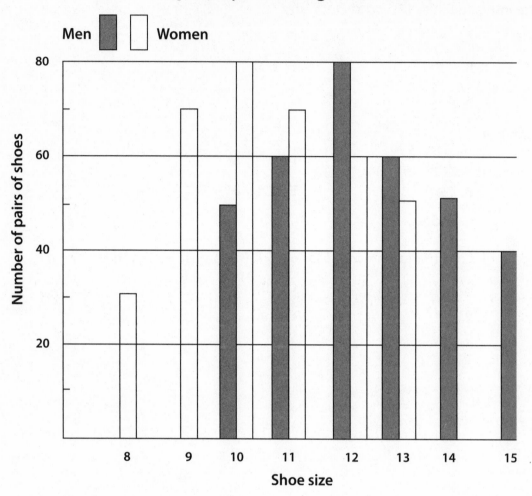

**Specialty Store Larger Shoe Sizes**

**Questions 21–25 refer to the chart on specialty large shoe sizes.**

21. The difference in the number of pairs of shoes between men's size 12 and men's size 10 is

    A. 0        D. 30

    B. 10      E. 60

    C. 20

22. Of all the shoes in stock, the percentage of men's shoes greater than size 13 is about

    A. 10%    D. 20%

    B. 13%    E. 42%

    C. 16%

23. If the average price of women's shoes increases 10% per size, and if the average price of a size 8 shoe is $200, all the women's size 10 shoes would sell for how much more than all the women's size 8 shoes?

      **A.** $40              **D.** $13,360

      **B.** $10,000       **E.** $13,660

      **C.** $13,200

24. What size shoe has the greatest difference in numbers in stock between men's and women's shoes?

      **A.** 10              **D.** 13

      **B.** 11              **E.** 14

      **C.** 12

25. If 40% of women's size 12 shoes are black and 25% of these have high heels, how many women's size 12 black shoes do not have high heels?

      **A.** 18              **D.** 32

      **B.** 24              **E.** 52

      **C.** 28

26. What is the minimum number of colors you can color a cube so that no two adjacent faces have the same color?

      **A.** 2               **D.** 5

      **B.** 3               **E.** 6

      **C.** 4

**Questions 27-28 refer to the Norman window shown here, which is a rectangle surmounted by a semicircle.**

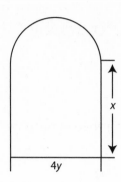

27.  Its perimeter is

A. $2x + 8y + 4\pi y$          D. $2x + 4y + \pi y$

B. $2x + 4y + 4\pi y$          E. $2x + y + \dfrac{\pi y}{2}$

C. $2x + 4y + 2\pi y$

28.  Its area is

A. $xy + \dfrac{\pi y^2}{2}$          D. $4xy + \pi y^2$

B. $4xy + 4\pi y^2$          E. $4xy + \dfrac{\pi y^2}{4}$

C. $4xy + 2\pi y^2$

29.  If $\dfrac{x - 6}{y + 4} = 0,$

A. $x = 0, y \neq 0$          D. $x = 6, y \neq -4$

B. $x = 6, y = -4$          E. $x \neq 6, y \neq -4$

C. $x \neq 6, y \neq -4$

30. If $\frac{2}{5}$ of $n$ is $\frac{7}{3}$, $\frac{2}{7}$ of $n$ is

   A. $\frac{3}{5}$         D. 35

   B. $\frac{5}{3}$         E. 210

   C. 6

# ANSWERS

## Part 1A

1. **(B)**  $3(3 \times 3) = 27, 3(3 + 27) = 90, 3(3 + 90) = 279$, so $A = 279$.

2. **(C)**  $m$ and $q = 0$.

3. **(C)**  Since (0,0) is the midpoint of $AB$, the value of $r$ is the negative of the value of $n$. For example, if $n = 4$, $r$ must be $-4$. Consequently, $-r$ would be $-(-4) = 4$.

4. **(B)**  $x^2 - 1 < x^2$

5. **(B)**  $B$ is much bigger than 1; $A$ is less than 1.

6. **(D)**  If $q = 0$, $A$ and $B$ are equal; If $p$ and $q$ are negative, such as $p = -10, q = -8, r = 3$, $A$ is bigger; if only $p$ is negative, such as $p = -10, q = 2, r = 3$, $B$ is bigger.

7. **(D)**  If $q = 0$ or if $q > 0$, $B$ is bigger; if $q < 0$ and $r < 0$, $A$ is bigger.

8. **(C)**  Circle $A$ has circumference $2\pi x$; circle $B$ has circumference $2\pi(2x)$. $2(2\pi x) = 2\pi(2x)$.

9. **(B)**  Twice the area of circle $A$ is $2\pi x^2$; the area of circle $B$ is $\pi(2x)^2 = 4\pi x^2$.

10. **(B)**  $A$ is less than $-1$, $B$ is greater than 1.

11. **(B)**  $\sqrt{181} < \sqrt{196} = 14 < 19$.

12. **(B)**  $A$ is less than 1; $B$ is greater than 1.

13. **(B)**  $A$ is negative; $B$ is positive.

14. **(C)**  $\dfrac{5}{8} = .6250$.

15. **(D)**  If $\dfrac{m}{n} < 1$; $B$ is bigger; if $\dfrac{m}{n} = 1$, the columns are equal; if $\dfrac{m}{n} > 1$, $A$ is bigger.

## Part 1B

16. **(C)**  The area of $\triangle AOB$ is 2; the area of equilateral $\triangle AOC$ is $\sqrt{3} \approx 1.7$; the sum is about 3.7.

17. **(E)**  I: odd to an even power is odd; II: odd + odd + odd = odd;, III: odd to an odd power is odd.

18. **(D)**  The secret is getting the age now. $m$ years in the future Jack will be $n$ years old, so now he is $n - m$. In p years, he will be $p + n - m$. If this doesn't work, substitute numbers like $m = 10, n = 30, p = 15$ (make the arithmetic easy for yourself).

19. **(E)**  $y = \sqrt{x} - 4$; $y + 4 = \sqrt{x}$; $x = (y + 4)^2$.

20. **(E)**  $x^4$ is largest since it is the only positive. $x^3 < x^5$; for example,

$$\left(-\frac{1}{2}\right)^3 = -\frac{1}{8} < \left(-\frac{1}{2}\right)^5 = -\frac{1}{32}.$$

21. **(E)**  For December, the average daily temperature of city $B$ is 60° and the average daily temperature of city $A$ is approximately 40°; their difference is 20°. The corresponding difference in temperatures between these two cities in January, February, March, and August are 16°, 14°, 16°, and 10°, respectively.

22. **(C)**  June, July, August, and September: $\dfrac{4 + 8 + 12 + 10}{4} = 8.5$.

23. **(C)**  $\dfrac{16}{34} = \dfrac{8}{17} \approx 47\%$.

24. **(C)**  About $60 - 40 = 20$, and $\dfrac{20}{60} = \dfrac{1}{3}$.

25. **(C)**  $98 - 60 = 38$; $\dfrac{38}{5} = 7.6$; $7.6 \times 3 = 22.8 \approx 23$; $23 + 15 = 38$ SPF.

26. **(E)**  $2x =$ number of men, $3x =$ number of women. $2x + 3x = 365$; $x = 73$; $3x = 219$.

27. **(D)**  Area $= 1 = \pi r^2$; $r = \dfrac{1}{\sqrt{\pi}}$; $d = 2r = \dfrac{2}{\sqrt{\pi}}$.

28. **(E)**  Surface area $= 2\ell w + 2\ell h + 2wh = 2(2x)(5x) + 2(3x)(5x) + 2(3x)(2x) = 62x^2$.

29. **(C)**  Multiply by 6; $3x + 2x = 6$; $5x = 6$.

30. **(A)**  $2^n + 2^n = 1(2^n) + 1(2^n) = 2(2^n) = 2^1 2^n = 2^{n+1}$

## Part 2A

1. **(B)**  $A = .005, B = .05$, or $A = .5\%, B = 5\%$.

2. **(C)**  $M = \dfrac{(5 + x + 7)}{3}$; $x = 3M - 12$; $\dfrac{(5 + x + M + 7)}{4} = \dfrac{(12 + M + 3M - 12)}{4}$

$$= \dfrac{4M}{4} = M!!!$$

3. **(C)**  3% of 4% of 2 $= (.03)(.04)(2) = .0024$ and 2% of 3% of 4 $= (.02)(.03)(4) = .0024$

4.  **(D)**   We don't know the sign of $m$. If $m > 0$, $A$ is bigger; if $m < 0$, $B$ is bigger. Note: $m \neq 0$, since $-\dfrac{1}{m}$ would be undefined.

5.  **(B)**   $N^2 = y^2 - 2xy + x^2 < y^2 + x^2$, since $x$ and $y$ are positive.

6.  **(D)**   1 to any power is 1; so $m$ and $n$ could be anything.

7.  **(A)**   If $m = n$, $0^{60-60}$ or $0^{50-50} = 0^0$, which is indeterminate. If $m < n$, $0^{m-n}$ is undefined. So $m > n$, and $m$ must be 60 and $n$ must be 50.

8.  **(A)**   $2^{m-n} = 2^1$; $m - n = 1$; $m = n + 1$.

9.  **(C)**   $y^2 - 2y + 1 = (y - 1)^2 \neq = 0$.

10. **(B)**   $.314 < .9$

**Note**  For Questions 11–13, $x$ could be any negative number, $x < -1$, and the answers would be the same!

11. **(B)**   The reciprocal of a large positive numeral is smaller.

12. **(A)**   A is positive and B is negative.

13. **(A)**   The reciprocal of a larger negative numeral is smaller.

14. **(C)**   $4x = 2x + 50$, $x = 25$.

15. **(C)**   $2x + 30 + 4x = 180$, $x = 25$.

## Part 2B

16. **(C)**   $x - b = 2bx$, so $x - 2bx = b$, and $x(1 - 2b) = b$. Therefore, $x = \dfrac{b}{(1 - 2b)}$.

17. **(D)**   Half the percentage; double the amount; $2(37) = 74$.

18. **(D)**   $mn = \dfrac{1}{2}pq = 170$; $pq = 340$.

19. **(D)**   $(5^1 a^1 b^3)^3 = 5^3 a^3 b^9 = 125 a^3 b^9$

20. **(D)**   $5x + 6x + 7x = 180$; $x = 10$; $7x = 70°$.

21. **(D)** $80 - 50 = 30$.

22. **(B)** $\dfrac{90}{700} \approx 13\%$.

23. **(D)** Size 8 costs \$200; \$200 × 30 = \$6,000; Size 9 costs 200 + .10(200) = \$220; Size 10 costs 220 + .10(220) = \$242; 242 × 80 = \$19,360; \$19,360 − \$6,000 = \$13,360.

24. **(E)** $50 - 0 = 50$.

25. **(A)** $60 \times .4 = 24$; $24 \times .25 = 6$; $24 - 6 = 18$.

26. **(B)** Top and bottom can be one color; left and right can one other color; front and back can be one other color.

27. **(C)** $p = \dfrac{1}{2} \times 2\pi r + x + x + 4y$; $r = 2y$; $p = 2\pi y + 2x + 4y$.

28. **(C)** $A = \dfrac{1}{2}\pi r^2 + bh = \dfrac{1}{2}\pi(2y)^2 + 4y(x) = 2\pi y^2 + 4xy$.

29. **(D)** A fraction equals 0 if the top equals 0 and the bottom does not equal 0.

30. **(B)** If you do the arithmetic, the 5 and the 7 change places.
$$\frac{2}{5}n = \frac{7}{3}; \ n = \left(\frac{7}{3}\right)\left(\frac{5}{2}\right) = \frac{35}{6}. \text{ Thus, } \frac{2}{7}n = \left(\frac{2}{7}\right)\left(\frac{35}{6}\right) = \frac{5}{3}.$$

"*We are on the last leg of the journey. One more practice test may be all you need.*"

## Part 1A

**Directions:** Each of the Questions 1–15 consists of two quantities, one in Column A and one in Column B. You are to compare the two quantities and choose:

**A** if the quantity in Column A is greater;

**B** if the quantity in Column B is greater;

**C** if the two quantities are equal;

**D** if the relationship cannot be determined from the information given

**Note** *Since there are only four choices, NEVER MARK (E).*

|  |  | **Column A** | **Column B** |
|---|---|---|---|
| 1. |  | 50% | $\dfrac{1}{.02}$ |
| 2. |  | $\sqrt{36.1}$ | 6.1 |
| 3. |  | $x^2 = 49$ | $x = 7$ |
| 4. |  | $\dfrac{1}{3} \div 2$ | 15% |
| 5. | $\dfrac{1}{x} > 1$ | $x$ | 1 |
| 6. |  | $\dfrac{4}{5} - \dfrac{5}{6}$ | $\dfrac{1}{30}$ |
| 7. | $a \neq b$ | $\dfrac{a^2 - b^2}{a - b}$ | $a + b$ |

| | **Column A** | **Column B** |
|---|---|---|
| 8. $4y^2 + 3y + 6y^2 + 4y$ $= 2y^2 + 6y + 8y^2 + 5$ | $y^2$ | 25 |
| 9. $4a = 5b = 6c = 7d > 0$ | $a$ | $d$ |
| 10. | $a \times 3 \times 3$ | $a + 3 + 3$ |
| 11. $x < 0$ | $(x^3)^7$ | $(x^3)(x^7)$ |
| 12. | $(a + b)^2$ | $a(a + b) + b(a + b)$ |
| 13. | $\dfrac{20}{27 - 24}$ | $\dfrac{20}{31 - 24}$ |
| 14. $a \otimes b = \dfrac{b + a}{7ab}$ | $7 \otimes 9$ | $9 \otimes 7$ |
| 15. | Area of equilateral $\Delta$ of side 6 | Area of square of side 4 |

## Part 1B

**Directions:** Each of the Questions 16–30 has five choices. For each of these questions, select the best of the answer choices given.

16. An item cost $600 after a 25% discount. It originally cost

    **A.** $150         **D.** $750

    **B.** $200         **E.** $800

    **C.** $700

17. The area of the shaded portion of the circle is

    **A.** $9\pi$         **D.** $105\pi$

    **B.** $16\pi$        **E.** $121\pi$

    **C.** $33\pi$

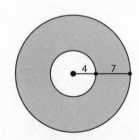

18. *A* and *B* (not shown) are on opposite sides of *P* on the line.

    $3AP = 4PB$. *M* is the midpoint of *AP*. $\dfrac{AM}{MB} =$

    A. $\dfrac{1}{4}$　　　　　　　D. $\dfrac{2}{5}$

    B. $\dfrac{2}{7}$　　　　　　　E. $\dfrac{4}{9}$

    C. $\dfrac{1}{3}$

19. Simplified, $\dfrac{\frac{1}{m^2} - \frac{1}{n^2}}{\frac{1}{m} - \frac{1}{n}}$

    A. 1　　　　　　　　　D. $mn + 1$

    B. $\dfrac{1}{mn}$　　　　　　　E. $\dfrac{1}{mn + 1}$

    C. $\dfrac{n + m}{nm}$

20. $100^x = 10^{100}$; $x =$

    A. 10　　　　　　　D. 50

    B. 20　　　　　　　E. 75

    C. 25

Total: 2000 Students

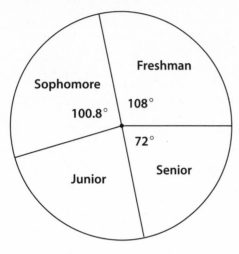

**Average June 2010 grades**

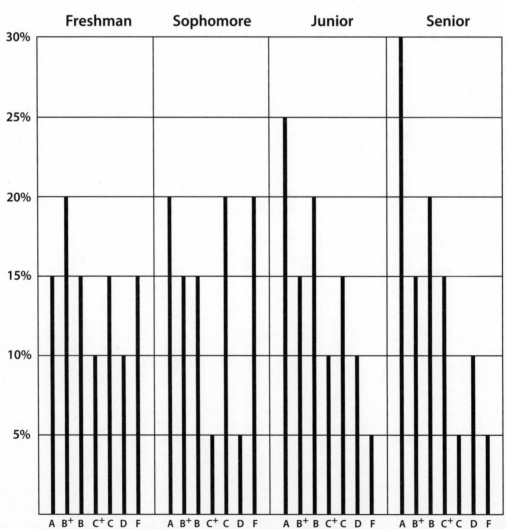

**Questions 21–25 refer to the chart of grades presented on page 216. The high school has 2000 students.**

21.  How many sophomores are there?

        **A.** 500               **D.** 560

        **B.** 540               **E.** 600

        **C.** 550

22.  The difference between the number of A's of the senior class and the number of A's of the freshman class is

        **A.** 9                **D.** 60

        **B.** 15               **E.** 90

        **C.** 30

23.  The number of students with at least a B average is

        **A.** 225               **D.** 1104

        **B.** 342               **E.** 1164

        **C.** 842

24.  If it takes at least a C to graduate, how many will graduate in 2010?

        **A.** 340               **D.** 1584

        **B.** 400               **E.** 2000

        **C.** 842

25. How many degrees on the pie chart would represent juniors?

        **A.** 70.2°           **D.** 99.2°

        **B.** 79.2°           **E.** 219.2°

        **C.** 82.2°

26.  $(x - 7)^2 = (x - 19)^2; x =$

        **A.** 9                **D.** 15

        **B.** 11               **E.** 17

        **C.** 13

27. On the number line, what number between 20 and 30 is twice as far from 20 as it is from 30?

    **A.** 26

    **D.** 27

    **B.** $26\frac{2}{3}$

    **E.** $27\frac{1}{2}$

    **C.** $26\frac{3}{4}$

28. If a box doubles its width, triples its length, and quadruples its height (multiplies it by 4), the new volume is how many times the old volume?

    **A.** 9

    **D.** 120

    **B.** 12

    **E.** 4,096

    **C.** 24

29. Referring to circle *O*, with radius *OT*, *TV* tangent to the circle, and the given lengths. The length of *UV* =

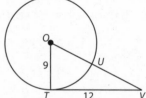

    **A.** 6

    **D.** 9

    **B.** 7

    **E.** 10

    **C.** 8

30. Bill is five times as old as Jim. Five years ago, Bill was nine times as old as Jim. Bill's age today is

    **A.** 5

    **D.** 50

    **B.** 10

    **E.** 60

    **C.** 20

## Part 2A

**Directions:** Each of the Questions 1–15 consists of two quantities, one in Column A and one in Column B. You are to compare the two quantities and choose:

**A** if the quantity in Column A is greater;

**B** if the quantity in Column B is greater;

**C** if the two quantities are equal;

**D** if the relationship cannot be determined from the information given

**Note** *Since there are only four choices, NEVER MARK (E).*

|  | **Column A** | **Column B** |
|---|---|---|
| 1. | $\dfrac{1}{10,000}$ | .01% |

2. $4x + 2y = 23$

   $3x + 5y = 26$    Mean of $x$ and $y$    3.5

3.    $a(a + b)$    $3(a^2 + ab) - 2a(a + b)$

4.    $97^2 - 5^2$    $(102)(92)$

5.    $\dfrac{94}{47 - 2}$    $\dfrac{86}{41 + 3}$

6.  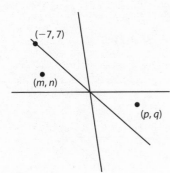    $\dfrac{m}{n}$    $\dfrac{p}{q}$

7.  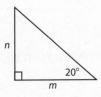    $m$    $n$

8.    Hours in a week    Minutes in $2\dfrac{5}{6}$ hours

9. $x^2 + 28x + 112 = 0$    $x^2 + 28x$    112

10. $abc = bcde > 0$    $a$    $d$

11.    $\dfrac{8}{\sqrt{2}}$    $4\sqrt{2}$

12. $-1, 0, 1, -1, 0, 1, \ldots$    86th term    0

13. $x'' 90$

Supplement of x° − complement of x°   90°

14.

Area of the Δ formed with the x-axis,   4

the y-axis, and the line $y = 2x + 4$

15. $4x − 2 = 6x + 6$          $2x − 1$                          $x + 1$

## Part 2B

**Directions:** Each of the Questions 16–30 has five choices. For each of these questions, select the best of the answer choices given.

16.  Define $a \otimes b = b + a^3$. $2 \otimes x^2 = 9x$ has solutions

    **A.** $x = 1$ and 0 only     **D.** $x = 0, 1,$ and 8 only

    **B.** $x = 8$ and 0 only     **E.** A 6th degree equation, which is unsolvable

    **C.** $x = 1$ and 8 only

17.  The area of *ABCD* is

    **A.** 24     **D.** 48

    **B.** 36     **E.** 54

    **C.** 42

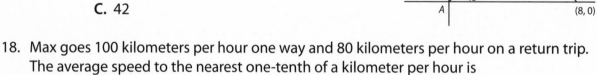

18.  Max goes 100 kilometers per hour one way and 80 kilometers per hour on a return trip. The average speed to the nearest one-tenth of a kilometer per hour is

    **A.** 85.3     **D.** 90.0

    **B.** 86.7     **E.** 92.3

    **C.** 88.9

19.  The sum of seven consecutive odd integers is −105. The product of the two largest ones is

    **A.** 99     **D.** 206

    **B.** 182     **E.** 399

    **C.** 225

20.  In this figure, the value of $x =$

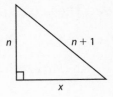

A. 1

D. $\sqrt{2n^2 + 2n + 1}$

B. $2n + 1$

E. $\sqrt{n + 1}$

C. $\sqrt{2n + 1}$

## Trade of Company X with Company Y, 1997–2008 (U.S. dollars)

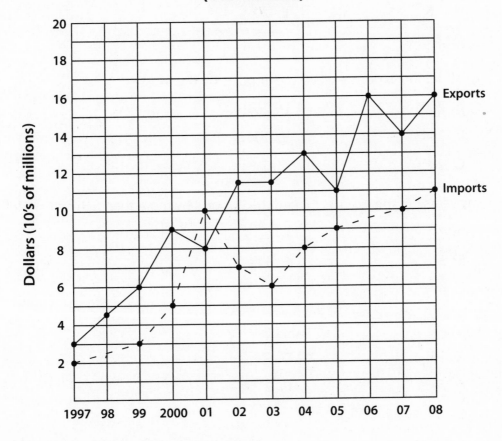

**For Questions 21–25, refer to the above graph.**

21.  In 2003, exports are about what percentage of imports?

A. 5.5

D. 190

B. 48

E. 204

C. 53

22. The largest percentage decrease in exports occurred from

    **A.** 2000 to 2001          **D.** 2006 to 2007

    **B.** 2002 to 2003          **E.** Both (C) and (D)

    **C.** 2004 to 2005

23. The difference between the rise in imports from 2003 to 2004 and the rise in imports from 2004 to 2008 in millions of dollars is

    **A.** 1                     **D.** 10

    **B.** 1.5                   **E.** 20

    **C.** 2

24. In what year did the exports exceed the imports by the most?

    **A.** 2001                  **D.** 2006

    **B.** 2003                  **E.** 2007

    **C.** 2004

25. How many years did the exports exceed the imports by more than five million dollars?

    **A.** 2                     **D.** 5

    **B.** 3                     **E.** 11

    **C.** 4

26. $M = 2^r. \ 8M =$

    **A.** $16^r$                **D.** $2^{r+1}$

    **B.** $64^r$                **E.** $2^{r+3}$

    **C.** $2^{r^3}$

27. If $m = \dfrac{p^6}{q^5}$ , which expression is equivalent to $\dfrac{qm}{p}$ ?

    **A.** $\dfrac{p^5}{q^4}$              **D.** $\dfrac{p^{12}}{q^3}$

    **B.** $\dfrac{p^7}{q^6}$              **E.** Cannot be determined

    **C.** $\dfrac{p^8}{q^7}$

28. The maximum value of $\dfrac{m + n}{m - n}$ with $8 \le m \le 10$ and $2 \le n \le 4$ is

   A. $\dfrac{3}{2}$          D. 3

   B. $\dfrac{5}{3}$          E. 6

   C. $\dfrac{7}{3}$

29. $0 < m < 1$

   I.  $m < \dfrac{1}{\sqrt{m}}$

   II. $\dfrac{1}{m} < \dfrac{1}{m^2}$

   III. $1 - m \le m$

   Which statements are always true?

   A. None                 D. II and III only

   B. I and II only         E. All three are always true

   C. I and III only

30. $\dfrac{x + 1}{x - 1} = \dfrac{x - 1}{x + 1}$. The solution is

   A. $x = 0$ only          D. $x = 4$ only

   B. $x = 0$ and 1 only     E. There are no solutions

   C. $x = 0$ and $-1$ only

# ANSWERS

## Part 1A

1. **(B)**   $A$ is $\dfrac{1}{2}$ and $B$ is 50.

2. **(B)**   Square both sides. The left side is 36.1 and the right side is 37.21.

3. **(D)**   $x$ could also be $-7$.

4. **(A)**   $A = .1666\ldots$

5. **(B)**   For this inequality to be true, $x$ has to be less than 1.

6. **(B)**   $A$ equals $-\dfrac{1}{30}$.

7. **(C)**   The top of $A$ factors into $(a + b)(a - b)$, then cancel.

8. **(C)**   Combine like terms to get $y = 5$, then square both sides.

9. **(A)**   $4a = 7d$, $a = \dfrac{7}{4}d$.

10. **(D)**   We need to know the sign and value of $a$.

11. **(B)**   $B$ is positive and $A$ is negative.

12. **(C)**   They both equal $a^2 + 2ab + b^2$.

13. **(A)**   If the numerators are the same, the smaller denominator gives the larger fraction.

14. **(C)**   Notice the order doesn't matter for addition and multiplication; do not do the arithmetic.

15. **(B)**   $A = 9\sqrt{3} \approx 9(1.73) < 16 = B$.

## Part 1B

16. **(E)**   Plug numbers into the answer choices, or use $x - .25x = 600$, so $\dfrac{3}{4}x = 600$, and $x = 800$.

17. **(D)**   The outside radius is 11 and the inside radius is 4, so the shaded portion is $121\pi - 16\pi = 105\pi$.

18. **(D)** Draw in hypothetical points $A$ and $B$, and point $M$ such that $AP = 4$ and $PB = 3$, as shown. $M$ is the midpoint. By counting, we see the answer is $\dfrac{2}{5}$.

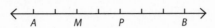

19. **(C)** $\dfrac{m^2 n^2 \left(\frac{1}{m^2} - \frac{1}{n^2}\right)}{m^2 n^2 \left(\frac{1}{m} - \frac{1}{n}\right)} = \dfrac{n^2 - m^2}{mn^2 - m^2 n} = \dfrac{(n+m)(n-m)}{mn(n-m)} = \dfrac{m+n}{mn}$. After doing this problem more than 100 times (since it requires a lot of skills in a relatively short problem), I found a shorter way to do it (for this test). Factoring the top of the original fraction (once we realize it is the difference of two squares), we get $\left(\dfrac{1}{m} - \dfrac{1}{n}\right)\left(\dfrac{1}{m} + \dfrac{1}{n}\right)$. Canceling both fractions with minus signs and adding the two fractions with the plus sign, we again get $\dfrac{n+m}{nm}$. It is never too late to find something new!

20. **(D)** $100 = 10^2$. So we have $10^{2x} = 10^{100}$, or $2x = 100$.

21. **(D)** $\left(\dfrac{100.8}{360}\right)(2000) = 560$.

22. **(C)** $= \left(\dfrac{72}{360}\right)(2000) = 400$ seniors; $400(.30) = 120$ A's. $\left(\dfrac{108}{360}\right)(2000) = 600$ freshman; $600(.15) = 90$ A's; $120 - 90 = 30$.

23. **(D)** There are $2000 - 600 - 560 - 400 = 440$ juniors. At least a B: $.50(600) + .50(560) + .60(440) + .65(400) = 1104$.

24. **(A)** $400(.85)$. Only seniors graduate. Actually this is a little fiction. No school really fails seniors anymore.

25. **(B)** $360 - (100.8 + 108 + 72) = 79.2$

26. **(C)** By sight, it has to be halfway between 7 and 19. You could also solve this algebraically. You would get $x^2 - 14x + 49 = x^2 - 38x + 361$. This simplifies to $24x = 312$, so $x = 13$.

27. **(B)** Let $x$ be the distance from the missing number to 30. Then $x + 2x = 30 - 20$; $x = 3\dfrac{1}{3}$. It's closer to 30; so $30 - 3\dfrac{1}{3}$ or $20 + 6\dfrac{2}{3}$ gives the answer.

28. **(C)**   The old box volume is $\ell wh$. The new box volume is $(3\ell)(2w)(4h) = 24\,\ell wh$.

29. **(A)**   The right triangle formed is a 9-12-15 triple; $OU = 9$; $UV = 15 - 9 = 6$.

30. **(D)**   $5x - 5 = 9(x - 5)$, so $x = 10$, and $5x = 50$.

## Part 2A

1. **(C)**   Both $= .0001$.

2. **(C)**   Adding we get $7x + 7y = 49$; so $x + y = 7$; and $\dfrac{x + y}{2} = 3.5$.

3. **(C)**   Both equal $a^2 + ab$.

4. **(C)**   $97^2 - 5^2$ is the difference of two squares, or $(97 + 5)(97 - 5)$.

5. **(A)**   A $> 2$ and B $< 2$. You don't have to get the exact values.

6. **(D)**   Both are negative fractions. $|m| > |n|$, so $\dfrac{m}{n} < -1$; $|p| > |q|$, so $\dfrac{p}{q} < -1$; and that's all we know.

7. **(A)**   The side opposite the larger angle (70°) is longer. The figure is not drawn to scale, but you should go by the given numbers, not what it "looks like."

8. **(B)**   $A = 24(7) = 168, B = 60\left(2\dfrac{5}{6}\right) = 170$.

9. **(B)**   $x^2 + 28x = -112$; you don't factor!

10. **(D)**   $a = de$; but $a$, $d$, and/or $e$ could be proper or improper fractions.

11. **(C)**   $\dfrac{8}{\sqrt{2}} \times \dfrac{\sqrt{2}}{\sqrt{2}} = \dfrac{8\sqrt{2}}{2} = 4\sqrt{2}$.

12. **(C)**   Cycle is 3: $\dfrac{86}{3}$ has a remainder of two. The second term is 0.

13. **(C)**   $(180 - x) - (90 - x) = 90$.

14. **(C)**   The $y$-intercept is 4; the $x$-intercept is $-2$; area $= \left(\dfrac{1}{2}\right)(2)(4)$; draw the picture!

15. **(B)**   Solving, $x = -4$; then substitute in each side. The left side is $-9$ and the right side is $-3$.

## Part 2B

16. **(C)**  $x^2 - 9x + 8 = (x - 8)(x - 1) = 0$.

17. **(C)**  Point $C$ is $(6, 6)$; so $h = 6$; $b_1 = 6$ and $b_2 = 8$; $A = \frac{1}{2}h(b_1 + b_2) = \frac{6}{2}(6 + 8) = 42$.

18. **(C)**  The LCM of 80 and 100 is 400. The time of the trip going is 5 hours; the return trip is 4 hours; $\frac{800}{9} \approx 88.9$.

19. **(A)**  $\frac{-105}{7} = -15$, the middle number; all are $-21, -19, -17, -15, -13, -11, -9$; $-11$ and $-9$ are the largest!

20. **(C)**  By the Pythagorean Theorem, $x = \sqrt{(n + 1)^2 - n^2} = \sqrt{n^2 + 2n + 1 - n^2} = \sqrt{2n + 1}$.

21. **(D)**  $\left(\frac{11.5}{6}\right)(100\%) =$ about $190\%$. You can forget about the zeroes, and $\frac{11.5}{6}$ is a little less than 2. So you shouldn't do the arithmetic.

22. **(C)**  For 2004–2005 and 2006–2007, the drop is the same. However, the totals from 2004 and 2005 are smaller, so the percentage drop, which is approx 15.4%, is higher for that period.

23. **(D)**  $8 - 6 = 2$; $11 - 8 = 3$; $3 - 2 = 1$; 1 group of 10,000,000; so 10 groups of 1 million.

24. **(D)**  $160$ million $- \$95$ million $= \$65$ million in 2006.

25. **(E)**  Since the chart is in tens of millions, 2001 is the only year it doesn't happen.

26. **(E)**  $M = 2^r$; $M = 8(2^r) = 2^3 2^r = 2^{r+3}$.

27. **(A)**  $m = \frac{p^6}{q^5}$; $\frac{qm}{p} = \frac{qp^6}{pq^5} = \frac{p^5}{q^4}$.

28. **(D)**  The maximum occurs when $m = 8$ and $n = 4$.

29. **(B)**  Statement I is always true: $\frac{1}{\sqrt{m}} > 1$ because if you square both sides, $\frac{1}{m} > 1$ is always true for $0 < m < 1$. Statement II is always true: $\frac{1}{m} > 1$; if you square it, it becomes larger. Statement III is sometimes true: it is true for $m \geq \frac{1}{2}$ only.

30. **(A)**  Cross-multiplying results in $x^2 + 2x + 1 = x^2 - 2x + 1$. Simplifying, we get $4x = 0$, so $x = 0$.

# CHAPTER 19: *Extra, Extra! Extra!!!!!*

*"Always be prepared."*

**Five** hours after I finished the original manuscript, the GRE board decided to add new material to the test. It decided to add questions on functions. It also added fill-in questions on the CAT version. I've added this new section in the form of the CAT version, but everyone needs to read this section!!!!!

On the paper-and-pencil GRE, these questions would be multiple-choice. However, on the new part of the computer-based tests, you must get your own answer without any choices. Fill-in spaces are provided in two formats: One is a box for a numerical answer; the other is a box for an answer that is a fraction. You fill in your answers by using the computer keyboard.

Be careful that your answer is in the correct units. If the question asks for cents, for example, 275 cents would be correct, whereas $2.75 would be wrong. Also, be aware that fractions do not have to be in the lowest terms. An answer of $\frac{120}{240}$ is as correct as $\frac{1}{2}$.

This chapter provides some examples and then presents a 20-item test for you to practice your skills.

**Example 1:** A taxi charges $3.00 for the first half mile and $0.40 for each additional quarter mile. The total taxi ride cost $10.20. Exactly how many miles did the cab travel?

(    ) miles

**Solution:** The cost of the first half mile is $3.00. That leaves $10.20 − $3.00 = $7.20 for the remaining quarter miles. $7.20 ÷ .40 = 18 quarter miles = 4.5 miles. 4.5 + the initial 0.5 mile = exactly 5 miles.

**Example 2:** In 2007, the first-class postage is 41 cents up to one ounce and 19 cents for each additional ounce or part of an ounce. A letter was $\frac{1}{4}$ ounces more than a half pound. How much did the letter cost to mail first class?

( ) cents

**Solution:** A half pound = 8 ounces. 8 ounces plus $\frac{1}{4}$ ounce puts the letter into the 9-ounce rate. So the charge is the one for 9 ounces. The first ounce is 41 cents and the remaining 8 ounces each cost 19 cents. Thus, 41 + 8(19) = 41 + 152 = 193. Notice that we are working with cents, since that is what the question asks for.

**Example 3:** Twelve of 35 people didn't enjoy the movie. What percentage, to the nearest tenth, enjoyed the movie?

( ) percent

**Solution:** 35 − 12 = 23 of 35 liked the movie. $\frac{23}{35}$ = 65.71. Put 65.7 in the box since the answer is to the nearest tenth of a percent.

**Example 4:** In a large vase, 3 of 20 balls are red. Drew draws 2 balls simultaneously without looking. What is the probability that neither ball is red?

( _____ )

**Solution:** Notice that the answer has to be a fraction. The probability that Drew does not pick a red twice is $\left(\frac{17}{20}\right)\left(\frac{16}{19}\right) = \frac{272}{380}$.

**Note** *It is not necessary to reduce this fraction. Any correct fraction will do.*

**Example 5:** A $20 book was sold for $15.25. What was the percentage discount?

( ) percent

**Solution:**  The discount is $4.75; divide 4.75 by 20 to get 23.75 percent. Easier yet is a trick. Multiply the top and bottom of the fraction by 5 to get $\dfrac{23.75}{100}$, which is 23.75 percent.

**Example 6:**  The product of ten million and ten million is how many billions?

$$(\quad) \text{ billions}$$

**Solution:**  $10,000,000 \times 10,000,000 = 100,000,000,000,000$. A billion is $\dfrac{100,000,000,000,000}{1,000,000,000} = 100,000$ billions.

**Example 7:**  A quarterly water bill was $80.75. It contained a fixed charge of $20.75 plus $0.0075 per gallon. How many gallons were used?

$$(\quad) \text{ gallons}$$

**Solution:**  $\$80.75 - \$20.75 = \$60$ for the per gallon charge. $\dfrac{60}{.0075} = 8,000 = 8,000$ gallons. Here's another arithmetic trick: Multiply the top and bottom of the fraction by 10,000; to get $\dfrac{600,000}{75}$. Now multiply the top and bottom by 4, to get $\dfrac{2,400,000}{300}$, and divide by 100 to get $\dfrac{24,000}{3} = 8,000$ gallons.

**Example 8:**  For the set 3,3,4,4,5,6,7,7,7,8, find the sum of the median, mean, and mode.

$$(\quad)$$

**Solution:**  The median is the mean of the middle two terms, or $= \dfrac{5+6}{2} = 5.5$. The mean is $\dfrac{54}{10} = 5.4$. The mode is 7. The sum of the three is 17.9.

**Example 9:**  Six people shake each other's hand exactly once. How many different handshakes are there?

$$(\quad) \text{ handshakes}$$

**Solution:**   $5 + 4 + 3 + 2 + 1 = 15$. Another way to get this is through combinations: $_6C_2 = \dfrac{6 \times 5}{2 \times 1} = 15$.

**Example 10:**   Three yards four feet five inches is how many inches?

$$(\quad) \text{ inches}$$

**Solution:**   $3(36) + 4(12) + 5 = 161$ inches

The new part of the computer-based GRE also includes some questions on functions.

## Ⓠ **Let's look at some of these.**

**Example 11:**   Suppose $f(x) = x^2 + 3x + 10$. What is

    **a.**  $f(6)$?

    **b.**  $f(-5)$?

$$\textbf{a.} (\quad) \quad \textbf{b.} (\quad)$$

**Solutions:**   **a.**  $f(6) = 6^2 + 3(6) + 10 = 64$;

    **b.**  $f(-5) = (-5)^2 + 3(-5) + 10 = 20$

**Example 12:**   Suppose $f(x) = x^2 + 8x$.

    **a.**  What is the minimum value for $c$ such that $f(c) = 9$?

    **b.**  Find the sum of the values such that $f(c) = 9$?

$$\textbf{a.} (\quad) \quad \textbf{b.} (\quad)$$

**Solutions:**   **a.**  $f(x) = x^2 + 8x$; $f(c) = 9$ means $c^2 + 8c = 9$ or $c^2 + 8c - 9$
       $= (c + 9)(c - 1) = 0$; so $c = -9$ or 1. The answer is $-9$,

    **b.**  $-9 + 1 = -8$.

On the paper-based GRE, such equations would be multiple-choice. The question might be:

What are the values such that $f(c) = 9$? (The correct answer is d.)

- **a.** $-9$ only
- **b.** 1 only
- **c.** 0 only
- **d.** $-9$ and 1 only
- **e.** $-1, 0,$ and 9

**Example 12:**  Let $f(x) = \dfrac{x^2 - 4x}{x^2 - 4}$.

- **a.** What is the product of the values such that $f(x) = 0$?

- **b.** What is the sum of the values such that $f(x)$ is undefined?

a. (  )  b. (  )

**Solutions:**    **a.** $f(x) = \dfrac{x^2 - 4x}{x^2 - 4} = \dfrac{x(x - 4)}{(x + 2)(x - 2)}$. $f(x) = 0$ means $x(x - 4) = 0$, so $x = 0$ and 4, and the product is 0.

**b.** $f(x)$ undefined means $(x + 2)(x - 2) = 0$ (the denominator is 0). Thus, $x = 2$ and $-2$, and the sum is 0.

As you might be able to tell, nearly every multiple-choice question with a numerical answer could be in this section. The only difference is you probably can't guess the answers to these problems. For some, this is a good thing; for others, not so good.

 **Let's do a practice test for the fill-ins on the computer-based GRE.**

## Directions:

For a single answer box, type a number in the box using the keyboard.

1. First, click on the answer box—a cursor will appear in the box—and then type a number.

2. To erase a number, use the BACKSPACE key.

3. For a negative sign, type a HYPHEN. For a decimal point, type a PERIOD.

4. To remove a negative sign, type the hyphen again and the minus sign will disappear; the number will remain.

5. ROUND YOUR ANSWER IF THE QUESTION ASKS SO; otherwise, ENTER AN EXACT ANSWER

For a fraction, type the numerator and denominator in their respective boxes.

1.  For a negative sign, type a HYPHEN. A decimal point can NOT be used in a fraction.

2.  Fractions do NOT need to be reduced to lowest terms.

## Fill-in Questions

1.  If $f(x) = 2x + 7$ and $g(x) = x^2 + 8x$. What is the smallest value such that $f(c) = g(c)$?

2.  What is the mean of $\frac{1}{5}$ and $\frac{1}{7}$?

3.  What is the median of $\frac{1}{5}$ and $\frac{1}{7}$?

4.  If $f(x) = |2x - 7|$ and $g(x) = 3$, what is the largest value such that $f(c) = g(c)$?

5.  22% of what is 44?

6.  If 4 oranges and 6 apples cost $1.12, how much do 10 oranges and 15 apples cost?  cents

7.  A large jar contains 5 brown balls and 4 yellow balls. Three balls are taken from the jar without replacement. Find the probability that all three are yellow.

8.  If $f(x) = \dfrac{x - 8}{x + 3}$, $g(x) = 8$ and $f(c) = g(c)$, what is $c$?

9.  The area of a rectangle is 100 square feet. A triangle with base 25 feet has the same area. The height of the triangle is what?  feet

10. 2% of 4 is what % of .02?

11. $\dfrac{1}{16}$ to the nearest thousandth is what?

12. The area of a circle is numerically equal to its circumference. What is the radius of this circle?

13. If 8 ounces = one cup, 2 cups = 1 pint, 2 pints are in a quart and 4 quarts are in a gallon, how many ounces are in a half gallon?  ounces

14. If $|2x - 3| = |5x - 2|$, what is the sum of the solutions?

15. $f(x) = 5x - 4$, $f(6) - f(8)$ is what?

16. If $8^{3x + 2} = 4^{2x + 3}$, what is $x$?

17. If $3x - 5 = 11$; $6x - 23$ is what?

18. $f(x) = 3x + 20$ and $g(x) = 2x + 6$; $f(c) = g(c + 4)$. What is $c$?

19. Find a fraction between $\dfrac{44}{47}$ and $\dfrac{45}{47}$ with the denominator less than 100.

20. A fair coin is flipped four times. What is the probability that you don't get 4 heads?

## ANSWERS

1.  $f(x) = 2x + 7$; $f(c) = 2c + 7$; $g(x) = x^2 + 8x$; and $g(c) = c^2 + 8c$.
    So $c^2 + 8c = 2c + 7$, or $c^2 + 6c - 7 = (c + 7)(c - 1) = 0$.
    The smallest value for $c$ is $-7$ (the other value is 1).

2.  $\dfrac{1}{2}\left(\dfrac{1}{5} + \dfrac{1}{7}\right) = \dfrac{1}{2} \times \dfrac{12}{35} = \dfrac{6}{35}$

3.  It is the same as the answer to question 2!

4.  $f(c) = |2c - 7|$ and $g(c) = 3$. This means $2c - 7 = 3$ or $2c - 7 = -3$, so $c = 2$ or 5.
    The answer is 5.

5.  $\dfrac{44}{.22} = 200$.

6.  $4x + 6y = 112$ cents, where $x$ is oranges and $y$ is apples. Then $2x + 3y = 56$ cents (divide by 2), and $10x + 15y = 5(56) = 280$ cents. Note that \$2.80 is not the answer that is called for here.

7.  $Pr(Y) = \dfrac{4}{9} \times \dfrac{3}{8} \times \dfrac{2}{7} = \dfrac{1}{21}$. The fraction doesn't have to be reduced, but
    canceling works well with the numbers here and avoids tedious multiplication.

8.  $\dfrac{c - 8}{c + 3} = 8$, or $c - 8 = 8c + 24$. Then $7c = -32$, and $c = -\dfrac{32}{7}$.

9.  $\dfrac{1}{2}bh = 100$; so $bh = 200$. Since $b = 25$, $h = 8$ feet.

10. 2% of 4 is .08; $\dfrac{.08}{.02} \times 100\% = 400\%$.

11. Divide 16 into $1 = .0625 = .063$.

12. $\pi r^2 = 2\pi r$. Canceling $\pi$ and $r$ (since $r$ can't be 0) yields $r = 2$.

13. $\dfrac{8 \times 2 \times 2 \times 4}{2} = 64\,\text{ounces}$.

14. $2x - 3 = 5x - 2$, or $2x - 3 = 2 - 5x$. Then $x = -\dfrac{1}{3}$ or $\dfrac{5}{7}$; their sum is $\dfrac{8}{21}$.

15. $f(6) = 26$ and $f(8) = 36$; the difference is $-10$.

16. $(2^3)^{3x+2} = (2^2)^{2x+3}$; so $3(3x + 2) = 2(2x + 3)$. Then $9x + 6 = 4x + 6$, and $x = 0$.

17. $3x = 16$, so $6x = 32$. Then $6x - 23 = 32 - 23 = 9$. Notice that you do not have to find $x$.

18. $f(c) = 3c + 20$; $g(c + 4) = 2(c + 4) + 6 = 2c + 14$. So $3c + 20 = 2c + 14$, and $c = -6$.

19. Multiply each fraction by $\frac{2}{2}$; to get $\frac{88}{94}$ and $\frac{90}{94}$. Between these is $\frac{89}{94}$. The average, or the mean, is always between (a little poem).

20. $Pr(4 \text{ heads}) = \left(\frac{1}{2}\right)^4 = \frac{1}{16}$. $Pr(\text{Not 4 heads}) = 1 - \frac{1}{16} = \frac{15}{16}$.

# CHAPTER 20: *Epilogue*

*"If you feel more is needed, you may need a little more for your confidence. But if our journey together has been complete, you have all you need for success."*

**Again,** congratulations. Now that you've finished the book, you should review any section that has caused you difficulty.

Remember, again, that you do not need a perfect score. You need only a score that will get you into the graduate school of your choice.

Good luck with the rest of your college education and the rest of your life.

# GRE General Test

# ANSWER SHEETS

# ANSWER SHEET: *Practice Test 1*

1. Ⓐ Ⓑ Ⓒ Ⓓ Ⓔ
2. Ⓐ Ⓑ Ⓒ Ⓓ Ⓔ
3. Ⓐ Ⓑ Ⓒ Ⓓ Ⓔ
4. Ⓐ Ⓑ Ⓒ Ⓓ Ⓔ
5. Ⓐ Ⓑ Ⓒ Ⓓ Ⓔ
6. Ⓐ Ⓑ Ⓒ Ⓓ Ⓔ
7. Ⓐ Ⓑ Ⓒ Ⓓ Ⓔ
8. Ⓐ Ⓑ Ⓒ Ⓓ Ⓔ
9. Ⓐ Ⓑ Ⓒ Ⓓ Ⓔ
10. Ⓐ Ⓑ Ⓒ Ⓓ Ⓔ
11. Ⓐ Ⓑ Ⓒ Ⓓ Ⓔ
12. Ⓐ Ⓑ Ⓒ Ⓓ Ⓔ
13. Ⓐ Ⓑ Ⓒ Ⓓ Ⓔ
14. Ⓐ Ⓑ Ⓒ Ⓓ Ⓔ
15. Ⓐ Ⓑ Ⓒ Ⓓ Ⓔ
16. Ⓐ Ⓑ Ⓒ Ⓓ Ⓔ
17. Ⓐ Ⓑ Ⓒ Ⓓ Ⓔ
18. Ⓐ Ⓑ Ⓒ Ⓓ Ⓔ
19. Ⓐ Ⓑ Ⓒ Ⓓ Ⓔ
20. Ⓐ Ⓑ Ⓒ Ⓓ Ⓔ
21. Ⓐ Ⓑ Ⓒ Ⓓ Ⓔ
22. Ⓐ Ⓑ Ⓒ Ⓓ Ⓔ
23. Ⓐ Ⓑ Ⓒ Ⓓ Ⓔ
24. Ⓐ Ⓑ Ⓒ Ⓓ Ⓔ
25. Ⓐ Ⓑ Ⓒ Ⓓ Ⓔ
26. Ⓐ Ⓑ Ⓒ Ⓓ Ⓔ
27. Ⓐ Ⓑ Ⓒ Ⓓ Ⓔ
28. Ⓐ Ⓑ Ⓒ Ⓓ Ⓔ
29. Ⓐ Ⓑ Ⓒ Ⓓ Ⓔ
30. Ⓐ Ⓑ Ⓒ Ⓓ Ⓔ

31. Ⓐ Ⓑ Ⓒ Ⓓ Ⓔ
32. Ⓐ Ⓑ Ⓒ Ⓓ Ⓔ
33. Ⓐ Ⓑ Ⓒ Ⓓ Ⓔ
34. Ⓐ Ⓑ Ⓒ Ⓓ Ⓔ
35. Ⓐ Ⓑ Ⓒ Ⓓ Ⓔ
36. Ⓐ Ⓑ Ⓒ Ⓓ Ⓔ
37. Ⓐ Ⓑ Ⓒ Ⓓ Ⓔ
38. Ⓐ Ⓑ Ⓒ Ⓓ Ⓔ
39. Ⓐ Ⓑ Ⓒ Ⓓ Ⓔ
40. Ⓐ Ⓑ Ⓒ Ⓓ Ⓔ
41. Ⓐ Ⓑ Ⓒ Ⓓ Ⓔ
42. Ⓐ Ⓑ Ⓒ Ⓓ Ⓔ
43. Ⓐ Ⓑ Ⓒ Ⓓ Ⓔ
44. Ⓐ Ⓑ Ⓒ Ⓓ Ⓔ
45. Ⓐ Ⓑ Ⓒ Ⓓ Ⓔ
46. Ⓐ Ⓑ Ⓒ Ⓓ Ⓔ
47. Ⓐ Ⓑ Ⓒ Ⓓ Ⓔ
48. Ⓐ Ⓑ Ⓒ Ⓓ Ⓔ
49. Ⓐ Ⓑ Ⓒ Ⓓ Ⓔ
50. Ⓐ Ⓑ Ⓒ Ⓓ Ⓔ
51. Ⓐ Ⓑ Ⓒ Ⓓ Ⓔ
52. Ⓐ Ⓑ Ⓒ Ⓓ Ⓔ
53. Ⓐ Ⓑ Ⓒ Ⓓ Ⓔ
54. Ⓐ Ⓑ Ⓒ Ⓓ Ⓔ
55. Ⓐ Ⓑ Ⓒ Ⓓ Ⓔ
56. Ⓐ Ⓑ Ⓒ Ⓓ Ⓔ
57. Ⓐ Ⓑ Ⓒ Ⓓ Ⓔ
58. Ⓐ Ⓑ Ⓒ Ⓓ Ⓔ
59. Ⓐ Ⓑ Ⓒ Ⓓ Ⓔ
60. Ⓐ Ⓑ Ⓒ Ⓓ Ⓔ

# ANSWER SHEET: *Practice Test 2*

1. Ⓐ Ⓑ Ⓒ Ⓓ Ⓔ
2. Ⓐ Ⓑ Ⓒ Ⓓ Ⓔ
3. Ⓐ Ⓑ Ⓒ Ⓓ Ⓔ
4. Ⓐ Ⓑ Ⓒ Ⓓ Ⓔ
5. Ⓐ Ⓑ Ⓒ Ⓓ Ⓔ
6. Ⓐ Ⓑ Ⓒ Ⓓ Ⓔ
7. Ⓐ Ⓑ Ⓒ Ⓓ Ⓔ
8. Ⓐ Ⓑ Ⓒ Ⓓ Ⓔ
9. Ⓐ Ⓑ Ⓒ Ⓓ Ⓔ
10. Ⓐ Ⓑ Ⓒ Ⓓ Ⓔ
11. Ⓐ Ⓑ Ⓒ Ⓓ Ⓔ
12. Ⓐ Ⓑ Ⓒ Ⓓ Ⓔ
13. Ⓐ Ⓑ Ⓒ Ⓓ Ⓔ
14. Ⓐ Ⓑ Ⓒ Ⓓ Ⓔ
15. Ⓐ Ⓑ Ⓒ Ⓓ Ⓔ
16. Ⓐ Ⓑ Ⓒ Ⓓ Ⓔ
17. Ⓐ Ⓑ Ⓒ Ⓓ Ⓔ
18. Ⓐ Ⓑ Ⓒ Ⓓ Ⓔ
19. Ⓐ Ⓑ Ⓒ Ⓓ Ⓔ
20. Ⓐ Ⓑ Ⓒ Ⓓ Ⓔ
21. Ⓐ Ⓑ Ⓒ Ⓓ Ⓔ
22. Ⓐ Ⓑ Ⓒ Ⓓ Ⓔ
23. Ⓐ Ⓑ Ⓒ Ⓓ Ⓔ
24. Ⓐ Ⓑ Ⓒ Ⓓ Ⓔ
25. Ⓐ Ⓑ Ⓒ Ⓓ Ⓔ
26. Ⓐ Ⓑ Ⓒ Ⓓ Ⓔ
27. Ⓐ Ⓑ Ⓒ Ⓓ Ⓔ
28. Ⓐ Ⓑ Ⓒ Ⓓ Ⓔ
29. Ⓐ Ⓑ Ⓒ Ⓓ Ⓔ
30. Ⓐ Ⓑ Ⓒ Ⓓ Ⓔ

31. Ⓐ Ⓑ Ⓒ Ⓓ Ⓔ
32. Ⓐ Ⓑ Ⓒ Ⓓ Ⓔ
33. Ⓐ Ⓑ Ⓒ Ⓓ Ⓔ
34. Ⓐ Ⓑ Ⓒ Ⓓ Ⓔ
35. Ⓐ Ⓑ Ⓒ Ⓓ Ⓔ
36. Ⓐ Ⓑ Ⓒ Ⓓ Ⓔ
37. Ⓐ Ⓑ Ⓒ Ⓓ Ⓔ
38. Ⓐ Ⓑ Ⓒ Ⓓ Ⓔ
39. Ⓐ Ⓑ Ⓒ Ⓓ Ⓔ
40. Ⓐ Ⓑ Ⓒ Ⓓ Ⓔ
41. Ⓐ Ⓑ Ⓒ Ⓓ Ⓔ
42. Ⓐ Ⓑ Ⓒ Ⓓ Ⓔ
43. Ⓐ Ⓑ Ⓒ Ⓓ Ⓔ
44. Ⓐ Ⓑ Ⓒ Ⓓ Ⓔ
45. Ⓐ Ⓑ Ⓒ Ⓓ Ⓔ
46. Ⓐ Ⓑ Ⓒ Ⓓ Ⓔ
47. Ⓐ Ⓑ Ⓒ Ⓓ Ⓔ
48. Ⓐ Ⓑ Ⓒ Ⓓ Ⓔ
49. Ⓐ Ⓑ Ⓒ Ⓓ Ⓔ
50. Ⓐ Ⓑ Ⓒ Ⓓ Ⓔ
51. Ⓐ Ⓑ Ⓒ Ⓓ Ⓔ
52. Ⓐ Ⓑ Ⓒ Ⓓ Ⓔ
53. Ⓐ Ⓑ Ⓒ Ⓓ Ⓔ
54. Ⓐ Ⓑ Ⓒ Ⓓ Ⓔ
55. Ⓐ Ⓑ Ⓒ Ⓓ Ⓔ
56. Ⓐ Ⓑ Ⓒ Ⓓ Ⓔ
57. Ⓐ Ⓑ Ⓒ Ⓓ Ⓔ
58. Ⓐ Ⓑ Ⓒ Ⓓ Ⓔ
59. Ⓐ Ⓑ Ⓒ Ⓓ Ⓔ
60. Ⓐ Ⓑ Ⓒ Ⓓ Ⓔ

# ANSWER SHEET: *Practice Test 3*

1. Ⓐ Ⓑ Ⓒ Ⓓ Ⓔ
2. Ⓐ Ⓑ Ⓒ Ⓓ Ⓔ
3. Ⓐ Ⓑ Ⓒ Ⓓ Ⓔ
4. Ⓐ Ⓑ Ⓒ Ⓓ Ⓔ
5. Ⓐ Ⓑ Ⓒ Ⓓ Ⓔ
6. Ⓐ Ⓑ Ⓒ Ⓓ Ⓔ
7. Ⓐ Ⓑ Ⓒ Ⓓ Ⓔ
8. Ⓐ Ⓑ Ⓒ Ⓓ Ⓔ
9. Ⓐ Ⓑ Ⓒ Ⓓ Ⓔ
10. Ⓐ Ⓑ Ⓒ Ⓓ Ⓔ
11. Ⓐ Ⓑ Ⓒ Ⓓ Ⓔ
12. Ⓐ Ⓑ Ⓒ Ⓓ Ⓔ
13. Ⓐ Ⓑ Ⓒ Ⓓ Ⓔ
14. Ⓐ Ⓑ Ⓒ Ⓓ Ⓔ
15. Ⓐ Ⓑ Ⓒ Ⓓ Ⓔ
16. Ⓐ Ⓑ Ⓒ Ⓓ Ⓔ
17. Ⓐ Ⓑ Ⓒ Ⓓ Ⓔ
18. Ⓐ Ⓑ Ⓒ Ⓓ Ⓔ
19. Ⓐ Ⓑ Ⓒ Ⓓ Ⓔ
20. Ⓐ Ⓑ Ⓒ Ⓓ Ⓔ
21. Ⓐ Ⓑ Ⓒ Ⓓ Ⓔ
22. Ⓐ Ⓑ Ⓒ Ⓓ Ⓔ
23. Ⓐ Ⓑ Ⓒ Ⓓ Ⓔ
24. Ⓐ Ⓑ Ⓒ Ⓓ Ⓔ
25. Ⓐ Ⓑ Ⓒ Ⓓ Ⓔ
26. Ⓐ Ⓑ Ⓒ Ⓓ Ⓔ
27. Ⓐ Ⓑ Ⓒ Ⓓ Ⓔ
28. Ⓐ Ⓑ Ⓒ Ⓓ Ⓔ
29. Ⓐ Ⓑ Ⓒ Ⓓ Ⓔ
30. Ⓐ Ⓑ Ⓒ Ⓓ Ⓔ

31. Ⓐ Ⓑ Ⓒ Ⓓ Ⓔ
32. Ⓐ Ⓑ Ⓒ Ⓓ Ⓔ
33. Ⓐ Ⓑ Ⓒ Ⓓ Ⓔ
34. Ⓐ Ⓑ Ⓒ Ⓓ Ⓔ
35. Ⓐ Ⓑ Ⓒ Ⓓ Ⓔ
36. Ⓐ Ⓑ Ⓒ Ⓓ Ⓔ
37. Ⓐ Ⓑ Ⓒ Ⓓ Ⓔ
38. Ⓐ Ⓑ Ⓒ Ⓓ Ⓔ
39. Ⓐ Ⓑ Ⓒ Ⓓ Ⓔ
40. Ⓐ Ⓑ Ⓒ Ⓓ Ⓔ
41. Ⓐ Ⓑ Ⓒ Ⓓ Ⓔ
42. Ⓐ Ⓑ Ⓒ Ⓓ Ⓔ
43. Ⓐ Ⓑ Ⓒ Ⓓ Ⓔ
44. Ⓐ Ⓑ Ⓒ Ⓓ Ⓔ
45. Ⓐ Ⓑ Ⓒ Ⓓ Ⓔ
46. Ⓐ Ⓑ Ⓒ Ⓓ Ⓔ
47. Ⓐ Ⓑ Ⓒ Ⓓ Ⓔ
48. Ⓐ Ⓑ Ⓒ Ⓓ Ⓔ
49. Ⓐ Ⓑ Ⓒ Ⓓ Ⓔ
50. Ⓐ Ⓑ Ⓒ Ⓓ Ⓔ
51. Ⓐ Ⓑ Ⓒ Ⓓ Ⓔ
52. Ⓐ Ⓑ Ⓒ Ⓓ Ⓔ
53. Ⓐ Ⓑ Ⓒ Ⓓ Ⓔ
54. Ⓐ Ⓑ Ⓒ Ⓓ Ⓔ
55. Ⓐ Ⓑ Ⓒ Ⓓ Ⓔ
56. Ⓐ Ⓑ Ⓒ Ⓓ Ⓔ
57. Ⓐ Ⓑ Ⓒ Ⓓ Ⓔ
58. Ⓐ Ⓑ Ⓒ Ⓓ Ⓔ
59. Ⓐ Ⓑ Ⓒ Ⓓ Ⓔ
60. Ⓐ Ⓑ Ⓒ Ⓓ Ⓔ

# GRE General Test

# INDEX

# INDEX

# NOTES

NOTES

**NOTES**

NOTES

**NOTES**

NOTES

# Also
# available
## from
# REA

*For more information visit us online at*
## www.rea.com/GRE